Developing Leadership

Professional Learning

Series Editors: Ivor Goodson and Andy Hargreaves

The work of teachers has changed significantly in recent years and now, more than ever, there is a pressing need for high-quality professional development. This timely new series examines the actual and possible forms of professional learning, professional knowledge, professional development and professional standards that are beginning to emerge and be debated at the beginning of the twenty-first century. The series will be important reading for teachers, teacher educators, staff developers and policy makers throughout the English-speaking world.

Published and forthcoming titles:

Developing Leadership
Creating the schools of tomorrow

Martin J Coles and
Geoff Southworth

Open University Press

Open University Press
McGraw-Hill Education
McGraw-Hill House
Shoppenhangers Road
Maidenhead
Berkshire
England
SL6 2QL

email: enquiries@openup.co.uk
world wide web: www.openup.co.uk

and Two Penn Plaza, New York, NY 10121–2289, USA

First published 2005

A catalogue record of this book is available from the British Library

ISBN 0 335 21542 4 (pb) 0 335 21543 2 (hb)

Library of Congress Cataloging-in-Publication Data
CIP data applied for

Typeset by RefineCatch Limited, Bungay, Suffolk
Printed in the UK by Bell & Bain Ltd, Glasgow

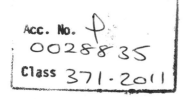

Contents

List of contributors

Raymond Bolam is Emeritus Professor of Education in the School of Social Sciences at Cardiff University and a Visiting Professor in the Departments of Education at the Universities of Bath and Leicester. He has also held Chairs in Education at Cardiff and Swansea Universities, He has acted as consultant to the UNESCO, the OECD, the British Council, and the European Commission as well as to governments and national and international agencies in Africa, Asia, Australia, Europe and North America. His research and publications have focused on school leadership, professional development, school improvement and the management of change. He is currently co-directing a nationally funded study on 'Creating and Sustaining Effective Professional Learning Communities' in schools.

Amy F. Coldren is a doctoral candidate in the graduate program in Human Development and Social Policy at Northwestern University. She is currently writing her dissertation on how elementary school teachers construct and reconstruct understandings of reform initiatives in Mathematics and Literacy instruction.

Gary M. Crow is Professor and Chair in the Department of Educational Leadership at The University of Utah (USA). His research interests include work socialization of school site leaders and school reform. His most recent, co-authored, book is *Being and Becoming a Principal*. He is president-elect of the University Council for Educational Administration.

John B. Diamond is an Assistant Professor at the Harvard Graduate School of Education. His interests include the sociology of education, school and community relations, race and class stratification, African American and Latino/a student achievement, and leadership and organizational change.

Clive Dimmock is Professor of Educational Leadership and Director of the Centre for Educational Leadership and Management, University of Leicester. He has published extensively in the areas of cultural and cross-cultural approaches to leadership and school improvement, and has an abiding interest in Asian education and the leadership of multi-ethnic schools in both Anglo-American and Asian contexts.

Dean Fink is a former superintendent and principal in Ontario, Canada, an associate of the International Centre for Educational Change at the University of Toronto, and a visiting fellow of the International Leadership Centre at the University of Hull. His most recent book is *It's About Learning and It's About Time* (with Louise Stoll and Lorna Earl).

Dr. Andy Hargreaves is the Thomas More Brennan Chair in Education at the Lynch School of Education, Boston College. Prior to that, he was Professor of Educational Leadership and Change at the University of Nottingham, England, and Co-director of and Professor in the International Centre for Educational Change at the Ontario Institute for Studies in Education of the University of Toronto. He is holder of the Canadian Education Association/ Whitworth 2000 Award for outstanding contributions to educational research. Andy Hargreaves is the author and editor of more than twenty books in the fields of teacher development, the culture of the school and educational change. His most recent book, *Teaching in the Knowledge Society: Education in the age of insecurity*, was given the 2004 Outstanding Book Award in curriculum studies by the American Educational Research Association.

Bill Mulford, Professor and Director of the Leadership for Learning Research Group in the Faculty of Education at the University of Tasmania. Bill is a former teacher, school principal, Assistant Director of Education and Past President of both national and international professional associations in educational administration. He is an adviser to state and national Departments of Education and a consultant to international organizations.

Dr. Fred Paterson is Senior Research Officer for the National College for School Leadership and 'lead enquirer' for the New Visions programme. Previously, Fred worked as an educational researcher at the Universities of Leicester and Nottingham, an advisory teacher and a primary practitioner in Nottinghamshire.

Tony Richardson is Director of Online Learning at The National College for School Leadership (NCSL). Tony has been a primary headteacher, an education adviser specializing in Information and Communications Technology, a senior primary adviser and most recently Chief Education Adviser and Head of Northamptonshire LEA Inspection and Advisory Service (NIAS). Tony has lead responsibility for the NCSL's virtual presence and online learning.

Professor Jennifer Z. Sherer is a doctoral candidate in the graduate program in Learning Sciences at Northwestern University. She is currently writing her dissertation on distributed leadership practice and how the subject matters.

Professor Lee Sing Kong is the Dean of Graduate Programmes and Research at the National Institute of Education, Nanyang Technological University. Professor Lee has spearheaded several innovation projects in the fields of education and science, and has received several national and international awards in recognition of his achievements.

Halia Silins is an internationally recognized researcher in educational leadership. She has led numerous programmes on managing change in Australia, UK, USA and Malaysia. Her consultancies bring her research and practical skills together to help leaders achieve personal goals and improved organizational outcomes. Halia is an Associate Professor at Flinders. University of South Australia.

James P. Spillane is Associate Professor of Education and Social Policy, and a Faculty Fellow at the Institute for Policy Research, Northwestern University, where he teaches in both the Learning Sciences and Human Development and Social Policy graduate programmes. His most recent book is *Standards Deviations: How Local Schools Misunderstand Policy* (Harvard University Press, 2004).

Louise Stoll is an educational consultant, President of the International Congress for School Effectiveness and School Improvement, and Visiting Professor at the Institute of Education, University of London and at the University of Bath. Her research, development work and writing focus on school improvement, leadership and capacity for learning and change.

Dr. Ken Stott is an Associate Dean at Nanyang Technological University in Singapore, where he is in charge of school leadership development programmes. He has written a wide range of books and articles on management and leadership, and his work on management teams is well known internationally.

Allan Walker is professor and Chair of the Department of Educational Administration and Policy at the Chinese University of Hong Kong. He is also Associate Director of the Hong Kong Centre for the Development of Educational Leadership. His research interests include principalship preparation and development, cultural influence on school leadership and leadership needs analysis.

John West-Burnham is a Senior Research Adviser at NCSL. Having worked in schools, further and adult education for fifteen years, John's work has taken him to the Open University, Crewe and Alsager College, University of Leicester, University of Lincoln, and University of Hull. John's current research and writing interests include transformational leadership, leadership learning and development, and educational leadership in the community.

Series editors' preface

Teaching today is increasingly complex work, requiring the highest standards of professional practice to perform it well (Goodson and Hargreaves 1996). It is the core profession, the key agent of change in today's knowledge society. Teachers are the midwives of that knowledge society. Without them, or their competence, the future will be malformed and stillborn. In the United States, George W. Bush's educational slogan has been to leave no child behind. What is clear today in general, and in this book in particular, is that leaving no child behind means leaving no teacher or leader behind either. Yet, teaching is also in crisis, staring tragedy in the face. There is a demographic exodus occurring in the profession as many teachers in the ageing cohort of the Boomer generation are retiring early because of stress, burnout or disillusionment with the impact of years of mandated reform on their lives and work. After a decade of relentless reform, in a climate of shaming and blaming teachers for perpetuating poor standards, the attractiveness of teaching as a profession has faded fast among potential new recruits.

Teaching has to compete much harder against other professions for high calibre candidates than it did in the last period of mass recruitment – when able women were led to feel that only nursing and secretarial work were viable options. Teaching may not yet have reverted to being an occupation for 'unmarriageable women and unsaleable men', as Willard Waller described it in 1932, but many American inner cities now run their school systems on high numbers of uncertified teachers. The teacher recruitment crisis in England has led some schools to move to a four-day week; more and more schools are run on the increasingly casualized labour of temporary teachers from overseas, or endless supply teachers whose quality busy administrators do not always have time to monitor (Townsend 2001).

Meanwhile, in the Canadian province of Ontario in 2001, hard-nosed and hard-headed reform strategies led in a single year to a decrease in applications to teacher education programmes in faculties of education by 20–25 per cent, and a drop in a whole grade level of accepted applicants.

Amid all this despair and danger though, there remains great hope and some reasons for optimism about a future of learning that is tied in its vision to an empowering, imaginative and inclusive vision for teaching as well. The educational standards movement is showing visible signs of over-reaching itself, as people are starting to complain about teacher shortages in schools and the loss of creativity and inspiration in classrooms (Hargreaves 2003). There is growing international support for the resumption of more humane middle-years philosophies in the early years of secondary school that put priority on community and engagement, alongside curriculum content and academic achievement. School districts in the United States are increasingly seeing that high-quality professional development for teachers is absolutely indispensable to bringing about deep changes in student achievement (Fullan 2001). In England and Wales, policy documents and White Papers are similarly advocating more 'earned autonomy', and schools and teachers are performing well (e.g. DfES 2001). Governments almost everywhere are beginning to speak more positively about teachers and teaching – bestowing honour and respect where blame and contempt had prevailed in the recent past.

The time has rarely been more opportune, or more pressing, to think deeper about what professional learning, professional knowledge, and professional status should look like for the new generation of teachers who will shape the next three decades of public education. Should professional learning accompany increased autonomy for teachers, or should its provision be linked to the evidence of demonstrated improvements in pupil achievement results? Do successful schools do better when the professional learning is self-guided, discretionary, and intellectually challenging, while failing schools or schools in trouble benefit from required training in the skills that evidence shows can raise classroom achievement quickly? And does accommodating professional learning to the needs of different schools and their staffs constitute administrative sensitivity and flexibility (Hopkins *et al.* 1997), or does it constitute a kind of professional development apartheid (Hargreaves 2003). These are the kinds of questions and issues which this series on professional learning sets out to address.

How effectively teachers pursue their own professional learning depends, of course, on their own interest and initiative. But the extent and effectiveness of professional learning is also influenced by the school communities in which teachers work. The leaders of these communities create the climate of encouragement and expectation in which teachers do or do not learn how to improve professionally. Helping teachers learn well so they can help pupils to learn well is one of the fundamental responsibilities of leadership – and one of the essential elements of professional learning among leaders themselves.

Coles and Southworth's book *Developing Leadership*, examines the significant role of leaders individually, and leadership collectively, in improving the quality of learning among everyone in the school. Bringing together some of the world's leading writers and researchers on educational leadership from Britain, America, Australia, Europe and Asia, Coles and Southworth's edited collection sets out visions for leadership learning and leadership development that focuses not merely on passing along existing leadership knowledge, but on developing the future leadership capacities that will be needed in the schools of tomorrow. Their collection deals with how to distribute learning and leadership among the entire educational community, rather than concentrating it in the hands of a few highly-placed individuals, and how to pass on leadership learning across the generations through improved processes of leadership succession. Mentoring, coaching, networking and training are all dealt with in this state-of-the-art text, along with more complex issues of how to create and sustain entire cultures of learning and leadership.

Coles and Southworth, the editors of this collection, are themselves distinguished researchers and writers in the fields of professional learning and educational leadership. They also direct the research department, and help steer the agenda of leadership research, in England's new and highly-influential National College of School Leadership (NCSL). Established by the UK National Government and opened by Tony Blair in 2002, NCSL is a unique national organization that tries to ensure that school leaders are supported, developed and have access to research and leading-edge thinking on leadership from across the world. The College organizes and orchestrates all the major development and accredited training for all kinds of educational school leaders, from emergent to advanced, through face-to-face, school-based and on-line learning, and through networked learning and inquiry among leaders themselves.

This key book on leadership and leadership learning, therefore, represents the kind of research and thinking on leadership that is most respected in one of the world's most influential institutions of leadership learning and development. Michael Fullan (2001) has argued that if the closing years of the twentieth century were marked by a focus on standards, then the opening decade of the twenty-first century is, in many ways, the decade of leadership. In this decade, the improvement and renewal of leadership is being increasingly connected to the improvement of pupil learning and achievement. Intellectually and strategically, *Developing Leaders* places itself squarely in the centre of this vital agenda connecting leadership to learning. Years of official obsession with the management of standards and targets in tested achievement are giving way to a new era of leadership that will create learning for all in a creative and complex knowledge society. In this respect, *Developing Leaders* takes us significantly forward in understanding how teachers learn and how leaders can and should learn better still.

Andy Hargreaves
Ivor Goodson

References

Department for Education and Skills (2001) *Achieving Success*. London: The Stationery Office.

Fullan, M. (2001) *Leading in a Culture of Change*. San Francisco: Jossey-Bass/Wiley.

Fullan, M. (2004) *Leadership and Sustainability: System thinkers in action*. Thousand Oaks, CA: Corwin Press.

Goodson, I. and Hargreaves, A. (1996) *Teachers' Professional Lives: Aspirations and actualities*. New York: Falmer Press.

Hargreaves, A., Earl, L., Moore, S. and Manning, S. (2001) *Learning to Change: Teaching beyond subjects and standards*. San Francisco: Jossey-Bass/Wiley.

Hopkins, D., Harris, A. and Jackson, D. (1997) Understanding the schools capacity for development: Growth states and strategies. *School Leadership and Management*, 17(3), 401–11.

Townsend, J. (2001) 'It's bad – trust me, I teach there,' *Sunday Times*. 2 December, p. 10.

List of figures and tables

Introduction:
Developing Leadership – creating the schools of tomorrow

Good leadership is critical to a school's success. The quality of leadership can make a difference between a school which struggles and one which strives for the highest levels of attainment, between a school where pupils and staff are pulling in different directions and one where everyone collaborates and works towards a shared purpose.

Fundamentally it can make a difference between success for the few and success for everyone. But how do we develop good school leaders, able to make the schools of tomorrow the best they can be?

This book is not about prescriptions or blueprints. It is about opening up debate and describing possibilities. The idea for the book grew out of an international conference organized by the National College for School Leadership (NCSL) entitled *Learning from best practice worldwide*. The conference was designed to explore innovative and significant aspects of educational leadership and bring together international colleagues to generate new understandings. The conference brought together researchers, academics and policy-makers with practitioners and proved a dynamic forum for debate. That debate is reflected in this book.

The study of leadership as a formal discipline is a relatively recent phenomenon of course, and in the literature about leadership it is usual to suggest that as vital a notion as leadership undoubtedly is, there is little agreement around the concept:

> There has been an enormous outpouring of writing on leadership since the 1940s but there is little consensus on what counts as leadership, whether it can be taught, even how effective it might be.
>
> (Call for papers: 'Studying leadership': EIASM Workshop on Leadership Research, University of Oxford. 16 and 17 December 2002)

But it became clear during the NCSL conference that there was a consensus of understanding around certain key themes that crossed national boundaries – themes and ideas that are integral to the different chapters in this book. This book is designed to explore this consensus, to promote our best present understanding of good school leadership, and to inform school leaders, policy-makers and other educationalists about leading edge thinking which bears on the development of school leaders.

The principal themes, which will be highlighted at various points throughout the book, are built around the concepts and practice of: professional learning communities; distributed leadership; sustainability; internship; mentoring and coaching; and strategic thinking about ICT.

Dean Fink's opening chapter, *Developing leaders for their future not our past*, considers a looming crisis in education – the recruitment, induction and professional growth of future leaders. He suggests that years of 'naming, shaming, and blaming' educators for the real and imagined problems of education have made positions of leadership unattractive to many potential leaders. This reluctance to step forward coincides with significant demographic shifts among educators and the increasing demands of a knowledge society. He argues that what is required for the future is an on-going investment in leadership potential, and develops this argument with reference to succession planning in both the private and public sectors.

Andy Hargreaves draws on his current work for the second chapter, developing ideas on *Leadership succession*. He points out that one of the most significant events in the life of a school is a change in its leadership; yet few things in education succeed less than leadership succession. In part, he says, we mismanage succession because our most basic assumptions about leadership are flawed. Drawing on evidence from a Spencer Foundation funded study in eight US and Canadian high schools, he demonstrates how successful succession depends on sound succession planning, on limiting the frequency of succession events, on preserving the idea of leadership in the face of pressures towards more management and on the successful employment of leadership knowledge which is focused as much on preserving past successes and keeping improvements going, as on change or turning things around.

Chapter Three by James Spillane and colleagues, *Developing distributed leadership*, revises and updates his previous writing on the distribution of leadership. The past decade has witnessed extraordinary efforts to improve the quality of teaching in classrooms with raised expectations for student's academic work leading to increased expectations for teacher's practice. This chapter provides evidence and examples of how schools that cultivate certain in-school conditions including shared visions for instruction, norms of collaboration, and collective responsibility for student's academic success create incentives and opportunities for teachers to improve. School leadership is recognized as important in promoting these conditions.

Chapter Four, *Developing leadership for learning communities*, describes work that Stoll and Bolam have been involved in recently to do with creating and sustaining effective professional learning communities. The chapter explores the issues around leadership in professional learning communities. What is a professional learning community? What makes it effective? How is such a community created and sustained? What is the role of school leader in these communities? Such questions imply the need for leaders who are 'capacity builders', promoting ongoing and sustainable learning among the entire school community.

Gary Crow has evaluated for the Department for Education and Science in England an internship programme for aspiring headteachers in schools facing challenging circumstances. The project placed experienced deputies in secondary schools facing challenging circumstances for a period of one year. This chapter, *Developing leadership for schools facing challenging circumstances*, does not describe that evaluation, but draws lessons and recommendations for preparing innovative school leaders to work in schools facing challenging circumstances, and analyses the pros and cons of internship as a leadership development practice.

Walker and Dimmock's chapter, *Developing leadership in context*, follows up the theme of the Crow chapter. The Hong Kong Government has recently introduced a new policy to revitalize the professional development of aspiring, newly appointed and experienced principals. The chapter outlines the new principal professional development policy and highlights some of the successes and problems of the policy to date. Among the positive outcomes is the increased responsibility being taken by principals themselves for developing new and future leaders, and it is this theme which Walker and Dimmock develop.

In Chapter Seven, *Developing innovative leadership*, Ken Stott and Lee Sing Kong offer an analysis of the principles behind and benefits of another leadership development programme, the National Institute of Education in Singapore's new Principalship Preparation Programme highlighting the intention to develop innovative leaders. With a focus on knowledge creation and innovation, the six months full-time learning experience for talented educators includes a varied menu of learning opportunities, including an overseas visit and an extensive innovation project in schools. The authors discuss the principles which underpin a programme designed to develop school leaders with the capability to operate innovatively in a complex, competitive, fast-changing environment.

Chapter Eight offers an analysis of a third leadership development programme. Launched in 2002, New Visions is a National College for School Leadership programme that supports the development of new headteachers. The programme combines a variety of innovative learning processes and uses the perspective of experienced school leaders. Participants are organized into networks that combine peer support, problem-solving and study groups. In this chapter, *Developing beginning leadership*, Fred Paterson and John West-Burham draw upon research undertaken to explore the learning processes associated with the programme, and the climate and programme processes that influence the learning and development of the participants. A discussion of implications for future leadership development programmes is a significant element of the chapter.

Tony Richardson's chapter, *Developing leadership for e-confident schools*, describes briefly the major technological changes that have been enacted recently in the mainstream schools system and predicts some of the innovations to come. It then considers the impact of such changes upon teaching and learning from the perspective of school leaders, and draws conclusions about the implications for the development of school leaders. It also develops an argument around the potential conflict between the development of truly independent learning enabled by the sophisticated use of ICT and externally imposed constraints, which cause tensions in the agenda for leadership development.

Bill Mulford has been leading a major research project in Australia, the 'Leadership for Organisational Learning and Student Outcomes (LOLSO) Research Project', which addresses the need to extend present understandings of school reform initiatives that aim to change school practices with the intention of supporting enhanced student learning. In this chapter, *Developing leadership for organisational learning*, results from LOLSO's teacher and student surveys are used to discuss some of the projects research questions: What leadership practices promote organizational learning in schools? In what ways do school leadership and/or organizational learning contribute to student outcomes? The answers to these questions lead to implications relating to distributive leadership, development, context, and a broader understanding of student outcomes. The answers also raise concerns about transactional leadership, that is, school leadership that over-emphasizes the managerial or strategic.

Geoff Southworth's *Overview and conclusions* chapter draws together the themes and issues raised in the previous chapters, examines what they mean for practitioners and researchers and links them to the work of the National College for School Leadership in England. In very broad terms there are two themes which run across all the chapters: leadership development, and creating schools of tomorrow. It is no surprise that these are the two major themes, given the title of this book. However, it is also clear from many of the chapters that the two themes together create a third one – developing leaders for tomorrow's schools. This final chapter discusses each of these three themes in turn, identifying the range of ideas which the writers of the previous chapters have focused on and considering the issues they have highlighted.

Over the last generation a body of evidence about what constitutes an 'effective' school has been accumulated, creating a more and more explicit set of reference points for the evaluation of leadership, and frameworks within which school leaders are expected to act. The role of school leaders in generating and sustaining such change has become the subject of intense debate, financial investment and public expectation. Today's school leaders occupy the same kind of pivotal position within their institution that schools have traditionally occupied in wider society. As the expectations of schooling, and the scrutiny and accountability given to their performance have grown, the visibility of leadership and the stakes attached to leadership strategies have become steadily higher. So how does school leadership need to develop for the future?

A publication from the National College for School Leadership, *Unique Creations* (2002) suggests that it is self-evident that the future matters to us. But it is difficult to plan for the future; some would say it cannot be planned for at all since the future unfolds through myriads of interactions, policies, inventions, agendas, opportunities taken and opportunities lost. But if the future cannot be controlled we can still make collective choices that make a difference. In fact, because the future is open, thinking clearly and rigorously about it is crucial if we want to have any chance of realizing our values and commitments, and wish to understand the choices we have individually and together. In confronting the possibility that schooling could evolve in several different directions, we must also admit that leadership will be instrumental in converting the possibilities into realities. The chapters which follow draw connections between different approaches to leadership development and the different possibilities for the way that we might create the schools of the future. They underline how vital it is that all those working in schools continue learning to refresh their knowledge, understandings and skills, and take charge of change.

one

Developing leaders for their future not our past

Dean Fink

Introduction

For most of my career in state education in the Canadian province of Ontario, I held some kind of leadership role. First as a department head in a secondary school, then successively as a deputy school head in a primary school, deputy head and head in a secondary school, a local inspector and later a regional inspector. It may sound simplistic and perhaps naïve, but I always believed and acted on the premise that my job as a leader was to ensure the learning of the students in my care. If this meant mobilizing community support for the school, raising funds to purchase computers, dismissing an incompetent teacher, modelling good class-room practices, taking on county hall on behalf of my school, or supporting a troubled colleague, it all added up to my trying to create a situation that enhanced the learning of my students. Just as I believed and acted on this image of leadership, I am even more convinced that now in an 'age of insecurity' (Hargreaves 2003), 'schools for tomorrow' will require leaders who are passionately, obsessively, creatively and stead-fastly committed to enhancing students' learning. This means more than just preparing students for the tests and exams that often pass for 'deep' learning, but rather leaders who focus the entire school on students' learning for understanding. As Andy Hargreaves and I have written elsewhere,

> Learning for understanding is not just a cognitive and psychological matter, though. It involves more than constructivism, multiple intelli-gences, metacognition, or problem-based learning. Deep learning and teaching are also cultural and emotional processes. They entail

contextualizing students' learning in what they have learned before, in what other teachers are also teaching them, and in student's own cultures and lives.

(2000: 30)

In my career, I was a distributive leader before anyone had coined the term. Not that I was particularly clairvoyant, but rather as a secondary school head, sharing leadership with my staff was not only common sense, it was an act of self preservation. These activities were means to an end, not ends in themselves. I make no claims to being 'heroic' or even a very special school leader. In fact, I have worked with many leaders in many countries who, if I am truly honest with myself, were far better leaders than I ever was. Now in my post-retirement years, I find myself on the fringes of academe. I am amazed that I did as well as I did, considering that many of my decisions and actions were based on intuition, common sense, acquired experience, reason and fairly strong convictions about what constituted good and ethical practice.

Leadership in recent years has become a growth industry. Politicians demand more of it, academics decry the lack of it, and potential school leaders are deciding 'to hell with it'. I would submit that we are making the business of leadership so complicated that we seem to need either John Wayne at his mythological best or Xena: Warrior Princess of television fame to run a school. A combination of disenchantment with leadership roles as a result of the standards/standardization agenda and demographic changes as the baby boom generation moves on, have produced, and will continue to produce, a rapid turnover of school heads and other educational leaders in the schools of most Western educational jurisdictions (Earley, Evans, Collarbone, Gold and Halpin 2002; Williams 2001). Not only do politicians and educators need to address this crisis of 'schools of today', but also they will have to develop creative and thoughtful ways to identify, recruit, prepare and support the kind of people who have the potential to become leaders of learning in the 'schools of tomorrow'.

In this chapter, therefore, I propose to address these problems of expectations and recruitment from both conceptual and policy perspectives. First I present a somewhat idiosyncratic review of the leadership literature and argue for the need to focus on future leaders' potential rather than the prevailing practice of reifying present and past leadership proficiencies. I will then suggest that this focus on potential must be imbedded in a coherent plan for leadership succession. To this end I briefly review some of the literature on the topic and suggest that the sustainability of change will be dependent on our ability to recruit, train and sustain a new generation of educational leaders. Perhaps in the process I can contribute to demythologizing leadership and encourage talented 'mortals' to aspire to leadership roles.

The importance of leadership

While I have stated that we seem to be making leadership into something beyond the capabilities of reasonably talented mortals, and certainly unattractive to potential leaders, this is not to suggest that leadership is unimportant. Indeed, the importance of leadership in an organization is one of the few ideas in the literature about change about which there is consistent agreement (Sammons et al. 1995; Fullan 1993; Stoll and Fink 1996). The major reform movements all identify leadership as an important ingredient of educational change. In recent years, the perceived failure of reform efforts inspired by these movements to alter rapidly and significantly the essential 'grammar of schooling' (Tyack and Tobin 1994) internationally has resulted in an increased interest, indeed preoccupation, with leadership as a key ingredient in school change. Policy makers in many jurisdictions have legislated long lists of leaders' competencies, mandated increased credentials for leaders and, in the United Kingdom, invested heavily in a National College for School Leadership. The creation of the College is a very forward-looking move. However, the degree of success of the College will depend on how successful it is in looking at leadership in the long term – focusing on leadership potential—rather than the 'short termism' that infects many politically motivated educational efforts.

When one looks at the lists of competencies required by school heads in various countries, the proficiencies that principals need in order to be successful in this age of rapid, complex reform are truly daunting. Principals are not only required to lead, manage and attend to culture along with structure (Davidson and Taylor 1999), but they must also unite their school through inspiring visions (Takahashi 1998), or less 'heroic' approaches (Copland 2001) that empower others (Caldwell 1998) by 'distributing' leadership among colleagues (Elmore 2000; Supovitz 2000; Blasé and Blasé 1999). This pressure has led to feelings of 'overwhelming responsibilities, information perplexity, and emotional anxiety' (Whitaker 1999). New heads are described as 'frightened' by the challenge of headship (Mansell 2002). An Ontario principal confessed that 'I feel like I am responsible for the whole world.' Paradoxically, at a time when policy makers place so much importance on leadership, it would appear that many of their reform policies actually inhibit leadership, and oblige school heads and other educational leaders to become little more than the managers of externally mandated changes.

Gronn (1996) indicates that 'whatever the cultural, ethnic, gender and social class component of the context concerned, the two attributes which best define a leader are influence and identification, while 'leading' is defined as 'the framing of meaning and the mobilization of support for a meaningful course of action'. This deceptively simple definition raises fundamental questions such as: How do leaders influence followers to pursue a course of action? Why do followers identify with leaders? How do leaders 'frame' meaning, mobilize followers, and define a 'meaningful' course of action? The leadership literature until the 1980s tended to see leadership and leaders as 'doing things right' (Bennis and Nanus 1985) – being efficient and managerial. This generation of 'theories and studies was driven by assumptions about scientific management, rational decision making, positivist epistemology, and behaviouristic psychology' (Starrett 1993). Burns (1978) defined this style of leadership as transactional. Leithwood (1992) explained that transactional leadership in education is 'based on an exchange of services (from a teacher, for example) for various kinds of rewards (salary, recognition, intrinsic rewards) that the leader controls, at least in part. Transactional leadership practices, some claim, help people recognize what needs to be done in order to reach a desired outcome and may also increase their confidence and motivation' (Leithwood 1992). As Sergiovanni (1992a) expressed it – 'what is rewarded gets done'.

Leithwood and his colleagues (1999) described seven major approaches to leadership that currently influence educational policy and practice – managerial, contingent, instructional, transactional, moral, transformational and participative. The first five models tend to be more 'instrumental' in design (Sergiovanni and Starratt 1988). In each model, formal leaders attempt to influence followers to achieve organizational goals by employing various sources of power – the positional power of the manager or contingent leader, the expertise of the instructional leader (Smith and Andrews 1989), or system values by the moral leader (Sergiovanni 1992a; 1992b). These goals or 'meaningful courses of action' include ensuring the efficient completion of specified tasks (managerial), responding effectively to organizational challenges (contingent), enhancing the effectiveness of teachers' classroom practice (instructional), and increasing the effectiveness of decisions and staff involvement in these decisions (moral). In spite of many alternative models of leadership these technocratic approaches still tend to dominate policy and practice (Saul 1993).

The other two styles described by Leithwood and his colleagues (1999), transformational and participative leadership, require formal leaders to involve the larger group in decision-making activities to ensure organizational improvement. These models are derived from Burns' (1978) concept of transformational leadership and subsume such models as 'visionary' leadership (Bass 1985) and 'charismatic' leadership (House and Shamir 1993). These more inclusive approaches to leadership focus on effectiveness – 'doing things right' (Bennis and Nanus 1985). Leithwood and his colleagues (1999) argue that transformational leadership moves schools beyond first-order or surface changes to second-order changes that alter the 'core technologies' of schooling. This leadership style includes the pursuit of common goals, empowerment, maintenance of a collaborative culture, teacher development and problem solving (Leithwood 1992). These qualities are reflected in teacher-led professional development committees, mentorship programmes, teacher-initiated curriculum innovation, and staff-led school planning teams. Both collaborative styles – transformational and participative – are intended to involve people in organizations in decisions that will increase the organization's capacity to improve and respond to changes in its context.

The clear implication in most of this work is that leaders should 'transform' their organizations through substantive models of leadership that focus on the meaning, mission and identity of the organization as a whole, as well they should. As I reflect on my own career, however, I find these categories artificial and disconnected from my reality. I was both a manager and a leader, transactional and transformational, contingent and participative. On occasions, such as with the teacher who habitually swore at children, I was quite authoritarian, and in issues that involved the entire staff, such as developing a school-wide development plan, quite democratic. Deal and Peterson (1994) among others have criticized the 'artificial debate' between management and leadership, and suggest that schools require leadership that blends both the technical skills of an engineer and the creative imagination of the artist. They declare that:

> High performing organisations have both order and meaning, structure and values. They achieve quality at reasonable costs. They accomplish goals while attending to core values and beliefs. They encourage both fundamentals and fun. They embrace the dialectic between expression of values and accomplishment of goals. They encourage both leadership and management, symbolic behaviour and technical activity.
>
> (Deal and Peterson 1994: 9)

The educational administration literature generally supports this view (Louis and Miles 1990; Stoll and Fink 1996). One only needs to look at the diversity of roles played by educational leaders to recognize that most leaders adopt many styles of leadership depending on the situation. Some critics have also argued that transformational leadership and similar participative approaches are really 'instrumental' in nature and just less overt 'techniques' or strategies to coerce teachers into co-operating with top-down changes in which they find little meaning (Alix 2000). Gronn (1996) contends that transformational leadership 'reduces leadership to something that goes on in the head of the leader: devoid of any recognition of follower attribution and implicit theories, nor is it aware that leadership is a socially constructed process'. It would appear that, at least in a school context, both transactional and transformational models of leadership have serious conceptual and practical flaws.

A third body of work on leadership is emerging that is influenced by complexity theory (Wheatley 1994: Morrison 2002) and the literature on school reculturing (Hargreaves 1994; Wonycott-Kytle and Bogoch 1997). Stacey (1993) for example suggests that instrumental views of leadership that are based on a rational, predictable, linear world are limited in times of diversity, complexity and unpredictability and that more democratic and inclusive models of leadership are required. Riley captures this idea in her description of 'distributive leadership'. 'It sees leadership as a network of relationships among people, structures and cultures (both within and across organizational boundaries), not just as a role-based function assigned to, or acquired by, a person in an organization, who then uses his or her power to influence the actions of others . . . Leadership is seen as an organic activity, dependent on interrelationships and connections' (Riley 2000: 47). Spillane and his colleagues' (2000) concept of 'distributed' leadership develops similar ideas. The concept of distributed or distributive leadership fundamentally changes the role of formal leaders. Block (1993) suggests that leaders in the future require stewardship not leadership – stewardship being defined as the willingness to be accountable for the wellbeing of the larger organization by operating in service rather than in control.

Elsewhere, my colleague Louise Stoll and I offer a compatible eclectic and holistic view of invitational leadership in schools based on the work of Purkey and Novak (1984): 'Leadership is about communicating invitational messages to individuals and groups with whom leaders interact in order to build on a shared and evolving vision of enhanced educational experiences for students' (Stoll and Fink 1996). We argued that authentic educational leaders are passionately and persistently focused on enhancing students' learning. This does not mean just adding a few points on a school's results on a standardized test; rather we mean attending to the kinds of learning captured by the UNESCO report of the International Commission on Education for the Twenty-first Century entitled *Learning: the treasure within*. In it, the report's international group of authors (1996) argued that 'traditional responses to the demand for education that are essentially quantitative and knowledge-based are no longer appropriate. It is not enough to supply each child with a store of knowledge to be drawn on from then on. Each individual must be equipped to seize learning opportunities throughout life, to broaden her or his knowledge, skills and attitudes, and to adapt to a changing, complex and interdependent world'. To this end, the Commission proposes 'four fundamental types of learning which, throughout a person's life, will in a way be the pillars of knowledge':

Learning to know – acquiring a broad general knowledge, intellectual curiosity, the instruments of understanding, independence of judgement, and the impetus and foundation for being able to continue learning throughout life.

Learning to do – the competence to put what one has learned into practice, even when it is unclear how future work will evolve, to deal with many situations and to act creatively on one's environment. This involves higher skills at all levels, being able to process information and communicate with others.

Learning to live together – developing understanding of and respect for other people, their cultures and spiritual values, empathy for others' points of view, understanding diversity and similarities between people, appreciating interdependence, and being able to dialogue and debate, in order to participate and co-operate with others, enhance relationships, and combat violence and conflict.

Learning to be – developing the 'all-round' person who possesses greater autonomy, judgement and personal responsibility, through attending to all aspects of a person's potential – mind and body, intelligence, sensitivity, aesthetic sense and spiritual values – such that they can understand themselves and their world, and solve their own problems.

Within each of these categories anyone involved in the education of our children and particularly 'leaders of learning' must pursue 'deep, powerful, high-performance learning-for-understanding that prepares young people to participate in today's knowledge or informational society' (Hargreaves and Fink 2000: 30).

How then do we prepare leaders for their future as leaders of learning? This may sound heretical, but others can do most of the stuff that presently consume a school leader's time and these 'others' can probably do it better. It is ironic that site-based management has meant decentralizing management issues like budgets, school repairs and transportation, and centralizing the 'what', 'how', 'why' and 'how do we know' of education to central bureaucracies quite removed from the learners. When one sees the kinds of tasks governments have offloaded to schools in the name of local decision-making, it is no wonder that some officials in the British government now consider non-educators such as accountants and business people to be quite suitable school heads. If all that your government wants are 'number crunchers', 'paper pushers' and 'intellectual accountants' then it is on the right track. If, however, it is serious about students' learning, I believe such a policy is misguided. At the same time, unless heads see themselves as educators and find ways to reinvent themselves as leaders of learning, then the new breed envisaged by some government officials will conduct the business of schooling more efficiently. I repeat, however, the only rationale for educational leadership is attending to those things that enhance students' learning. For those agencies such as the National College for

School Leadership in England charged with developing school leadership, I would suggest that any leadership development programme should address three interrelated concepts:

- the *qualities* that the potential or existing leaders bring with them when they walk through the door,
- the '*learnings*' required by leaders of learning when they return to their various leadership settings, and
- their career *trajectory*, and how it is influenced by their qualities and learning.

Qualities for leadership

What makes us unique as humans is our ability to consider and to make choices. We are not like Pavlov's salivating dog. We have the ability to shape events in our lives as opposed to being shaped by circumstances. The key word is ability. We may or may not use it – 'to embrace this ability we need tools – qualities – which allow us to free ourselves from our own psycho-drama at least long enough to consider real questions in real contexts' (Saul 2001). John Ralston Saul, Canada's foremost contemporary philosopher, has identified six interrelated 'qualities' or tools that we all possess – reason, ethics, imagination, intuition, memory and common sense.

In his book *On Equilibrium* (2001) he argues that we can learn to use each of our qualities simultaneously and effortlessly. 'We can normalize the use of them so that much of the time we hardly need to stop in order to consider.' Through these qualities we 'can shape and direct our talents and characteristics – both ours and society's'. Each of these qualities, he explains 'takes its meaning from the other – from the tension in which they exist with each other'. Isolated they can become distorted. Ethics can become unethical and reason can become unreasonable. Together and 'in equilibrium' they are powerful; isolated they become distorted into ideology. 'After all ideology is the easiest mechanism for leading the way. Why? Because it makes the large world small. And seemingly certain.'

For the most part the educational literature and management programmes focus on the primacy of reason over other ways of knowing. Not 'reason' as defined by Saul as 'thought and argument' but rather 'instrumental reason' that is concerned with form, function and measurement. This addiction to instrumental reason and rationality has created an educational environment of structures, measurements, targets and compliance. The obsession with testing, for example, in most western educational jurisdictions has distorted the purposes of effective evaluation and assessment in the learning-teaching process in the name of efficiency (Weeden, Winter and

Broadfoot 2002), and arguably, political expediency. It is just one example of instrumental reason in education gone mad. Like society's overuse of penicillin to the point that it has become less effective in treating certain viruses, testing has experienced a 'pathology of intensity' (Homer-Dixon 2001) – overuse to the point of irrationality. 'What makes instrumental reason (utilitarian, instrumental logic) so profoundly irrational is its devotion to mechanistic solutions conceived in limited time and space, as if the matter at hand were free standing. Instrumental reason is only used because we believe it to be a form of thought, when all we are dealing with is narrow logic built from within.' Reason unlimited by other qualities will become irrational because everything is related to everything else. Our central protection against irrationality, therefore, is the tension between reason and our other qualities – ethics, common sense, intuition, imagination, and memory.

Ethics: Reason unbalanced by ethics has produced holocausts, arms races and genocide (Saul 1993). Ethics answer the question, how should I live, given the context of the larger good? 'The larger good assumes the existence of the *other*, of the family, of the community, of the public good' (Saul 2001). Bishop Tutu expressed this concept well when he stated, 'I am because you are.' Even that demi-god of the political right Adam Smith said, 'The wise and virtuous man is at all times willing that his own private interest should be sacrificed to the public interest' (Smith). Ethics unbalanced by the other qualities, however, easily slip into extremism – 'good intentions are converted into misplaced certainty as to moral rectitude. This certainty convinces the holder of truth that he has the right to harm others' (Saul 2001). Ethics can lead to fanaticism when extreme ethical positions replace normal behaviour in normal times and are not balanced by reason (as thought and argument) and common sense.

Common sense is shared knowledge that carries us above self-interest. 'Shared knowledge by its very nature is a consideration of the whole. It is essentially inclusive and human.' Saul argues that there are two forms of common sense – shared knowledge within society (e.g. education is important) versus superstitions or truths (e.g. private is always superior to public) that are declared to be visible, evident and inevitable. If students are attending school, for example, they have a much better chance of learning – this is 'common sense'. Common sense is also the easiest quality to deform into nonsense – pretence of simplicity and truth can easily be presented as self-evident truth. Since the exclusion from school of some pupils makes life easier for teachers and heads, it might be argued that the exclusion is in everyone's best interest. This line of reasoning is an example of 'conventional wisdom' or at least unexamined practice that has become false common sense designed to ensure the passivity of others. Common sense unbalanced by other qualities can lead to thoughtlessness and control.

Imagination is the quality that allows us to picture a 'realistic' future because it most naturally draws all our qualities together. It protects us from premature conclusions – 'just when we think we understand it leaps ahead again into more uncertainty. And so imagination is naturally inclusive and inconclusive' (Saul 2001). 'Imagination is our primary force for progress because it is driven by ideas – incomplete, aggressive, inconclusive ideas.' Saul contends that policies can only survive if they continue to be led by ideas – by the imagination. 'The moment the direction slips into managerial logic, they begin to fall apart, because they are no longer linked directly to the reality and the collective unconscious of society.' As he explains,

> Those who believe in the dominance of understanding and method-ology seem to miss the obvious. The tools they consider marginal – those of the arts – are in fact the tools of story telling and reimagining ourselves which all humans use. And why do we use them? In order to convince ourselves that we exist as humans and as individuals in a society.
>
> (Saul 2001: 126)

Intuition is imagination in action. Great athletes, whether it is on a soccer pitch or an ice hockey arena, can intuitively anticipate where the ball or puck is *going* to be. As Saul explains, 'The offensive force is the swirling uncertainty of our imagination. Intuition is our reaction to the movement' (2001: 163). It is the basis of action that does not have the luxury of slow consideration. False intuition, however, leads to superstition by trying to turn uncertainty into certainty. 'Uncertainty is taken for normal, and the ability to embrace it as a sign of human consciousness as intelligence not fear' (2001: 211). We all possess this intuitive quality but often don't trust our instincts; yet successful leaders often have an instinctual ability to take the appropriate action at the right time.

Memory gives us the ability to shape our thinking and our actions in a balanced way. From it we grasp our context, our thoughts, our questions, our actions our lives. It is the platform from which we initiate thought – without memory there is a vacuum – propaganda thrives in a vacuum, as does ideology. 'Functioning individuals and functioning societies require the context of memory in order to shape their thinking and their actions.' Memory to the extreme, however, freezes our thoughts and actions in the past and distorts our other qualities. As Saul explains, 'A rigid memory pretends to guarantee the future by freezing that of the past.' As a result, habit can become 'a labour saving device' (Tyack and Tobin 1994) and a significant obstacle to change and improvement.

Each person who aspires to a leadership role possesses these qualities. Few leadership programmes that I am aware of overtly attempt to develop all of these qualities. The challenge for those who design leadership programmes is to engage these qualities of their potential leaders. Aspiring leaders need to contemplate the history of reform (memory), and address such ethical issues as coaching only those students who will alter a school's placement in league tables. They will need to engage their imagination in envisioning possible alternative structures to enhance learning in schools, and experience simulations that at once engage a person's intuition and common sense. Leadership development programmes must infuse opportunities to develop all of these qualities 'in equilibrium' throughout all their activities rather than perpetuating the present practice of focusing on instrumental rationality and memory to the virtual exclusion of other qualities. If these qualities are the vehicle through which we engage potential leaders in their learning, what do leaders of learning need to learn?

Learning (for leaders of learning)

I suggest that to prepare leaders for their future as leaders of learning we need to build our training programmes around a set of leaders' learnings that are not bounded by time and space. As my colleagues and I have written in a recent book:

> Leadership for learning is not a destination with fixed co-ordinates on a compass, but a journey with plenty of detours and even some dead ends. Effective educational leaders are continuously open to new learning because the journey keeps changing. Their maps are complex and can be confusing. What leaders require for this journey is a set of inter-related learnings looking at school leadership in a holistic rather than reductionist way. These learnings can be deepened, elaborated, nurtured, abandoned, and connected and related to other learnings as the journey progresses.
>
> (Stoll, Fink and Earl 2002)

We recommend the following 'learnings' for leaders as at least a starting point.

Understanding learning

To promote learning and support others' learning, leaders need to have a deep, current and critical understanding of the learning process. Not only do they need to have insight into 'deep' learning for students; but they must also have a 'deep' understanding of how adults learn if they are to support teachers' learning.

Making connections

It is leaders' role to see the entire organization and help stakeholders to view the school in a holistic way. Leaders provide coherence and make connections so others can see the interrelationships and interconnections of the many things happening in a school. The development of a school-wide perspective is an important 'learning' to promote positive change. To promote a holistic view, leaders must learn how to look at change in a multi-dimensional way – to look at change through multiple frames or lenses (Bolman and Deal 1997; Louis, Toole and Hargreaves 1999; Fink 2000).

Futures thinking

Successful leaders must also learn how to connect the past, the present and the future. Leaders' awareness and understanding of forces influencing the life of a school are crucial to shaping a school community's shared sense of vision in productive and inspiring ways. Leaders are also aware of shifting currents of local political, social and economic forces and help staff to understand the connections between and among global, national and local forces. Anticipating the future enables leaders to help colleagues act strategically rather than randomly as they journey into the future (Davies and Ellison 1999).

Contextual knowledge

Successful leaders make further connections by developing firm knowledge and understanding of their context. Context relates to the particular situation, background, or environment in which something is happening. Leaders must have strategies to analyse their contexts and respond to their unique characteristics. In addition to knowing about pupil achievement in total, they need to know how various sub-groups in the school are doing, for example, how girls compare to boys. Context-aware leaders know how the pupils, parents and staff feel about the school. They understand the deeper social context in which their school resides.

Critical thinking

What differentiates effective leaders and ineffective leaders is the quality of their judgements: whether their decisions work for the pupils in the long term. Knowing and remembering to ask the right questions depends on both wisdom and judgement (Secretan 1996). A significant part of formal leaders' job is to act as a gatekeeper, to ask the right questions, to know what initiatives to support, what to oppose and what to subvert. This questions-asking facility is a necessary 'learning' to enable leaders to help to develop a school's capacity to deal with change.

Political acumen

School leaders must represent the interests of their school with their governing bodies, community and government agencies. Politics is about power and influence, and to ignore political issues or consider that political activity is unworthy of a leader is to leave the school, its staff, pupils and parents vulnerable to competing social forces. At micro-levels, schools are filled with groups and individuals with different interests and power that occasionally lead to conflict. Leaders use political methods, such as negotiation and coalition building, to move schools towards agreed-upon goals.

Emotional understanding

To create an environment in which teachers find 'flow' (Csikszentmihalyi 1990) requires leaders with emotional understanding. Leaders with emotional understanding learn to read the emotional responses of those around them and create 'emotional engagements and bonds with and among those with whom they interact'. Andy Hargreaves (1998) explains that the emotions of educational change most commonly addressed are ones helping to defuse so-called 'resistance' to change like trust, support, involvement, commitment to teamwork and willingness to experiment. Leaders with emotional understanding do, however, lead their colleagues into uncharted territory on the change journey through the 'impassioned and critical engagement or critique' of ideas, purposes and practices.

Together these interconnected and interrelated 'learnings' exercised through the leader's inherent qualities of reason, ethics, imagination, intuition, memory and common sense provide the essence of leadership for learning regardless of career stage. These qualities, however, will interact differently as a leader's career proceeds. Similarly a leader's career stage will make some 'learnings' or applications of these 'learnings' more or less relevant to the leader.

Career trajectories

A useful way to examine career stages of leaders is through the concept of 'multiple trajectories' described by Etienne Wenger (1998) in his *Communities of Practice*. Wenger explains that,

> Developing a practice requires the formation of a community whose members can engage with one another and thus acknowledge each

other as participants. As a consequence, practice entails the negotiation of ways of being a person in that context ... the formation of a community of practice is also the negotiation of identities.

(Wenger 1998: 149)

Wenger suggests that 'our identities form in a ... kind of tension between our investment in various forms of belonging and our ability to negotiate the meanings that matter in those contexts'. Identity formation is the result of the interplay between one's *identification* with a community of practice and one's ability to *negotiate* meaning within that community. The capacity of school heads for example to identify with their schools (and the schools' staffs to identify with them) and their ability to negotiate a shared sense of meaning of the schools' directions affect the heads' trajectories and therefore their identities in relationship to their schools as 'communities of practice'. Identity is a 'constant becoming' and we 'constantly renegotiate through the course of our lives'. He identifies five different but interacting trajectories that apply to existing and potential leaders:

'Inbound' trajectories refer to individuals who join a community with the 'prospect of becoming full participants in its practice'. Their engagement may be peripheral in the beginning but in time they expect to be an 'insider'. This trajectory begs the question of what type of experience potential leaders require. In Ontario, deputy heads are usually expected to have experiences as a deputy in two or three different types of schools before they are promoted to a headship. This leads to deputies always being on the periphery of 'communities of practice', but this procedure does provide a breadth of experience in their 'inbound trajectory'.

'Peripheral' trajectories may never lead to full participation but are significant to one's identity. Ontario deputy heads fit this trajectory and only become part of a community of practice when they are established as heads. Even when they move into new settings as the head, they will spend a considerable amount of time on a peripheral trajectory. The larger the school the more difficult it is to identify with and negotiate into a community of practice. Even leaders who are promoted from within a school must renegotiate their new role within the existing community. This suggests that leaders will need to learn entry strategies that provide them with an understanding of their new context before they can become an influential part of it. One of the problems of rapid turnover of leaders is that school staff learn to recognize this impermanence and tend to exclude them from full participation in the school as a community of practice.

Insider trajectories grow and develop over time, as one becomes a full member of a community. It is from within a community of practice that leaders are at their most effective. The accepted wisdom in many North American jurisdictions is that heads lose their effectiveness after their seventh or eighth year in a school. It is for this reason that heads in both the US and Canada are routinely moved to new settings. This practice is not without its critics, especially in turbulent times (MacMillan 2000; Hargreaves et al. 2002). The question remains however – how can serving heads continue to learn and to grow as leaders? How can training institutions enhance the qualities and 'learnings' of incumbent heads and deputies? New events, practices and people are certainly occasions for renegotiating one's identity but in a climate in which schools are judged almost solely on test scores, there appears to be little incentive in schools with higher achieving students other than the leader's personal pride to continue to grow professionally. The most common complaint I hear from advisory staff is that they find it very difficult to engage the leaders of what Louise Stoll and I have called 'cruising' schools (Stoll and Fink 1996). These are schools that appear effective because of the quality of their student intake but have a limited capacity for growth and development.

Boundary trajectories develop as one spans and links various communities of practice. Consultants, advisors or senior officials of an LEA would develop their identities as they move from school to school. Similarly, special education teachers within schools often are 'network' leaders because they can cross boundaries that senior managers and department heads cannot traverse (Senge et al. 2001). School districts in North America base their policy of regularly rotating principals and assistant principals from school to school on the need for their leaders to span boundaries to gain a system's perspective. How do potential leaders learn the 'big' picture? Are there alternate routes to school leadership? Is leadership experience necessary before one becomes a teacher of potential leaders? Boundary trajectories are linked closely to inbound trajectories.

Outbound trajectories apply to those who plan or expect to move out of a community at some point. Their participation in one community is built on where they are going next. In some cases, leaders move to new settings and their outbound trajectory becomes part of the inbound trajectory in the new setting. For others they are departing school leadership permanently and in increasing numbers. Leaders on an outbound trajectory need to consider their leadership legacy and attend to issues of sustainability of educational change (Hargreaves and Fink 2003).

The essence then of a highly effective leadership development model is the ability to combine meaningfully the inherent *qualities* that all people possess with the '*learnings*' required for leaders of learning, and to apply them to fit the potential leader's *trajectory*. This requires a succession planning approach that systemically connects the identification, recruitment, preparation, induction and ongoing support of school leaders over time. The very clear picture in education is that most leadership preparation programmes are disjointed, episodic and geared very much to the delivery of the educational model propounded by the government of the day (Bush and Jackson 2002). Our best models come from those few businesses that have thought deeply about the problem of replacing the 'baby boom' generation of leaders.

Succession planning

With the impending retirements of 40 to 50 per cent of the existing leaders in the private sector, business leaders have identified leadership succession as a crucial problem that needs to be urgently addressed. Early retirements, downsizing and reorganizations have created critical shortages of middle and top leaders in the business community for the immediate future (Byham 2001). To attend to this pending problem, business observers contend that organizations must embark on systemic succession planning programmes to replace the departing leaders (Liebman, Bruer and Maki 1996; Schall 1997; National Academy of Public Administration 1997). While various authors emphasize different aspects of succession planning, there appears to be considerable agreement on the need to connect goal setting, recruitment, development, accountability practices and leadership succession. Rather than 'polishing yesterday's paradigm' (Peters 1999) they define leadership roles flexibly in terms of what will be required in the future rather than limit role descriptions to existing competencies.

Educators have much to learn from the practices of the more forward-looking businesses. The best businesses make connections among the various parts of its organization and their functions and practices. Educational systems tend to be very loosely coupled and can learn from some businesses to connect their goal setting, recruitment, development, accountability practices and succession plans. As I have argued throughout this chapter, school systems, like progressive companies, can define leadership roles flexibly in terms of what will be required in the future rather than limit role descriptions to existing competencies (Stoll, Fink and Earl 2002). The involvement of senior political and policy leaders in the processes of succession planning is as important in school jurisdictions as in private businesses. Perhaps the most significant finding from the business literature is that the succession plan must be 'tailored to the organization's unique needs, culture and history: there are no quick fixes' (Souque 1998).

While there is a great deal to learn about succession planning from the business community, it would be foolish to adopt business practices uncritically. Most succession plans in the business community are top-down, linear, managerial, and generally 'technicist' exercises that are long on paper but seemingly short on human interactions. One clear lesson from the best of the business community is that successful succession plans require the availability of the personnel to develop a succession plan and the time and money to recruit effectively, provide the development opportunities and ensure the effective accountability procedures necessary to make the plan work.

In the face of a growing leadership crisis in education, and the increasingly urgent demands for school improvement, students and their parents deserve (and schools of tomorrow will demand) leaders of learning in every school. Rather than searching for a template of best practices, this chapter has suggested that agents and agencies devoted to leadership development must focus their attentions on identifying, recruiting, and selecting leaders based on their potential to become 'leaders of learning', rather than recycling existing practices based on lists of proficiencies. They will also need to design their processes for the training, induction and on-going development of leaders to engage the innate qualities of potential leaders – reason, ethics, imagination, intuition, common sense and memory – as fully and imaginatively as possible. Moreover, leadership preparation must connect these processes to the career trajectory of each potential or practising leader. It is becoming increasingly clear that coercion, mandates and oppressive accountability schemes have failed to enhance the learning of students in meaningful ways and that educational change takes place school by school. In my view, the last best hope for school growth and development, now and in the future, is the creation of 'communities of learners' in each school, led by dynamic, dedicated and creative 'leaders of learning'.

Bibliography

Alix, N.M. (2000) Transformational leadership: Democratic or despotic, *Educational Management and Administration*, 28(1): 7–20.

Bass, B.M. (1985) *Leadership & Performance Beyond Expectations*. New York: The Free Press.

Bennis, W. and Nanus, B. (1985) *Leaders*. New York: Harper & Row.

Blasé, J. and Blasé, J. (1999) Shared governance principals: The inner experience, *NASSP Bulletin*, 83(606): 81–93.

Block, P. (1993) *Stewardship: Choosing service over self Interest*. San Francisco: Berrett Kohler.

Bolman, L.G. and Deal, T.E. (1991) *Reframing Organizations: Artistry, choice and leadership*. San Francisco: Jossey-Bass.

Burns, J.M. (1978) *Leadership*. New York: Harper & Row.

Bush, T. and Jackson, D. (2002) A preparation for school leadership: An international perspective, *Educational Management and Administration*, 30(4): 417–29.

Byham, W.C. (2001) Grooming next-millennium leaders, *Society for Human Resources*, www.shrm.org/articles.

Caldwell, B.J. (1998) Strategic leadership, resource management and effective school reform, *Journal of Educational Administration*, 36(5): 445–61.

Copland, M.A. (2001) The myth of super principal, *Phi Delta Kappan*, 82(7): 528–33.

Csikszenmihalyi, M. (1990) *Flow: The psychology of optimal experience*. New York: Harper & Row.

Davies, B. and Ellison, L. (1999) *Strategic Development and Direction of the School*. London: Routledge.

Davidson, B.M. and Taylor, D.L. (1999) The effects of principal succession in an accelerated school. Paper presented at the annual meeting of the American Educational Research Association. San Diego CA, April 13–17.

Deal, T.E. and Peterson, K. (1994) *The Leadership Paradox: Balancing logic and artistry in schools*. San Francisco: Jossey-Bass.

Delors, J., Al Mufti, I., Amagi, A., Carneiro, R., Chung, F., Geremek, B., Gorham, W., Kornhauser, A., Manley, M., Padrón Quero, M., Savané, M-A., Singh, K., Stavenhagen, R., Suhr, M.W. and Nanzhao, Z. (1996) *Learning: the Treasure within – Report to UNESCO of the International Commission on Education for the Twenty-first Century*. Paris: UNESCO.

Earley, P., Evans, J., Collarbone, P., Gold, A. and Halpin, D. (2002) *Establishing the Current State of School Leadership In England: Research report No. 336*. London: Department for Education and Skills.

Elmore, R.F. (2000) *Building a New Structure for School Leadership*. Washington DC: Albert Shanker Institute.

Fink, D. (2000) *Good Schools/Real Schools: Why school reform doesn't last*. New York: Teachers' College Press.

Fullan, M. (1993) *Change Forces: Probing the depths of educational reform*. London: Falmer Press.

Gronn, P. (1996) From transactions to transformations: A new world order in the study of leadership, *Educational Management and Administration*, 24(1): 7–30.

Hargreaves, A. (2003) *Teaching in the Knowledge Society: Education in the age of insecurity*. New York: Teachers' College Press.

Hargreaves, A. (1994) *Changing Teachers, Changing Times: Teachers work and culture in the postmodern age*. Toronto: The Ontario Institute for Studies of Education of the University of Toronto.

Hargreaves, A. (1998) The emotional politics of teaching and teacher development: Implications for leadership, *International Journal of Leadership in Education*, 1(4): 315–36.

Hargreaves, A., Shaw, P., Fink, D., Giles, C., Moore, S. (2002) *Secondary School Reform: The experiences and interpretations of teachers and administrators in six Ontario schools*. Toronto: Ontario Institute for Studies in Education/University of Toronto.

Hargreaves, A., Shaw, P., Fink, D., Retallick, J., Giles, C., Moore, S., Schmidt, M.

and James-Wilson, S. (2000) *Change Frames: Supporting secondary teachers in interpreting and integrating Secondary School Reform*. Toronto: Ontario Institute for Studies in Education/University of Toronto.

Hargreaves, A. and Fink, D. (2003) Sustaining leadership. In Davies, B. and West-Burnham, J. *Handbook of Educational Leadership and Management*. London: Pearson Education.

Hargreaves, A. and Fink, D. (2000) The three dimensions of educational reform, *Educational Leadership*, 57(7): 30–4.

House, R.J. and Shamir, B. (1993) Towards the integration of transformational, charismatic, and visionary theories. In Chemers, M. M. and Ayman R. (eds) *Leadership Theory and Research Perspectives and Directions*. San Diego CA: Academic Press: 81–107.

Homer-Dixon, T. (2000) *The Ingenuity Gap: Can we solve the problems of the future?* Toronto: Alfred A. Knopf.

Liebman, M, Bruer R.A., and Maki, B.R. (1996) Succession management: The next generation of succession planning, *Human Resource Planning*, 19(3): 16–29.

Leithwood, K.A., Jantzi, D., and Steinbach, R. (1999) *Changing Leadership for Changing Times*. Buckingham: Open University Press.

Leithwood, K. (1992). The move towards transformational leadership. *Educational leadership*, 49(5): 8–12.

Lemley, R. (1997) Thoughts on a richer view of principals' development, NASSP Bulletin, 81(585): 33–7.

Louis, K., Toole, J. and Hargreaves, A. (1999) Rethinking school improvement. In Louis, K., Toole, J., and Hargreaves, A. (eds), *Handbook in Research in Education Administration* 251–76, New York: Longman.

Louis, K.S. and Miles, M.B. (1990) *Improving the Urban High School: What works and why*. New York: Teachers' College Press.

Macmillan, R. (2000) Leadership succession, culture of teaching, and educational change. In Bascia, N. and Hargreaves, A. (eds), *The Sharp Edge of Educational Change*. London: Falmer Press.

Mansell, N. (2002) New heads frightened by top job, *Times Educational Supplement*, September 13: 7.

Morrison, K. (2002) *School Leadership and Complexity Theory*. London: Routledge/Falmer.

National Academy of Public Administration (1997) *Managing Succession and Developing Leadership: Growing the next generation of public service leaders*. Washington DC: NAPA.

Peters, T. (1999) *The Circle of Innovation: You can't shrink your way to greatness*. New York: Vintage.

Pitcher, P. (1997) *The Drama of Leadership: Artists, craftsmen and technocrats*. New York/Chichester: Wiley.

Purkey, W.W. and Novak, J. (1984) *Inviting School Success*, 2nd edn. Belmont CA: Wadsworth.

Riley, K. (2000) Leadership, learning and systemic change, *Journal of Educational Change*, 1(1): 57–75.

Rothwell, W.J. (2001) *Effective Succession Planning: Ensuring leadership continuity and building talent from within*, 2nd edn. New York: AMACOM.

Sammons, P, Mortimore, P. and Hillman, J. (1995) *Key Characteristics of Effective Schools: A review of school effectiveness research*. London: Office for Standards in Education.

Saul, J.R. (2001) *On Equilibrium*. Toronto: Penguin/Viking.

Saul, J.R. (1993) *Voltaire's Bastards: The dictatorship of reason in the West*. Harmondsworth: Penguin.

Schall, E. (1997) Public sector succession: A strategic approach to sustaining innovation, *Public Administration Review*, 57(1): 4–10.

Secretan, L. (1996) *Reclaiming the Higher Ground: Creating organizations that inspire the soul*. Toronto: Macmillan.

Senge, P., Kleiner, A., Roberts, C., Ross R., Roth, G. and Smith B. (1999) *The Dance of Change*. New York: Doubleday.

Sergiovanni, T. (1992a) *Schools as Moral Communities*. San Francisco: Jossey-Bass.

Sergiovanni, T. (1992b) *Moral Leadership*. San Francisco: Jossey-Bass.

Sergiovanni, T. and Starratt, R. (1988) *Supervision: Human perspectives*, 4th edn. New York: McGraw-Hill.

Smith, A. (1984) *The Theory of Moral Sentiments*. Indianapolis: Liberty Fund.

Smith, W.F. and Andrews, R.L. (1989) *Instructional Leadership: How principals make a difference*. Alexandria VA: Association for Supervision and Curriculum Development.

Souque, J.P. (1998) *Succession Planning and Leadership Development*. Ottawa ON: Conference Board of Canada.

Spillane, J.P., Halverson, R. and Drummond, J.B. (2001) Investigating school leadership practice: A distributed perspective, *Educational Researcher*, 30(3), 23–8.

Stacey, R. (1995) *Managing Chaos*. London: Kogan Page.

Starratt, R.J. (1993) *The Drama of Leadership*. London: Falmer.

Supovitz, J.A. (2000) Manage less: Lead more, *Principal Leadership*, 1(3): 14–19.

Stoll, L., Fink, D. and Earl, L., (2002) *It's About Learning (and It's About Time)*. London: Routledge/Falmer.

Stoll, L. and Fink, D. (1996) *Changing Our Schools. Linking school effectiveness and school improvement*. Buckingham: Open University Press.

Takahashi, S.S. (1998) The Keeper of the house: Principal succession and the mending of the hearts. Paper presented at the annual meeting of the American Educational Research Association, San Diego CA, April 13–17.

Tyack, D. and Tobin, W. (1994) The Grammar of Schooling: why has it been so hard to change? *American Educational Research Journal*, 31(3), Fall, 453–80.

Wheatley, M. (1994) *Leadership and the New Science*. San Francisco: Berrett-Koehler.

Whitaker, K.S. (1999) Principal role changes and implications for Principalship candidates, *International Journal of Educational Reform*, 8(4), 352–62.

Weeden, P., Winter, J. and Broadfoot, P. (2002) *Assessment: What's in it for schools*. London: Routledge/Falmer.

Wenger, E. (1998) *Communities of Practice*. Cambridge: Cambridge University Press.

Wonycott-Kytle, A.M. and Bogotch, I. E. (1997) Reculturing: assumptions, beliefs, and values underlying the processes of restructuring, *Journal of School Leadership*, 7(1), 27–49.

two

Developing leadership for succession

Andy Hargreaves

Introduction

The Emperor Caligula murdered half his children. England's ageing Queen will not cede the throne to her eldest child. Saturn ate his own son. What do all these people have in common? They refuse to face the facts of leadership succession.

No leader lasts forever. Few things are more tragic than leaders clinging grimly to power when their glory days are behind them. The best time for leaders to leave is when they are at the top of their game. And it is best for everyone else when capable successors have been prepared to follow them.

The prospect of leadership succession is a challenge to any leader's psyche and a source of struggle in his or her soul. It is the last challenge of leadership, and in many ways also the most difficult. There is a dark corner in most of us that secretly wants our own leadership achievements never to be surpassed; that hopes our successors will be a little less brilliant, not quite so well loved as ourselves. Moral leadership does not deny these feelings but rises above them to serve the good of all, long after we have gone.

One of the most significant events in the life of a school is a change in its leadership. Yet few things in education succeed less than leadership succession. Failure to care for leadership succession is sometimes a result of manipulativeness or self-centeredness; but more often it is oversight, neglect or the pressures of crisis management that are to blame.

In part, we mismanage succession because our most basic assumptions about leadership are flawed. People tend to equate leadership with administratively senior individuals (Leithwood, Jantzi and Steinbach 1999). Heroic leaders who turn failing schools around stand out most strongly in the public imagination. Transformational leaders rather than transformational leadership get the greatest attention in leadership research (Gronn 1996). The important idea of distributed leadership is starting to draw more attention to how leadership also spreads across organizations, without diminishing the importance of the principal's role within this overall distribution (Crowther, Kaagan, Ferguson and Hann 2002; Spillane and Halverson 2001). Yet leadership also exerts itself over time as well as across space.

Principals' and headteachers' (from now on I will use the word 'principals') impact on their schools is greatly influenced by people they have often never met – those who have died, or moved on to other institutions, or not yet even arrived. These are principals' predecessors and successors; principals of the school's past, and principals who have yet to come. Whether they are aware of it or not, principals stand on the shoulders of those who went before them and lay the foundation for those who will follow. Sustainable improvement that matters and lasts depends on understanding and managing this process of leading over time (Hargreaves and Fink 2003).

Reformers and change experts rarely grasp the long-term aspects of leadership. Quick-fix changes to turn around failing schools often exhaust the teachers or the principal and the improvement efforts are not sustained over time. The principal's success in a turnaround school may lead to his or her own rapid promotion, then regression among teachers who feel abandoned by their leader or relieved when the pressure is off.

Sustainable improvement and the contribution of principals to it must be measured over many years and several principalships, not just one or two. What legacy do principals leave on their departure? What capacities have they created among students, community and staff that will live beyond them? How can and should others build on what has been achieved? These questions of leadership over time are the central questions of leadership succession.

Few people in education are more aware of the impact of leadership succession than teachers. A leadership succession event is a highly emotionally charged one. There may be grieving for well-loved leaders who have retired or died, feelings of abandonment regarding leaders who are being promoted and moving on, or relief when teachers are finally rid of principals who are self-serving, controlling or incompetent. Incoming principals may be viewed as threats to a comfortable school culture, or as saviours of ones that are toxic. Whatever the response, leadership succession events are crucial to the ongoing success of the school.

Increasingly, leadership succession is more than just an episodic event: it is a regular and recurring part of school life. In the past decade, school districts have become increasingly demanding about assigning, replacing and sometimes rotating their school principals. The rapid demographic turnover of leaders due to the boomer generation retiring, the rush to early retirement precipitated by standardized reform pressures, and increasing pressures on school districts to bring about rapid improvement in underperforming schools are creating heightened instability in school leadership (Administrators 2001; Reform 2002).

Teachers develop long-term responses to these repeated successions. For them, successive successions feel more like a procession. These teachers may develop cynicism towards change efforts, devise strategies to wait their principals out, exploit changes of direction for their own ends, or become determined to survive a poor principalship in the belief that a better one will soon follow (MacMillan 2000). Leadership succession today is not just a temporary episodic problem in individual schools, but a pervasive crisis in the system. How should we address it? How can it be fixed?

Several colleagues and I have been investigating leadership succession as part of a Spencer Foundation funded study of *Change Over Time?* in eight US and Canadian high schools (Hargreaves, Fink, Moore, Brayman and White 2003). The database for this study includes over 250 interviews with teachers and administrators who worked in these schools in the 1970s, 80s and 90s. One of the five most significant changes affecting the life of a school and the sustainability or not of its improvement efforts over these three decades, we found, is leadership succession. Our results show that successful succession depends on sound succession planning, on the successful employment of *outbound* and not just *inbound* leadership knowledge, on limiting the frequency of succession events, and on preserving the idea of leadership in the face of movements towards more and more management. Let's look at each of these in turn.

Succession planning

A central issue in leadership succession is whether a transition in leadership establishes continuity or provokes *discontinuity* with past directions – and how far this is deliberately planned. The intersection of these different possibilities creates four cells of leadership succession (Figure 2.1).

Planned continuity occurs when the assignment of a new principal to a school reflects a well-thought-out succession plan that is meant to sustain and build further on the general directions and goals of his or her predecessor. Sustained school improvement over long periods and across multiple leaders depends on a lot of carefully planned continuity.

The most successful instances of planned continuity in our research were in the three purpose-built innovative schools in our sample, when insiders were groomed to follow their leader's footsteps as they tried to embed achievements more firmly within the culture of the school.

	Continuity	Discontinuity
Planned (purposeful)	Planned continuity	Planned discontinuity
Unplanned (accidental/ unintentional)	Unplanned continuity	Unplanned discontinuity

Figure 2.1 Planning and continuity

Blue Mountain School was explicitly established as a learning organization in 1994. Its principal realized that the first crisis for an innovative school is when the founding principal leaves (Sarason 1972). Ben McMaster therefore planned for his own successor from the outset. He anticipated his own departure by 'working hard' to create a school structure of professional learning teams and student councils that would perpetuate his devotion to the idea of a 'learning community' when he eventually left the school. While McMaster's imprint was everywhere – in the school's philosophy, organization, design and culture – he was very alert to the threats posed by the possibility of an ensuing principal importing a significantly different philosophy. He therefore canvassed the district to ensure he could groom a successor who would understand and be committed to the school's distinctive mission and be able to maintain its momentum. After four years, the district did in fact move him to a larger 'high profile' school in the district and promoted his assistant principal, Linda White, to replace him.

White continued to stress Blue Mountain's emphasis on relationships. She and her leadership team were described by many of the staff as 'wonderful', 'supportive', 'spectacular' and 'amazing' people who were 'still teachers at heart'. She was highly valued as being 'very caring', and as someone who recognized that 'family comes first'. White worked hard to be open and accessible as she dedicated herself to maintaining the originating philosophy of the school.

> Before [McMaster] was moved to another school we talked and we talked about how we could preserve the direction that this school was moving in. We were afraid that if a new administrator came in as a

principal that if he or she had a different philosophy, a different set of beliefs, then it would be quite easy to simply move things in that particular direction and we didn't want that to happen.

As principal, she stated that, 'I'm on the same road and any detours I take will only be for a few moments in the overall scheme of things before I come back onto the main road again.' Unlike the founding principal who had stressed the creation of new values, she emphasized the preservation of existing ones.

Planned continuity occurred only in our most innovative schools, and even there only in the case of isolated transitions rather than all successions. More usually, leadership successions were planned and intended to create discontinuity so as to move a school in strikingly different directions than under its predecessors. A new principal assigned to turn around a failing school, to give a jolt to a 'cruising' school (Stoll and Fink 1996), or to implement a 'top-down' reform agenda, all fit this category. Several leadership succession events in the Spencer project schools were ones of *planned discontinuity*. They represented efforts to get traditional schools that were resting on their laurels, or drifting a little, to meet their students' needs more effectively.

Bill Andrews was appointed to Stewart Heights Secondary School in 1998. Once a small district school serving a white, middle-class suburban and rural population, Stewart Heights was now surrounded by urban development and reflected the increasing cultural diversity of the region. The students were changing but the stable and long-serving staff stayed the same, pining nostalgically for the days when they had been a small 'village' school.

Bill Andrews' predecessor who had led the school for a decade since 1988, confessed that,

> One of the difficulties I found for my personal approach to leadership was that I didn't have a particular direction or goal for my school. I simply wanted to facilitate the relationship between teachers and students, and I thought my job was to take as much of the administrivia and annoyance and pressure from outside sources off the teachers so that they could work effectively with kids.

A policeman's son, Andrews was a tall, commanding and self-confident figure. His wide experience and extensive knowledge of the larger school district through two former principalships and time in the district office allowed him to move confidently, quickly and energetically to shake the school out of what he viewed as its historical lethargy.

Andrews articulated firm expectations for staff performance and student behaviour and showed them that change was possible. When guidance personnel complained that student schedules could not be completed in time for the beginning of school, Andrews personally attended to the timetables of the more than 80 affected students and demonstrated that their problems were, and from then on would be, soluble. He aggressively addressed management and building issues, making public spaces more welcoming for students and the community, and gradually mobilized the staff behind a coherent set of school goals. He was not reluctant to initiate, preside over and engage in the rough and tumble of difficult and lively staffroom debate. For example, to heighten staff awareness of student needs, he presented teachers with survey data showing that 95 per cent of staff was satisfied with the school even though only 35 per cent of students and 25 per cent of parents were. This created a common problem that staff had to solve together. An experienced teacher explained,

> He's brought a willingness to think about kids, to do things for kids and to make kids look good, as opposed to managing the status quo. And I think for a long time, this school had a good reputation . . . and so it just went along. In the meantime, its reputation in the community kind of went away, but nobody within this building really realized it. I think with the principal's arrival, he knew the problems, and he set out to deal with them and to make changes and I think, you know for the most part, it's been good.

Andrews ruffled quite a few feathers, however. 'I think he has ideas of where he wants to go and I think he's going to, but his overall style is almost an imposing kind of thing that will be — 'this is how it will be.' '[He has been] insisting that there's certain things he has to do because this is his mandate from the district.' 'He's a change agent and an instigator, but it sometimes is decreed to be done.'

Andrews pushed the school a long way forward during his brief tenure. Parent and student satisfaction levels soared. Plants and benches began to make the school feel less like a factory and more like a community. The School Improvement Team steamed ahead in its efforts to gain staff support for improving student learning. In this school and others like it, planned discontinuity served its intended purpose of bringing about much needed change.

Planned discontinuity was effective in shaking up schools in our study, but not in making changes stick. This succession strategy can yield rapid results but its leadership needs time to consolidate the new culture and heal the wounds that its disruption inevitably creates. Yet, because of his quick and visible success, Bill Andrews was lifted out of his school too early, after less than three years, to take up a promotion in the district office. Other leaders of planned discontinuity in our study were also transferred to struggling schools elsewhere that urgently needed their skills, long before their existing work had been completed. The result was a constant cycling of change throughout schools in the system, but little lasting improvement in any one of them.

In reality, most cases of succession therefore ended up being a paradoxical mix of *unplanned continuity and discontinuity*: discontinuity with the achievements of a leader's immediate predecessor, and continuity with (or regression to) the more mediocre state of affairs preceding that predecessor. In this carousel of principal succession, successful leaders are often lifted suddenly and prematurely out of the saddle of the school they are improving, in order to mount a rescue act in a school facing a crisis or a challenge elsewhere. Much less thought seems to be given to the appointment of their successors.

Charmaine Watson was appointed as the first-ever principal of Talisman Park collegiate high school in 1995. Situated in an affluent, well-established neighbourhood, and with an 80-year tradition, Talisman Park saw its mission as preparing students for post-secondary education. More than 70 per cent of its graduates were accepted into universities and colleges. Over the previous decade like Stewart Heights, Talisman Park's largely middle-class, white, Anglo-Saxon student population had become more racially and ethnically diverse. Watson's predecessor, Bill Andrews (who later reappeared in Stewart Heights after his spell in the district office), had already pushed Talisman Park's teachers to confront school change by advocating an inclusive approach to planning and problem-solving and by involving students in the process. Just as at Stewart Heights, teachers either loved Andrews because of his unwavering dedication to students or hated him because he seemed to play favourites among the staff.

When Andrews was suddenly transferred to the district office for personal reasons in 1995, Charmaine Watson was rushed in to replace him. Watson had little opportunity to interact with Andrews or the staff before assuming her new role. Having taught at Talisman Park earlier in her career, Watson understood the school's history and culture. Though widely seen as being caring and supportive by many staff, she did not hesitate to try and change this culture so it would benefit all students in the school.

Watson set out to democratize the school by taking major decisions to the staff as a whole, rather than depending on the previously powerful heads of department. Distributing leadership beyond existing formal structures, she initiated a whole-school strategic plan that focused on improving assessment strategies for student work and engaging students in instructional technology. Watson participated with staff in professional development activities and encouraged teachers to diversify their teaching to meet the changing nature and needs of the school's students. She also initiated a strategic plan that involved parents and others in the Talisman Park community and she engaged them in developing the purposes of the school.

After four years in the school, most staff members appeared to be supportive of Watson's approach, or at least willing to go along. In spite of her best efforts, however, a small but influential element of long-serving staff resisted her initiatives. Several were part of an embittered 'coffee circle' of influential teachers who met every morning before school to cast scorn on the government's latest reform initiatives, and undermine cross-department improvement efforts in the school.

While Watson presented a strong personal presence in the school, she was therefore only partly successful in her attempt to instil her vision of an inclusive learning community. Even though she had the credibility of teaching at Talisman Park during its 'glory' years, and was seen by most staff as a caring and capable leader, dissenting teachers did not want to share their difficulties with her because they did not want to upset her. Watson had not yet become an insider.

Unfortunately, Watson would never get the chance to lead from the inside out – to sail the school, steering from the stern rather than driving the school from the front as she had during most of her comparatively brief tenure (Hopkins 1992). In 1998, in response to a number of unexpected retirements among its school leaders, after schools had adjourned for the summer break, the district abruptly (and from Watson's point of view, traumatically) transferred her to a school that was experiencing serious leadership problems.

The district replaced Watson with Ivor Megson, a former assistant principal at the school. Megson's arrival coincided with significant government reforms impacting on teachers with full force. Megson's style was more managerial than Watson's. The sheer pressure of government reform initiatives and teachers' resentment towards them also forced him to move away from the school's reculturing programme that Watson and Andrews had each made their priority. Megson had to fall back on the traditionally influential department head's group to implement the reform agenda. Having once been closer to staff as their assistant principal, he tried to buffer them from the deluge of reforms. For instance, in response to the newly initiated, high-stakes, Grade 10 literacy test, Megson and his staff developed the short-term strategy of focusing their remedial efforts on students who came close to meeting the provincial norms. While this boosted overall student achievement scores and gained a higher ranking for the school, teachers had less time and energy to devote to those students most in need of intensive literacy support. All the results of the reculturing work that Andrews and Watson had begun to achieve over the past eight years were undone in a matter of months.

At about the same time, back at Stewart Heights, another first-time principal, Jerry West was rapidly promoted in mid-term to replace his take-charge predecessor, Andrews, who had been catapulted upwards into a superintendency. Facing a school that had experienced three principals in four and a half years, and an escalating government reform agenda, West had no time to establish himself as a leader and little opportunity to acquire knowledge about the school or his new role from other sources. His response was to make no changes in his first semester and to build relationships one at a time. Though understandable within an evolutionary climate of improvement, in a time of imposed change, this response led instead to a climate of apparent inertia and drifting. Just as in Talisman Park, departmental power structures reasserted themselves to fill the void, and staff on the School Climate Committee set about correcting student behaviour rather than continuing Andrews' commitment to whole-school change.

West's promotion occurred at the same time as the pressure to implement the government standards agenda was at its peak. As he stated,

> Sometimes the rules change, day by day by day in terms of what we can and can't do. As we were making our own changes, moving forward in the direction that we believed we need to go, other changes and outside pressures have been imposed on us as well. So things that you want to do have to take a back seat sometimes and that can be quite frustrating.

The take-charge style of Andrews, West's predecessor, had propelled significant progress in Stewart Heights' improvement. Undoubtedly, he irritated and sometimes alienated a faction of the staff, but the force of his leadership and personality kept pushing them forward. With more time, as the school achieved its goals, these cracks could have been filled and the school could have been pulled together. But Andrews' short tenure and premature replacement left his mission truncated, and the cracks he had opened widened into chasms when he left. The movement towards a school-wide learning community that Andrews had initiated now fragmented into a number of micro-political units that reasserted their traditional power. Rapid rotation of leadership, poor succession planning and the onset of an overwhelming and under-supported reform agenda, undermined two years of considerable improvement. After just three years, West himself was moved on to another school. Three days into his new principalship, he was committed to hospital with a suspected mental breakdown.

Successful planned continuity or discontinuity are the scarce commodities of educational leadership. This is part of a wider pattern in which succession planning in the public sector tends to be much less effective than in the corporate world. The corporate world tends to proactively recruit and encourage potential leaders in a formal process of long-term planning for future leadership capacities. By contrast, the public sector handles succession more informally to replace existing roles in the short term as a reaction to illnesses, promotions or other events (Jackson 2000).

On our evidence, leadership succession in schools is too often spoiled by poor planning. Succession plans either go awry, or there is no real planning at all. Recent success is discontinued, improvement gains are eliminated and continuity is re-established with earlier, more mediocre patterns. When the leadership pool is not consistently excellent, a common belief among school district administrators is that improvement goals can be achieved by moving the scarce pool of truly outstanding principals around a district, and replacing them in the schools they leave behind with the residue of less experienced or less effective leaders who will at least be able to maintain the gains that have already been made. The evidence from our schools is that, in most instances, these panic appointments and rotational practices are based on fantasies and fallacies of leadership and improvement. Principal rotation and repeated successions do not push schools along an upward curve of improvement but around a perpetual carousel in which all of them move up and down with depressing regularity.

Jurisdictions may not always rotate their leaders on a regular basis in this way. England has an open market of school leaders, for instance. But difficult urban schools, especially ones that are failing or underperforming, also tend to encounter similar patterns of rapid leadership turnover.

There is clearly a need for better succession planning in schools and school districts with adequate forewarning and proper time to prepare. Districts could begin by requiring succession issues and needs to be incorporated into every school improvement plan. There is also a compelling need for stronger and deeper leadership cultures within school districts of widespread talent that will make planning, selection, matching and rotation easier and more effective. Yet poor planning is not the only source of succession problems. Three other issues are also important – leaders' knowledge of improvement and succession processes, frequency and rates of succession, and the changing nature of leadership in times of large-scale reform.

Inbound and outbound knowledge

Etienne Wenger (Wenger 1998) describes several kinds of 'trajectories' that leaders can take as they move through their organization – these include *inbound, insider* and *outbound* trajectories. Drawing on Wenger's work, we have found that leaders and their systems in our study used three kinds of knowledge during the succession process.

Inbound knowledge is knowledge of leadership or of a particular school that is needed to change it, make one's mark on it, or turn it around. *Insider knowledge* is the knowledge one gains from and exercises with other members of the community to improve the school after becoming known, trusted and accepted by them. *Outbound knowledge* is what is needed to preserve past successes, keep improvement going, and leave a legacy after one has left.

Our research data show that schools and school systems are preoccupied with *inbound knowledge* – with initiating and imposing changes more than looking back and consolidating existing ones. This pattern is especially common among charismatic leaders. Lord Byron secondary school was established as one of the most innovative schools in Canada in 1974. A charismatic principal, Ward Bond, was appointed to set its distinctive direction. Bond's adoring teachers acknowledged that he was a 'hard act to follow' and, when he left after just three years, his lesser successors could never quite live up to this legend and the school began a long process of 'attrition of change' (Fink 1999). Mike Arness, a past principal of Talisman Park, possessed some of Bond's charismatic qualities. When he left his school, he took not only his charisma with him but also many of his key middle level leaders as well. Charismatic leaders get their staff members to believe in the leader's own mystical qualities rather than believing in themselves. These leaders' inbound knowledge can inspire great change in a school but cannot sustain it after they have gone.

Inbound knowledge is also overemphasized in circumstances of planned discontinuity. Andrews and Watson at Stewart Heights and Talisman Park fulfilled their district's inbound faith that they could turn their 'cruising' school around. But their district did not allow them to remain long enough to solidify a new culture and embed their improvements in it. In the most recent years covered by our work, almost no principal stayed long enough (at least five years) to acquire the status of trusted insider.

'Failing' schools are also prone to quick-fix obsessions with inbound knowledge. Sheldon School, in New York State, is currently faced with being designated as 'in need of improvement' under *No Child Left Behind* legislation. Once known as the 'jewel' of its urban district, Sheldon went into decades of decline due to the impact of race riots in the 1970s, subsequent 'white and bright flight' to the suburbs, the ensuing establishment of a magnet school that took Sheldon's best students from it, and the loss of its connection to its local community when the magnet initiative closed a school on the opposite side of the city and some of its most difficult students were bussed into Sheldon (Baker and Foote, in press).

One of Sheldon's earlier principals, in the school's better days, Len Adomo, was regarded as energetic, but also quite autocratic. His attitude was that 'I'm the boss and I'm going to decide how to do things.' Blocked from involvement in decisions that affected their lives, teachers increasingly turned to their union as an outlet for their frustrations and leadership impulses. The more fractious the union became, the more Adomo 'dug in'. As one teacher recalled, 'Len Adomo likes to fight with the union.' Unwilling to negotiate or compromise, virtually every issue, large and small, became a bone of contention. Over time, as the staff became more militant, and the school's students became more demanding, the district escalated the conflict by appointing principals they thought would 'stand up to' the union. A teacher described one of Adomo's successors as a 'vassal' of the school district, and the teaching staff as 'the serfs'. Yet each successively more autocratic principal only reinforced the militancy of the teachers so that 'Sheldonism' became a district synonym for unbridled union resistance to change. This ongoing standoff resulted in the school's almost complete inability to address its changing student population. Sheldon shows the fundamental flaw of 'inbound', top-down forcefulness as a succession strategy to rectify school underperformance. Instead of inspiring improvement, it only entrenches existing resistance to change.

All these dysfunctional scenarios of leadership succession exemplify how the short-term inbound knowledge of school systems repeatedly eclipses any consideration of the outbound knowledge that is needed to secure sustainable improvement.

Outbound knowledge was only fully considered in three of the innovative schools in the Spencer Project – Durant, Lord Byron and Blue Mountain – when each groomed an assistant principal as a likely successor to the incumbent principal to continue promoting the leader's and school's vision. Creating extensively distributed leadership (Spillane and Halverson 2001) also added to these principals' successful outbound trajectories. For instance, teachers at Durant Alternative school remembered its early days when 'we were all administrators and we all shared the administration'. One of them recalled how their founding leader was:

> the worst administrator ... because he never did his paperwork, he never submitted budgets and he was always behind on everything, but since we were a community, we had no problems reminding him or helping him, and in a sense bail him out. I think we all admired David's intellect so much, we could grumble initially and say 'Damn it David, why didn't you handle this. This is your job.' And then we would go ahead in the faculty meeting and work on it.

In this and other exceptional cases, it was the whole staff, not just one successor, who were able to move the school into its next phase of development. In the majority of schools, though, the sustainability of school improvement and reform initiatives is repeatedly undermined by excessive emphasis on the inbound knowledge of leadership at the expense of equally important outbound concerns. Principals who are making strides in school improvement really need to remain or be kept in their schools for more than five years if their changes are going to stick – otherwise schools become like early flying machines – repeatedly crashing just before take off.

Accelerating succession

A third factor affecting the success of succession is the rate or frequency of cumulative successions. Demographically-driven retirement, the difficulty of retaining leaders in urban schools, and the increasingly popular practice of moving principals around more and more frequently to plug the leaks in failing schools, mean that principal turnover is accelerating dramatically. While Talisman Park had six principals in its first 68 years, it had another five in scarcely a fifth of the time (14 years). From 1970, Stewart Heights had just four principals in 28 years, then three in quick succession in the next five. Lord Byron School had four principals in its first 14 years after opening in 1970, then just as many in the past five.

This 'revolving door' principalship only breeds staff cynicism, which subverts long-term, sustainable improvement. Jerry West at Stewart Heights observed how 'it's only been one-plus year (of his time in the school) but teachers are coming to me already and asking how long am I going to be here'. Part of the quest for future leadership must be defined less by how to remove principals from or rotate them between schools, than by how to retain them in schools longer when they are doing well.

The changing nature of leadership

Growing teacher cynicism about principals and principalships is to do with not only increasing frequency of changes from leader to leader but also changes in the nature of leadership as well. A department head at Talisman Park who had worked under five different principals spoke for many when he said that the school's principals in the 70s and 80s

> were totally committed to the overall programme of the school. When they went into the hiring process they knew exactly what they wanted and what they needed. Their number one focus was the school. As time went on and principals changed, the principal was less interested in the school and more interested in his own personal growth. You could tell as some of these other principals came in, they spent more time outside the school than they did inside the school. I get to Bill Andrews and his number one focus wasn't on Talisman Park. It was on the next step to be a superintendent and that's what he is right now.

A long-serving colleague remarked how current principals

> are forced into an administrative role and are becoming more detached from what we do in the classroom . . . They're getting dumped on too. Principals generally come in and they have grand visions and plans and somewhere along the line . . . they seem to always have an ulterior motive . . . Maybe they want to go to another school or be a superintendent.

Over the three decades covered by the *Change Over Time?* study, leadership has changed a lot. Until the mid to late 1970s, leaders were remembered as larger-than-life characters (in a good or a bad way), who knew people in the school, were closely identified with it, made their mark on it, and stayed around for many years to see things through.

By the mid to late 1990s, teachers were seeing their leaders as being more like anonymous managers, who had less visibility in and attachment to the school, seemed to be more wedded to the system or their own careers and, because of accelerating succession, rarely remained long enough to ensure their initiatives would last. The pressures on the urban principalship of *No Child Left Behind*, where one of the prescribed options for repeated annual failure to improve involves removal of the principal, will only exacerbate these tendencies. The threats to sustainable improvement posed by poorly managed leadership succession raise fundamental questions about the nature of educational leadership today.

Our research suggests that the recent standards/standardization agenda has contributed to an emerging model of leadership that is reactive, compliant and managerial. This discourages and deters potential leaders from becoming principals who might be capable of inspiring the learning communities that promote deeper and higher learning for all students. Depleted pools of outstanding leadership restrict the resources and options at times of succession. Better leaders rather than embattled managers belong in and are attracted to systems that let leaders lead. Sustainability of improvement and leadership therefore requires less rather than more micromanagement and standardization in educational reform.

Conclusion

There are many ways to improve leadership succession in education.

- Succession needs to be planned much more thoughtfully and ethically. It needs to be an integral part of every school improvement and district-wide improvement plan. Deeper and wider pools of leadership talent have to be created so that succession issues are easier to resolve.
- Distributing leadership more effectively makes the success of successors less dependent on the talents or frailties of particular individuals.
- From the first day of their appointment, leaders themselves need to give as much thought to the leadership capacity they will build and legacies they will leave as to the changes they will bring about. Incorporating content on succession issues into all leadership training and development programmes will help them do this.
- The alarming rise in rates of succession should be reversed immediately, and principals should be kept in schools for longer than five years when their efforts at improvement are doing well.

For any, or all of this to make a difference, we must pull back from the precipice to which top-down, over-standardized reform has brought us, where motivational leaders who are wedded to the long-term success of their schools are being reduced to managerial vassals of a standardized system, which moves them with mounting desperation around the accelerating carousel of principal succession. Sustainable leadership depends on successful succession. This struggle for successful succession calls for more than improved succession planning. It comes down to a battle for the soul of leadership itself.

Bibliography

Association of California School Administrators (2001) *Recruitment and Retention of School Leaders: A critical state need*. Sacramento: ACSA Task Force on Administrator Shortage.

Baker, M. and Foote, M. (in press). Changing spaces: Urban school interrelationships and the impact of standards-based reform, *Educational Administration Quarterly*.

Crowther, F., Kaagan, S., Ferguson, M. and Hann, L. (2002) *Developing Teacher Leaders: How teacher leadership enhances school success*. Thousand Oaks CA: Corwin Press.

Fink, D. (1999) *The Attrition of Change*. New York: Teachers College Press.

Gronn, P. (1996) From transactions to transformations: A new world order in the study of leadership, *Educational Management & Administration*, 24(1): 7–30.

Hargreaves, A. (in press). Educational change over time, *Educational Administration Quarterly*.

Hargreaves, A. and Fink, D. (2003) Sustaining leadership, *Phi Delta Kappan*, 84(9): 693–700.

Hargreaves, A., Fink, D., Moore, S., Brayman, C. and White, R. (2003) *Succeeding leaders? A study of secondary principal rotation and succession: Final Report for the Ontario Principals Council*. Toronto: Ontario Principals' Council.

Hopkins, D. (ed.) (1992) *School Improvement in an Era of Change*. London: Cassell.

Jackson, K. (2000) *Building New Teams: The next generation*. Paper presented at the Future of Work in the Public Sector, School of Public Administration, University of Victoria, British Columbia.

Leithwood, K., Jantzi, D. and Steinbach, R. (1999) *Changing Leadership for Changing Times*. Buckingham: Open University Press.

MacMillan, R. (2000) Leadership succession: Cultures of teaching and educational change. In Bascia, N. and Hargreaves A. (eds) *The Sharp Edge of Educational Change: Teaching, leading and the realities of reform*. London and New York: RoutledgeFalmer: 52–71.

National Clearinghouse for Comprehensive School Reform (2002) Planning for the succession of leadership, NCCSR Newsletter 3(8), August.

Sarason, S. (1972) *The Creation of Settings and the Future Societies*. San Francisco: Jossey-Bass.

Spillane, J.P. and Halverson, R. (2001) Investigating school leadership practice: A distributed perspective, *Educational Researcher*, 30(3): 23–8.

Stoll, L. and Fink, D. (1996) *Changing Our Schools: Linking school effectiveness and school improvement*. Buckingham: Open University Press.

Wenger, E. (1998) *Communities of practice: Learning, meaning and identity*. Cambridge: Cambridge University Press.

three

Distributing leadership

James P. Spillane, John B. Diamond, Jennifer Z. Sherer and Amy Franz Coldren

Introduction

Leadership practice has not figured prominently in scholarship on school leadership. Scholars have concerned themselves mostly with leadership structures, roles, routines and arrangements. In this chapter we attempt to make school leadership practice more transparent by putting it centre stage in our discussion of school leadership. We do so in a particular way. We have developed elsewhere a distributed perspective on leadership (Spillane, Halverson and Diamond 2001; 2004). Our distributed leadership framework argues that leadership activity is *distributed* in the interactive web of leaders, followers and situation, which form the appropriate unit of analysis for studying leadership practice. Leadership practice is defined and takes shape in the interaction of leaders, followers and their situation (Gronn 2000).

In arguing that leadership is distributed we mean more than acknowledging that typically the work of leadership in schools involves multiple individuals. In arguing for a distributed view, we mean to convey that leadership practice as *stretched over* leaders, followers and their situation. In this chapter, we consider how leadership might be stretched over two or more leaders and their tools. To do this, we use data from the Distributed Leadership Study (Spillane *et al.* 2001) to construct vignettes of leadership practice that identify and illustrate the ways in which leadership is stretched over leaders and their tools.

Leadership as stretched over leaders

Taking a distributed perspective on leadership, one has to consider the relations among the leadership practices of different leaders. A distributed perspective on leadership practice involves more than developing models that capture the amount of leadership or number of leaders in an organization. A distributed perspective also involves more than mapping which leaders are responsible for which leadership functions. Studying leadership as a distributed practice involves unpacking the idea of distribution by exploring relations among the practices of multiple leaders. We use 'stretched over' to highlight that the distribution of leadership involves not only a consideration of who takes responsibility for which leadership functions, but also a consideration of how leadership tasks are co-enacted by two or more leaders. In this way, leadership practice might be 'in between' (Salomon and Perkins 1996) the practice of two or more leaders. Specifically, we unpack leadership practice as stretched over leaders by analysing interdependencies in and between leadership activities.

Our thinking here has been informed by the work of organizational theorists (March and Simon 1958; Thompson 1967; Malone *et al.* 1999). Thompson (1967) argues that interdependencies between activities can be viewed as:

(a) Reciprocal, where each activity requires inputs from the other. For example, in basketball, players must interact with each other, passing to teammates when they stop dribbling, and working to set one another up to shoot.
(b) Pooled, where the activities share or produce common resources but are otherwise independent. An example here is baseball, or cricket, where players in to bat perform alone but their practice has collective effects.
(c) Sequential, where some activities depend on the completion of others before beginning. For example, a relay on the track or in swimming involves a sequential interdependency.

Thompson's work, along with the work of Malone and his associates, has been especially helpful in our thinking about interdependencies between leaders' practices.

Collaborated leadership practice

When leadership practice is co-enacted by two or more leaders interacting together we term it 'collaborated leadership'. We use the term collaborated to denote that the leaders have to work simultaneously with each other on the leadership activity. In this way, the leadership activity is distributed over the group. Collaborated leadership involves a 'reciprocal' interdependency where the practice of different leaders requires input from one another to produce a particular leadership practice. Consider an example from a literacy committee meeting at Adams School.

Leaders at Adams believe that focusing on reading across the subject areas is critical to improving students' literacy performance. For this reason, the principal, Dr. Williams, and literacy coordinator, Ms. Tracy, have invited all the teachers to this particular literacy committee meeting. In addition to Dr. Williams and Ms. Tracy, Ms. Baize, the African-American Heritage Teacher, and Ms. Grovenor, a teacher leader, are also key leaders at this meeting. The interplay of these leaders' actions illustrates how in interaction they produce a particular leadership practice, an example of collaborated leadership.

Dr. Williams, widely admired for her success in turning Adams around and acknowledged by staff for her expertise in the area of literacy teaching, is well respected by her staff. Ms. Tracy is her right-hand person. She comes to the literacy coordinator role with over 20 years of literacy experience, bringing to her role experience as a classroom teacher as well as a stint as representative for a language arts textbook series. Ms. Tracy is soft-spoken, unwaveringly pleasant, and politically savvy. This meeting is representative of how Dr. Williams and Ms. Tracy play off each other, as well as draw others in to emphasize their points and enable improvement in literacy practice at Adams. Ms. Baize wears many hats; she considers herself a literacy coordinator in addition to her role as African-American Heritage Teacher. She runs Read 180, a programme that works with poorly performing middle school students on reading skills. Ms. Graham, a third-grade language arts teacher, is a member of the literacy core team at Adams and is often sought out by her peers for her expertise in literacy teaching.

Analysing the discourse and interactions during this meeting reveals that the four leaders play different roles and engage in different types of practices that weave together – collaborate – to enact a particular leadership practice. In their meeting interactions, Dr. Williams and Ms. Tracy's roles converge and diverge. Both leaders move the meeting along, praise and encourage their staff, present specific expectations of the teachers and invite teacher input and sharing. Dr. Williams is the big picture person. She periodically summarizes or synthesizes what has been said by others in order to share a powerful insight or strategy. In response to a teacher's example of her classroom practice, Williams states, 'That's the framework: model, guided practice, independent work, and *then* give the strategy.' She announces the most important elements of the discussion. Twice during this meeting Williams announces, 'We want to be proactive.' She also serves as the voice of the future, reporting critical and relevant district information.

Ms. Tracy, on the other hand, acts as the detail person. She identifies specific problems, offers solutions and resources for these concerns. Several times in the meeting she teaches or reinforces concepts for the teachers. For example, Tracy explains that a teacher's example of her classroom practice involves meta-cognition, a concept that she is trying to get her teachers to understand. She also brings up Bloom's Taxonomy and briefly explains how to use it in classroom practice. When the teachers answer this with silence, she plays it back to Dr. Williams, jokingly wondering why she is getting silence. In this way, she evokes the principal's power, as well as her close relationship with Williams, to make her point: this is important—if you don't know what I'm talking about, learn it. Tracy also directly and indirectly pulls other informal leaders into the conversation. Ms. Tracy, for example, pointedly asked another leader to introduce an important part of the book that she had previously given to each teacher. In this role, Ms. Baize pulled components from the text and talked about how she used these in her own classroom, illuminating how the particular component might work in practice. In this way, Ms. Baize's classroom expertise blends with the components that Ms. Tracy thinks are important, and the message is shared with other teachers in this way.

A similar situation emerges when Ms. Grovenor introduces an example from her own teaching. She describes to her colleagues an activity she used with her students, and subsequent activities that tie directly into the state literacy standards, which Ms. Tracy latches on to and sets out as a requirement for all teachers at Adams. Ms. Tracy explicitly asked Ms. Grovenor to try this strategy in her classroom and, because it met with success, it is rolled out to the rest of the school as a strategy everyone should use. Ms. Grovenor sets up the successful strategy with description of her own teaching, and Ms. Tracy uses this example to set up the expectation that all teachers will use this in the next five weeks, giving them an assignment to go along with this expectation. Williams and Tracy explicitly made time in the agenda for teachers to share examples of their literacy practice and Tracy uses some of these examples as an opportunity to press teachers to consider particular changes for their literacy teaching.

The leadership practice in this literacy committee is collaborative in that it lies and takes shape in the interplay between the four leaders. Williams presses the big picture; she moves the meeting forward at critical points and, in many respects, is insistent about what teachers should do in their classrooms. Tracy points out specific areas of need and concern, offers resources and strategies, encourages others to talk, and builds on the key points raised by practitioners to move the staff forward in its efforts to improve literacy teaching across the subject areas. This meeting is representative of how Ms. Tracy and Dr. Williams interact with each other as well as how they interact with other informal leaders (and indeed teachers) to lead improvement efforts at Adams. They both believe in giving teachers ownership as illuminated in their efforts to encourage teacher voice and build on teachers' ideas to improve practice. Williams depends on Tracy's literacy expertise, as well as convincing manner and wealth of information and resources, while Tracy depends on Williams' broader vision of the school and the district, as well as her positional authority. They both, but Tracy in particular, rely on teachers for classroom examples that illustrate in actual classroom practice their agenda for literacy teaching.

We argue that the leadership practice in the literacy committee meeting depended on the interplay between multiple actors. There is a reciprocal relationship between the practice of these four leaders, each requiring input from others. In reciprocal interdependencies, individuals play off one another, with the practice of person A enabling the practice of person B and vice versa. The co-enacted leadership evident in this meeting depended on the resources of multiple leaders working collaboratively, each bringing somewhat different resources – skills and knowledge – to bear. This reciprocal interdependency is visually represented in Figure 3.1.

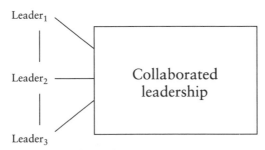

Figure 3.1 Reciprocal interdependency

Collective leadership practice

Leadership practice can also be stretched across the practice of two or more leaders who work separately but interdependently in pursuit of a common goal. Leadership for classroom teaching, for example, might target either different or the same aspects of teaching – students, materials and the teacher. In this situation, there is a 'pooled' interdependency, in which independent activities produce a common resource.

Consider as an example the work of teacher evaluation at another school in our study, Ellis Elementary. Both the principal and assistant principal believe that evaluating teaching is a critical tool in their efforts to forge instructional change. The principal at Ellis School believes that two visits to a classroom – the legal requirement – are simply inadequate to fully understand and evaluate a teacher's practice. She remarked:

> It's mandated by law; the principal must go in the classroom once a year, and see the horse and pony show. And I notify them and they [teachers] put on a show. And I'm supposed to, based upon that observation and another informal observation, rank them . . . It does not work.

One solution that the principal and assistant principal have adopted is to work together to evaluate instruction. The assistant principal, who maintains a friendly and supportive relationship with teachers, visits classrooms frequently, engaging in formative evaluation by providing regular feedback to teachers. As he describes it, he 'makes the rounds' two or three times a day, often sitting in on a lesson and giving the teacher feedback on what he observed.

In contrast, the principal engages in summative evaluation. Teachers at Ellis see her very much as an authority figure, referring to her as 'Doctor'. She visits classrooms once or twice per year and makes final determinations about the quality of teachers' instructional practices. Through formal and informal meetings the assistant principal and principal pool their insights using their collective observations to develop an understanding of teachers' practices and ensure what they believe is a more comprehensive evaluation of teaching practice. The assistant principal explained:

> So through a formative process and a summative process we take a look at all of our teachers. I'm more involved in the formative evaluation of teachers. Where I will observe teachers, talk to them prior to an observation. Observe teachers, and then they might tell me certain things to look for, that they need help in this area or that area. And then we'll meet after . . . So I try to visit every classroom every day . . . I do my best, you know, to be visible, 'cause you can pick up a lot just by those informal type observations, of just seeing what's going on . . . So, you know, that helps improve instruction.

These separate but interdependent practices allow the principal to avoid making judgements based on 'horse and pony shows'.

This vignette illuminates how two leaders, working separately but interdependently, construct a leadership practice through the evaluation of teaching practice that has collective effects. While they work on the same element of the instructional unit, with the shared goal of instructional improvement, they practice separately but interdependently. This practice of leading instructional change through the teacher evaluation process is stretched across the separate but interdependent work of these two leaders. In this way, teacher evaluation at Ellis Elementary School, involves a 'pooled' interdependency, in which independent practices produce a common leadership practice, producing a more substantive teacher evaluation process.

Moreover, their work is coordinated because they share a common goal (improved instruction), seek to reach it through a common approach (teacher evaluation), target the same element of the instructional unit (teachers) and communicate with each other about their work. Figure 3.2 shows how this type of interdependency might be represented. In this case, the interdependency is between two leaders whose leadership practice is enabled through its co-construction.

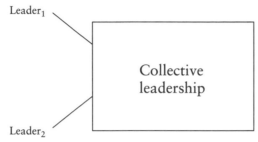

Figure 3.2 Pooled interdependency

Coordinated leadership practice

A third way in which leadership practice can be stretched over leaders involves what we term 'coordinated leadership' in which leaders work separately or together on different leadership tasks that are arranged sequentially. We use the term coordinated to underscore that the leadership practice is stretched over the different tasks that must be performed in a particular sequence for the enactment of the leadership practice. This involves a third type of interdependency; that is, a sequential or flow inter- dependency. In this case, leadership practice depends upon the completion of prior tasks. In this situation, multiple interdependent tasks, arranged sequentially, are critical to the enactment of leadership practice.

Consider an example from Carson Elementary School. School leaders at Carson use student test scores to focus their instructional improvement efforts. This strategy involves a number of interdependent steps, each build- ing on resources produced through the completion of prior steps. First, the tests must be administered to students, requiring scheduling and coordin- ation. Second, the test results must be received, analysed and interpreted by school personnel. Third, based on this analysis, instructional priorities are identified and disseminated and their implementation monitored through- out the school. This effort involves a number of separate but coordinated activities – administering the test, interpreting student test data through an item analysis of the test scores, establishing instructional improvement priorities, identifying instructional strategies to address deficiencies and implementing professional development sessions around those issues. Reflecting their different knowledge and expertise, different leaders take responsibility for executing the various tasks. At Carson, the use of student test scores to lead instructional improvement is stretched over the work of multiple leaders who, sometimes working together, other times separately, enact a series of tasks necessary for the execution of this leadership practice.

Step 1: Administering the tests. At Carson, the school counsellor, Ms. Roland, takes responsibility for the logistics of the testing process. The administration of the test involves an array of subtasks from making sure teachers and students have the appropriate materials to ensuring that the staff follow proper procedures.

Step 2: Receiving and interpreting test results. Once test results are returned to the school, Ms. Roland, Dr. Johnson (the school principal) and Ms. Brown (the assistant principal) work on interpreting the data. These three leaders bring different skills and knowledge to the task. Ms. Roland possesses substantial knowledge of the exam data. Dr. Johnson shares much of this knowledge but also understands the school's overall instructional programme, which she has played an integral role in building over the past five years. Finally, as a former elementary school teacher with more than 20 years of experience, Ms. Brown brings her knowledge of classroom practice to the discussion of the results. Together, these leaders study the 'item analysis' for each grade level and use it to determine the skills students have mastered and not mastered.

Step 3: Determining instructional priorities. Having received and interpreted the test score data, these leaders make determinations about particular areas of instructional focus. The principal explained that the school's plan for improvement was based on the analysis of test scores. She remarked,

> With the math I found that . . . our children tend to do well in computation, pencil and paper, figuring out the problem 2 + 2 . . . but when it comes down to the concepts . . . [when] they need to use higher order thinking skills, they tend to not do as well. Last year we started focusing in on higher order thinking skills because [the tests] are moving more and more in that direction.

At Carson, the development of instructional priorities is dependent on the execution of two other tasks – the administration of the test and the interpretation of the test results.

Step 4: Engaging in professional development. Having completed these first three steps, the school engages in professional development sessions designed to address problematic areas identified through the analysis of test data. Having restructured its school day, the time has been allocated for the staff to meet every Friday for an hour and a half for professional development. These sessions typically involve the principal, the school counsellor and sub-district personnel who lead a professional development session around focal areas identified by school leaders such as higher order thinking skills in math and literacy. The Carson example highlights how leadership can be stretched temporally over sequenced and coordinated tasks, illuminating how the enactment of certain leadership tasks depends upon resources generated from prior tasks.

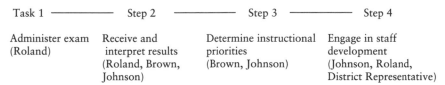

Figure 3.3 Sequential interdependency

Leadership as stretched over leaders and leadership tools

As we argued at the outset the situation together with leaders and followers is a critical element in defining leadership practice. Material artefacts and tools (e.g. teacher observation protocols) are one important part of the situation. Leaders not only typically work with others they also work with tools of various sorts. Schools and districts are awash with tools and artefacts that leaders use in their work. Yet tools do not figure prominently in most popular and empirical accounts of school leadership. When tools do feature, more often than not they are treated as incidentals. Leadership practice is viewed chiefly as a function of the skills and expertise of the leaders and if tools are mentioned they are typically viewed as accessories.

We find it difficult, though, to talk about leadership practice without reference to tools. As illustrated in the vignettes from Adams and Carson Schools, tests and test scores were an important tool in leadership practice. Moreover, these tools are not just accessories that influence leadership practice. Rather, tools in interaction with leaders and followers define leadership practice; they are a fundamental constituting or defining element in leadership practice.

Consider an example from another school in the Distributed Leadership Study. Hillside School is large, serving 1,300 students who are predominantly Mexican-American and with a low income. Believing that the ability to write and communicate clearly was critical to the success of Mexican-American students, Principal Miller has spearheaded improvement efforts in writing instruction at Hillside over the past decade. At the core of this effort to lead change in teaching was Mrs. Miller's monthly review of students' writing folders: from October through April, every teacher submitted monthly a folder that contained one composition written by each student in the class. Mrs. Miller read each student's work and provided the teachers and students with written feedback. She explained:

> I can tell a lot of what's happening in the classroom by just reading folders and providing feedback to teachers. I can see people who maybe need to work a little on certain things . . . It forced teachers to actually teach writing as a subject and not just as a homework assignment and encouraged them to use the writing as an integrated thing, not as a stand-alone.
>
> (Interview, 6 April 2000)

By looking at students' writing Mrs. Miller was able see what was happening in writing instruction at Hillside school. Moreover, she provided written feedback to both students and teachers about their work. She praised students and pointed out areas of their writing that needed more work. Based on her analysis of their students' writing, she provided each teacher with specific guidance about their teaching of writing, identifying skills they should cover and commenting on their grading of students' work, among other things.

Hillside teachers reported that the school principal's practice of reviewing writing folders was especially influential on their teaching. Ms. Crawford, for example, described how the writing folder review practice changed her approach to writing instruction,

> I switch my whole day around so they get almost an hour to work on [writing] . . . I have received notes from Mrs. Miller. We have to turn in compositions monthly . . . But that is what I've had to change in my approach this year is giving them more time to think, more time to work, more time to review the process. You know, review the criteria. You have to have this, this, and this.
>
> (Interview with K.C., 9 May 2000)

Mrs. Miller's feedback on the writing folders prompted Ms. Crawford to increase the amount of time she devoted to writing instruction and to what she covered in writing instruction. Other Hillside teachers offered similar accounts.

Mrs. Miller's monthly writing folders review is an important leadership practice for writing teaching at Hillside. This practice was not simply a function of Mrs. Miller's skill and expertise, though that was very important. Rather, this leadership practice took shape in the interaction of

Mrs. Miller and the writing folder – a key leadership tool. While the writing folder was a tool developed to support classroom teaching and learning, Mrs. Miller appropriated this tool, remaking it as a leadership tool. The writing folder shaped the leadership practice in this instance in a number of ways. First, the writing folder grounded this leadership practice in classroom teaching and learning; it focused leadership practice on what students were learning (or not learning) about writing. Second, by focusing on classroom teaching and learning, the writing folders enabled Mrs. Miller to offer very concrete and timely guidance to teachers about their ongoing efforts to teach writing. Third, the writing folder enabled Mrs. Miller to provide feedback to both students and teachers simultaneously. In this way Mrs. Miller was working to motivate and engage both teachers and students in the improvement of writing instruction at Hillside. Often efforts to lead change in classroom teaching focus exclusively on the teacher and in the process fail to take into account the fact that students together with teachers co-produced classroom teaching.

The writing folder, as appropriated by Mrs. Miller as a leadership tool, was not simply an aid in the leadership practice reflected in the monthly writing folder review activity. Rather, the writing folder in interaction with Mrs. Miller fundamentally shaped the leadership practice for writing teaching at Hillside. If Mrs. Miller had used a different tool, such as a series of model lessons on the writing process, then the leadership practice for writing at Hillside would have looked different. Leadership tools in interaction with leaders and followers define leadership practice.

Conclusion

Pressing on what a distributed perspective on leadership practice might entail, we explored how leadership activity is stretched over leaders and leadership tools in this chapter. We argue that combined properties of a group of leaders (and indeed followers) working together to enact a particular task leads to leadership practice that is more than the sum of each individual's practice. Consequently, to understand the knowledge needed for leadership practice in these situations, one has to move beyond an analysis of individual knowledge and consider what these leaders know and do together. Depending on the particular leadership task, school leaders' knowledge and expertise may be best explored at the group level rather than at the individual leader level. The interplay between the practices of multiple leaders is essential to understanding how leadership is stretched over leaders. We identified and elaborated on three ways in which leadership might be stretched over leaders – collaborated leadership, collective leadership, coordinated leadership – and considered how the interdependencies among leaders practices differ in each case. Our analyses also suggest that in attempting to understand school leadership as a distributed practice we need to also take into account how leadership might be stretched over the situation and especially over tools of various sorts.

Our distributed leadership perspective has implications for efforts to improve the practice of leadership in order to create better schools for tomorrow. Better schools for tomorrow will depend significantly on school leadership that enables and supports teacher learning. This is an enormous challenge that will depend on the work of multiple formal and informal leaders. The distributed leadership perspective suggests that leadership practice at the level of the school, rather than at the level of an individual leader, is the appropriate unit for thinking about creating better schools for tomorrow. Specifically, we need to analyse those leadership practices in our school, examining which functions these activities are designed to address and who takes responsibility for which activities. We can then begin to analyse the ways in which leadership practice for these activities is stretched over leaders – collaborated, collective and coordinated – and begin to identify the types of expertise that various leaders bring to this shared work and how these different co-enactments work (and don't work) in a particular school. At another level, we can begin to examine the tools that are used in the enactment of different leadership activities, identifying how different tools enable or constrain the leadership practice necessary to support teacher learning. In this way, the distributed leadership perspective provides a frame that can help practitioners interpret and think about their efforts to create better schools.

Bibliography

Malone, T.W. *et al.* (1999) Tools for inventing organizations: Toward a handbook of organizational processes. *Management Science*, 45: 425–43.

Malone, T.W. and Crowston, K. (1994) The interdisciplinary study of coordination. *ACM Computing Surveys*, 26: 87–119.

March, J.G., and Simon, H.A. (1958) *Organizations*. New York: Wiley.

Perkins, D.N. (1996) Person-plus: a distributed view of thinking and learning. In G. Salomon (ed.) *Distributed Cognition: Psychological and educational considerations* , Ch 3. New York: Cambridge University Press.

Salomon, G. (1996) No distribution without individual cognition: A distributed interactionist view. In G. Salomon (ed.) *Distributed Cognition: Psychological and educational considerations*. G. Salomon, New York: Cambridge University Press.

Spillane, J.P., Halverson, R. and Diamond, J.B. (2001) Investigating school leadership practice: A distributed perspective, *Educational Researcher*, 30(3): 23–8, 2001.

Spillane, J., Halverson, R., Diamond, J. (in press). Towards a theory of school leadership practice: Implications of a distributed perspective, *Journal of Curriculum Studies*.

Thompson, J.D. (1967) *Organizations in Action: Social science bases of administrative theory*. New York: McGraw Hill.

A version of this chapter was presented at the American Educational Research Association Annual Meeting in New Orleans, April 2000. Work on this chapter was supported by the Distributed Leadership Project, which is funded by research grants from the U.S. National Science Foundation and the Spencer Foundation. Northwestern University's School of Education and Social Policy and Institute for Policy Research also supported the work. All opinions and conclusions expressed in the chapter are those of the authors and do not necessarily reflect the views of any funding agency.

four

Developing leadership for learning communities

Louise Stoll and Ray Bolam

Introduction: the learning imperative

Schools are bombarded with changes from all sides. They exist in a political context in which external reform, initiated by national, state or local authorities to raise standards of achievement, and often in response to concerns about economic competition, attempt to exert priority over schools' own vision of needed improvements. Relentless and often dramatic global change forces also create enormous pressures for education from 'out there', leading Hargreaves to conclude:

> The drivers of educational change are not always those of governmental policy; rather, it is rapid and continual change in the wider society that makes an impact on education.
>
> (1998: 10)

Papert (1996) suggests that three change forces exert particular influences on schools. First, a powerful industrial sector associated with new technologies views education as a market place, developing new online learning technologies, connecting schools, homes and other agencies. Second, understandings about broader theories of intelligence and the constructive nature of learning lead to growing awareness of the need for new learning approaches. This is accompanied by realization that, ultimately, the only genuinely marketable skill is that of learning itself, and that learning and learning how to learn are essential future life skills. Furthermore, readily available knowledge through technology in the home, libraries and other public places means that school no longer controls 'an accepted canon of knowledge'.

Third, Papert views 'child power' as the most powerful change force. In the developed world, children appear to have increasingly less regard for school as it lags behind the society it serves. Surveys in the UK, for example, demonstrate that approximately a quarter of students are at least dissatisfied with their schooling (McCall *et al.* 2001), and some are actually disaffected or 'disappeared' (Barber 1996). Traditional 'respect for adults' no longer exists. Children and young people are also now much more aware of their world, while still needing space to develop within a secure and safe environment. Such external change forces have massive implications for schools and leaders in schools. In short, they provide imperatives for learning.

Leading for learning under such pressures is particularly complex because it means engaging in activities that often feel contradictory. On one hand, school leaders are looking outside and making decisions about the changes they feel can best promote learning and how to bring these about: they are trying to guide their internal communities towards an evolving common vision of a better future and ensure its achievement. On the other hand, they also sometimes have to lead things they don't want to lead but have to, unless it is appropriate and feasible to hold these external demands at bay. Through it all, they are trying to find ways to connect everything coherently to make it meaningful for themselves and their relevant stakeholders.

Our central argument is that, to address this dilemma and these tensions, school leaders should aim to develop the capacity of their school for responding to these external imperatives within a framework of values and procedures designed to achieve the goals for and of the pupils in their particular school community. We see the idea of a professional learning community as the foundation of such capacity. The strategic role of school leaders in creating and sustaining professional learning communities as part of their overall strategy of capacity building for school improvement is clearly crucial. Finally, we argue that these ideas should be a central focus of leadership development programmes.

Capacity and capacity building

Schools embark on their improvement journeys from different starting points, related to the context in which they work and their particular growth state (Hopkins *et al.* 1997). Some don't have the capacity to deal with and work through the challenges improvement efforts bring. Others have the motivation, skill, resources, resilience and conditions to more readily engage in and sustain the continuous learning necessary for improvement. In a school with such capacity, all these features are configured in a positive way, helping everyone tackle the complexities of learning, achieve their goals and sustain learning over time. Successful educational reform also appears to depend on: teachers' individual and collective capacity (Lieberman 1995; Little 1999); school capacity (Stoll 1999; King and Newmann 2001); and system capacity (Elmore 2002; Fullan 1993). Capacity building is, therefore, central to leading for learning and is needed at and for all levels of the system, although we are mainly looking in this chapter at capacity building within schools. The focus of capacity building is:

- creating and maintaining the necessary conditions, culture and structures;
- facilitating learning and skill-oriented experiences and opportunities;
- ensuring interrelationships and synergy between all the component parts.

Professional learning communities

Professional learning communities seem to hold promise for enhancing the capacity of schools and individual teachers. It is important to investigate their practical use for schools because of major international policy issues of ageing workforces, teacher retention and recruitment. Investing in creating a rewarding and satisfying working environment may contribute to resolving these issues. It is thought that in professional learning communities, teachers and school leaders, collaborating with and supported by support staff, exercise professional judgements, for example about the best use of evidence and research for improving learning and teaching, within an agreed accountability framework. There also appears to be a strong belief that professional learning communities have a positive impact on pupils, although at this point the evidence is still relatively limited (Lee and Smith 1996; Louis and Marks 1998; Wiley 2001).

In England, the Department for Education and Skills (DfES), the National College for School Leadership (NCSL) and the General Teaching Council (GTC) have funded a two-and-a-half year research study, in which we are involved, to explore the creation, development and sustainability of professional learning communities in different school settings. Its aim is to identify and provide practical examples of: the characteristics of effective professional learning communities in different kinds of schools; key factors inside and outside schools which seem to help or hinder the development of these communities; and innovative practices for ongoing professional learning and development (see Stoll *et al.* 2003 and McMahon *et al.* 2004). Emerging themes from this project appear to support conclusions of previous research and writing suggesting that the following six themes are important for leading communities of learning:

- creating a culture for learning;
- ensuring learning for pupils and adults alike;

- attending to the human side of change;
- ensuring enquiry-based practice;
- making connections;
- creating external conditions in which professional learning communities can thrive.

The first five themes highlight actions of those within schools, while the sixth focuses on those outside schools.

Creating a culture for learning

Attempts to improve a school that neglect school culture are unlikely to succeed because school culture influences readiness for change. School culture's essence can be described as the deeper level of basic assumptions and beliefs shared by an organization's members, operating unconsciously, and defining the organization's view of itself and its environment (Schein 1985). Culture therefore describes how things are, and acts as a screen or lens through which the world is viewed, defining reality for those within the school, giving them support and identity, and influencing how each school community goes about its business.

Schools' cultures often vary dramatically in their learning orientation. Some have a significantly greater focus than others on learning for both pupils and adults (MacGilchrist *et al.* 1995). Rosenholtz (1989) found that some are 'learning enriched' while others are 'learning impoverished' for their teachers; and she discovered links between this and student outcomes. The norms in some schools emphasize a collaborative culture, underpinned by a shared learning vision and values and collective responsibility for success (Stoll and Fink 1996). Appropriately high expectations are a key feature of such a culture. In one Scottish study, there was a significant difference between the expectations of staff in two primary schools, both of which were located in similarly deprived areas. While in one, there was a widespread belief that the pupils' ability to learn in the school was affected by their background and external conditions and that there was little the school could do, in the other 'can do' beliefs came through strongly:

> . . . a teacher commented '. . . there are no limitations. You can come in this door and the world is your oyster . . . the children will be encouraged. Nothing is holding us back', while another told of how 'the school is always trying to better itself'. The headteacher was clear: 'Children come first . . . Pupils expect to be taught and taught appropriately and stretched.'
>
> (Stoll *et al.* 2001: 181)

The leadership challenge here may be one of reculturing: 'the process of developing new values, beliefs and norms. For systematic reform it involves building new conceptions about instruction . . . and new forms of professionalism for teachers' (Fullan 1996). In addition, leadership in improving schools is pervasive and does not just reside with formal leaders, but is a shared activity (Gronn 2003). Schools which reculture successfully develop educational meaning. This is the shared sense that staff members know where they are going, and is present throughout the school. This is no easy challenge, especially in schools where there are a number of temporary or supply staff and in situations of considerable staff turnover. It also requires simultaneous management attention to school structures – for example use of time, space for people to meet, etc. – to ensure that they support the learning culture.

Ensuring learning for pupils and adults alike

Learning is at the heart of what schools must be about. Leading communities of learning means ensuring opportunities to learn for all members of the community. In this section, we particularly focus on pupils, teachers and support staff.

Pupils' learning

Schools have a brief to prepare pupils for the changing world. Their ultimate goal must be to enhance pupils' progress, achievement and development in the broadest sense, to capture the breadth of what it is likely to take to flourish in the twenty-first century.

Reforms diverting attention away from teacher learning related directly to improved classroom practice in favour of management solutions, including school development plans, performance tables and whole school target setting, generally fail to penetrate into the classroom (Dimmock 2000). Over the last few years in England, introduction of national strategies in England at Key Stage 2 (7–11 year olds) and Key Stage 3 (11–14 year olds) have directly addressed teachers' practice. Many policy changes, however, are still based on research that only relates teaching behaviours, skills and strategies to better outcomes in basic skills. Such outcomes are not the entire story, especially in preparing young people for a changing world. Learning is also still perceived by many to mean learning *outcomes*. Over the last 30 years, research has generated new conceptions of learning. Summarizing research on major factors influencing learning and achievement, the American Psychological Association (1995) identified 14 core principles, applicable to learners of all ages, organized into four major categories: cognitive and meta-cognitive factors; motivational and affective factors; developmental and social factors; and individual differences factors. Based on such research and from studies of the brain, arguments have increasingly been offered for shifting the orientation to learner- and learning-centred education (Lambert and McCombs 1998; Darling Hammond 1997; Watkins 2003). Leaders need to understand what effective learning is and how best to promote this, which is only possible if their time is not taken up with administration and bureaucracy, fund raising because of insufficient resources, pupil behaviour management and parental crisis management.

Ongoing professional learning for individual staff members

Those working in schools also have to keep up and deal with the complexity and influence of a plethora of changes that impact on their work daily. For them, learning is also essential. Indeed, Fullan (1995) portrayed teachers as not only crucial to successful improvement efforts but also as key initiators, arguing that the rapid pace of change today imposes upon teachers moral and cultural imperatives compelling them to be active change agents. In a sample of OECD countries, professional development was said to be

> ... central to the way principals manage schools, in at least two respects: first, as instructional leaders, principals may be expected to coordinate professional progression of their staff; second, they need to manage the learning community as a whole, using development as part of school change.
>
> (CERI 2001: 27)

There are many different models of professional development in the literature. We find it helpful to begin with Sparks and Hirsh (1997) who asserted that sustained implementation of new practices requires a new form of professional development affecting not only the knowledge, attitudes and practices of individual teachers and school leaders but also the cultures and structures of the organizations in which they work. They argued that teachers must have opportunities to discuss, think about, try out and hone new practices by taking new roles, creating new structures, working on new tasks and creating a culture of inquiry; hence, staff development linked to a reform agenda must support a learner-centred view of teaching and a career-long conception of teachers' learning. This includes all the informal learning opportunities not officially falling within the frame of continuous professional development; for example, being a member of a school improvement planning team or participating in a group developing the school's learning and teaching policy. Leithwood and colleagues (1999) see this as 'creating the conditions for growth in teachers' professional knowledge'. They argue that this is best accomplished by embedding professional development in practical activities, what they call 'situated cognition', concluding that leaders should do this by: ensuring that the necessary funding and resources are available; helping teachers to share a common vision; helping teachers to engage in self-diagnosis with access to internal and external support; building self-efficacy; developing a collaborative culture; and sharing responsibility for teacher development throughout the school. The professional learning communities approach emphasizes that support staff should also have appropriate development opportunities because they can contribute to promoting student learning. Significantly, in their study, McMahon *et al.* (2004) found that 94 per cent of primary and 97 per cent of secondary school respondents said that 'teaching assistants have opportunities for professional development', while the corresponding figures for non-teaching support staff were 85 per cent and 88 per cent respectively.

Attending to the human side of change

Leading for learning is a very human enterprise. Leaders are continuously faced with the necessity of helping others see the reason for change, deal with it, manage it where necessary and actively take charge of it. For anyone, change is a very personal experience, and engaging in learning with colleagues can be risky. Teachers are unlikely to open themselves up to learning and participating in activities such as mutual inquiry, classroom observation and feedback, mentoring partnerships and discussion about pedagogical issues and innovation, unless they are confident it is safe to do this. Trust is key to this. Indeed, Bryk and colleagues (1999) found that social trust among members of staff was considerably the strongest facilitator of professional community.

Attending to people's sense of self appears to be key to bringing about successful change; yet until recently, most educational reforms and much of the change literature tended to ignore the human side of change (Evans 1996). This has significant implications for leadership, particularly given that factors within schools have a greater influence than externally instigated and centrally imposed factors on levels of primary teachers' job satisfaction, as well as their morale and motivation (Evans 1999). There is also a particular emotional cost in challenging areas, where the social context can inhibit people's best efforts to improve schools.

The human side of leadership also highlights leadership's moral nature (Sergiovanni 1992; Hodgkinson 1991). How leaders blend together their focus on promoting learning and enquiry, building community, and making connections depends on their values about the enterprise in which they are engaged, as well as beliefs about the basis on which they relate to the entire school community.

Emotional intelligence and its application to leadership and the workplace (Goleman 1998) has received a considerable amount of interest. Self awareness, self management, social awareness and social skills are important for leaders. While it is argued that emotional intelligence can be learned, for many people this requires real change. The jury is still out on the benefits of emotional intelligence. On the one hand, concern has been raised about its manipulative use. Elsewhere, however, empirical evidence: 'clearly endorses emotional intelligence as a legitimate part of effective leadership' (Day *et al.*, 2000).

Ensuring enquiry-based practice

Enquiry-based, or evidence-informed, practice is increasingly seen as an important feature of professional learning and effective leading for learning. In an overview, Earl and Katz (2002) argued that: 'data have the potential to be very powerful and useful mechanisms for helping schools change in productive ways' (2002: 1004). However, they introduce several notes of caution: against regarding data as 'precise, objective and unassailable'; about the sometimes demoralizing consequences of publishing school data; and the dangers of causing teachers to teach to the tests and of thus not enhancing learning. They urge school leaders to develop an 'inquiry-oriented habit of mind', to become data literate and to create a culture of enquiry in their schools. To do so, they need to work collaboratively with colleagues and to seek and use external support from local authorities [districts], universities and consultants.

In England, there has been an increased focus on evidence-informed practice and a major part of its rationale is the belief that teaching should emulate medicine, aiming to be a research-informed profession (Hargreaves 1996). Cochran-Smith and Lytle (2001) proposed that a legitimate and essential purpose of professional development is the development of a critical and transformative enquiry stance on teaching, linked not only to high standards for the learning of all students but also to social change and social justice and to the individual and collective professional growth of teachers. According to Stoll and colleagues (2002), three broad, interconnected approaches are open to school leaders wishing to promote evidence-informed practice:

- To promote systematic research and evaluation in the school, in departments and by individual classroom teachers.
- To adopt a more systematic approach to the collection, analysis and use of 'routine' data, for example, in relation to students' examination results, value-added data and external school inspection reports.
- To search for and use externally generated research.

None of these modes is unproblematic. Nevertheless, it is clear that school leaders in England are becoming increasingly confident in using these approaches. Thus, McMahon and colleagues (2004) found that almost four-fifths of primary/nursery and just over two-thirds of secondary respondents reported that 50 per cent or more of staff informed their practice through the routine collection, analysis and use of data, and both groups thought that the number of staff who did so had increased in the previous two years.

Making connections

School communities frequently struggle with a lack of coherence:

> . . . the main problem is not the absence of innovations but the presence of too many disconnected, episodic, piecemeal, superficially adorned projects.
>
> (Fullan 2001: 109)

Learning involves making connections (Brandsford *et al.*, 1999), but learning in organizations is frequently so individualistic that, even if individuals learn, this does not add up to collective learning and understanding throughout the organization. This is because: 'no single teacher knows, or could know, the totality of the staff's professional knowledge' (Hargreaves 1999a). Through collective knowledge creation (Louis 1994), school communities 'join up' their individual knowledge and, through processing it together, come up with new and shared knowledge and understanding.

A key feature of organizational learning is systems thinking, looking at the whole and seeing the relationships and patterns between the parts. It appears essential for leaders to understand how the school as a whole (the system) and its constituent parts (the sub-systems) are relating to each other. Senge (1990) describes systems thinking as 'a discipline for seeing wholes'. It is a framework for seeing interrelationships rather than linear cause-effect chains, and for seeing patterns and processes of change rather than static 'snapshots'. The capacity to see patterns and discern connections between seemingly unconnected events is a key feature of organizational learning.

One way of making connections is through networking between schools. Fullan argues that:

> Schools are beginning to discover that new ideas, knowledge creation, inquiry and sharing are essential to solving learning problems in a rapidly changing society.
>
> (2001: xi)

Some practitioners develop their own networks, for example teacher subject groups, or networks of schools working together, sharing quality learning and teaching practices that can be adapted within their own contexts, visiting each other with focused pedagogical questions, taking an enquiry stance to exploring common issues and generating new knowledge:

> A network increases the pool of ideas on which any member can draw and as one idea or practice is transferred, the inevitable process of adaptation and adjustment to different conditions is rich in potential for the practice to be incrementally improved by the recipient and then fed back to the donor in a virtuous circle of innovation and improvement. In other words, the networks extend and enlarge the communities of practice with enormous potential benefits.
>
> (D. Hargreaves 2003: 9)

Information technology has also expanded networking possibilities, as schools in isolated areas and different countries connect with each other. It has been suggested that: 'the best way to encourage teachers to share knowledge within a school is also to get them to share knowledge with others outside the school' (NCSL 2002). Evidence on this kind of impact of networked learning communities is still being collected, but if this is true, it has important implications for leading and developing professional learning communities.

Creating external conditions in which professional learning communities can thrive

The emphasis so far has been on the role of the school, its staff and leaders in seeking and using external support and linkages of various kinds. However, it is clear that developing internal capacity depends on both those inside and outside schools. In this section we consider implications and requirements for creating supportive external arrangements and conditions to make this possible and encourage it to happen.

Experience in England offers an illuminating example of the changing roles of external agencies in continuing professional development and school improvement. Initially, increased marketization of continuing professional development provision was accompanied by a reduction in the roles of Local Education Authorities (school districts) and universities, the demise of teachers' centres and a substantial increase in the numbers of private trainers and consultants. In the 1990s, there were major developments at national level with the establishment of the Teacher Training Agency, national standards of professional practice for teachers and headteachers, the National College for School Leadership and a range of national schemes and incentives for teachers to engage in research, development, networking and continuing professional development to promote school improvement and enhanced student learning. A tension arises, however, when continuing professional development at a national or state level is geared too heavily towards 'performance training initiatives' or 'sects' because:

> Over time, teachers inducted into performance training sects can lose the capacity or desire to make professional judgements and become more reflective.
>
> (A. Hargreaves 2003: 142)

The need for external support is evident in other developed countries. Thus, in the USA, Elmore and colleagues (1999) emphasized the importance of proactive district level contribution under seven headings: ensuring all schools focus on instruction; instructional change as a long multi-stage process; shared expertise as a driver of change; focusing on system (i.e. district) wide improvement; supporting people working together; setting clear expectations while decentralizing responsibility for action; and promoting collegiality, caring and respect. Fullan (2003) has proposed a four-level model of the 'moral imperative' if school leaders are to make a difference – individual, school, regional and societal. Fullan argues:

> On the positive side, a picture of the critical role of the district in going to scale is becoming clearer. Without the districts, reform across many schools will not happen.
>
> (2003: 55)

He concludes:

> The final component for transforming the system involves strengthening the infrastructure for developing school leadership. You can't get large-scale, sustainable reform by devolving development. The infrastructure – the policies and programs at the local and state level aimed at developing leadership – is crucial.
>
> (2003: 78)

Implications for leadership development

Realizing these themes has significant implications for leadership development. Here, we suggest ten particular implications:

• Leading communities of learning means focusing energies on capacity building throughout the school and the wider system. Fundamentally, leadership needs to be distributed, not only throughout schools but also system wide. Those working at a system level, whether nationally or locally, whether in government offices, local education authorities, higher education or other agencies, have a leadership responsibility to provide an infrastructure of support and encouragement for learning, participating in a system learning community. This means that development of leadership is necessary at all levels of the system, as well as throughout schools.

- Capacity building and, more specifically, creating and sustaining a professional learning community aimed at enhancing pupil learning, will depend in the long run on those in senior school roles being prepared to implement policies of distributed leadership, and this needs to be promoted within leadership development.
- Leadership development needs to pay attention to helping leaders understand the change forces that affect their work and work to create their preferable futures (Beare 2001).
- Leadership development needs to ensure that leading learning for all is at the heart of leadership activity, including implications for leading teaching. In relation to this, knowledge about effective learning – including the importance of experiential learning – must be taken into account in designing leadership development experiences.
- To take the human side of change seriously, leadership development needs to address the affective dimensions of leadership (Hallinger 2003), emphasizing self development and working with others.
- Supporting development of inquiry habits of mind at all levels of leadership means focusing leadership development on activities that will help promote professional accountability throughout the profession.
- Leadership development needs to provide opportunities to build on and develop prior experiences of collaboration through teamwork and developing community partnerships, including those with other schools.
- Developing the necessary organizational management skills that can facilitate the other themes will also be an important feature of related leadership development.
- Given that the first five themes highlight within school actions that need to be adapted for each particular school context, leadership development needs to help school leaders understand their context and how best to determine and meet its needs.
- Leadership development needs to help leaders make connections between all of the initiatives in which they are involved and, itself, needs to be coherently planned to ensure connections between the different levels of leadership and leadership development.

Many of these implications can be found in the various programmes of the National College for School Leadership, its strategic plans and the accompanying national standards for headteachers in England (see www.ncsl.org), although questions remain about leadership development for extended professional learning community at different levels in the system.

Bibliography

American Psychological Association Board of Educational Affairs (1995) *Learner-centred Principles: A framework for school redesign and reform* [On-line]. http://www.apa.org/ed/lcp.html

Barber, M. (1996) *The Learning Game: Arguments for an education revolution.* London: Victor Gollancz.

Beare, H. (2001) *Creating the Future School.* London: Routledge Falmer.

Brandsford, J.D., Brown, A.L. and Cocking, R.R. (1999) *How People Learn: Brain, mind, experience, and school.* Washington DC: National Academy Press.

Bryk, A., Camburn, E. and Louis, K.S. (1999) Professional community in Chicago elementary schools: facilitating factors and organizational consequences, *Educational Administration Quarterly,* 35 (Supplement): 751–81.

Centre for Educational Research and Innovation (CERI) (2001) *New School Management Approaches.* Paris: OECD.

Cochran-Smith, M. and Lytle, S.L. (2001) Beyond certainty: taking an enquiry stance on practice, in A. Lieberman and L. Miller (eds) *Teachers Caught in the Action: Professional development that matters.* New York: Teachers College Press.

Darling-Hammond, L. (1997) *The Right to Learn: A blueprint for creating schools that work.* San Francisco: Jossey Bass.

Day, C., Harris, A., Hadfield, M., Tolley, H. and Beresford, J. (2000) *Leading Schools in Times of Change.* Buckingham: Open University Press.

Dimmock, C. (2000) *Designing the Learning-Centred School: A cross-cultural perspective.* London: Falmer Press.

Earl, L. and Katz, S. (2002) Leading schools in a data-rich world, in K. Leithwood and P. Hallinger (eds) *The Second International Handbook of Research on Educational Leadership and Administration.* Dordrecht: Kluwer.

Elmore, R. (2002) *Bridging the Gap Between Standards and Achievement.* Washington DC: Albert Shanker Institute.

Elmore, R. and Burney, D. (1999) Investing in teacher learning. In L. Darling-Hammond and G. Sykes (eds) *Teaching as the Learning Profession.* San Francisco: Jossey-Bass.

Evans, L. (1999) *Teacher Morale, Job Satisfaction and Motivation.* London: Paul Chapman.

Evans, R. (1996) *The Human Side of School Change: Reform, resistance, and the real-life problems of innovation.* San Francisco: Jossey-Bass.

Fullan, M. (2001) *Leading in a Culture of Change.* San Francisco: Jossey-Bass.

Fullan, M. (1993) *Change Forces: Probing the depths of educational reform.* London: Falmer Press.

Fullan M. (1995) The limits and the potential of professional development. In T.R. Guskey and M. Huberman (eds) (1995) *Professional Development in Education: New paradigms and practices.* New York and London: Teachers College Press.

Fullan, M. (2003) *The Moral Imperative of School Leadership.* London: Corwin Press.

Goleman, D. (1998) *Working with Emotional Intelligence.* London: Bloomsbury.

Gronn, P. (2003) *The New Work of Educational Leaders: Changing leadership in an era of school reform*. London: Paul Chapman and Thousand Oaks, CA: Sage.

Hallinger, P. (2003) School leadership preparation and development in global perspective, in P. Hallinger (ed.) *Reshaping the Landscape of School Leadership Development: A global perspective*. Lisse, The Netherlands: Swets & Zeitlinger.

Hargreaves, A. (2003) *Teaching in the Knowledge Society: Education in the age of insecurity*. Buckingham: Open University Press.

Hargreaves, A. (forthcoming) The emotional geographies of teachers and their colleagues. *International Journal of Educational Research*.

Hargreaves, D.H. (2003) *From Improvement to Transformation*. Keynote address to the annual conference of the International Congress for School Effectiveness and Improvement. Sydney, Australia, January.

Hargreaves, D.H. (1998) *Creative Professionalism: The role of teachers in the knowledge society*. London: DEMOS.

Hargreaves, D.H. (1996) *Teaching as Research-Based Profession: Possibilities and prospects*. The Teacher Training Agency Annual Lecture 1996, London: TTA.

Hodgkinson, C. (1991) *Educational Leadership: The moral art*. Albany, NY: SUNY Press.

Hopkins, D., Harris, A. and Jackson, D. (1997) Understanding the school's capacity for development: growth states and strategies, *School Leadership and Management*, 17(3): 401–11.

King, M.B. and Newmann, F.M. (2001) Building school capacity through professional development: conceptual and empirical considerations, *The International Journal of Educational Management*, 15(2): 86–93.

Lambert, N.M. and McCombs, B.L. (1998) *How Students Learn: Reforming schools through learner-centred education*. Washington DC: American Psychological Association.

Lee, V.E. and Smith, J.B. (1996) Collective responsibility for learning and its effects on gains in achievement for early secondary students, *American Journal of Education*, 104 (February): 103–47.

Leithwood, K., Jantzi, D. and Steinbach, R. (1999) *Changing Leadership for Changing Times*. Buckingham: Open University Press.

Lieberman, A. and Grolnick, M. (1996) Networks and reform in American education, *Teachers College Record*, 98(1), 7–45.

Little, J.W. (1999) *Teachers Professional Development in the Context of High School Reform: Findings from a three-year study of restructuring schools*. Paper presented at the Annual Meeting of the American Educational Research Association, Montreal, April.

Louis, K.S. and Marks, H. (1998) Does professional community affect the classroom? Teachers' work and student experience in restructured schools, *American Journal of Education*, 106(4): 532–75.

MacGilchrist, B., Mortimore, P., Savage, J. and Beresford, C. (1995) *Planning Matters: The impact of development planning in primary schools*. London: Paul Chapman.

McCall, J., Smith, I., Stoll, L. *et al.* (2001) Views of pupils, teachers and parents: vital indicators of effectiveness and improvement, in J. MacBeath and

P. Mortimore (eds) *Improving School Effectiveness*. Buckingham: Open University Press.

McMahon, A., Thomas, S., Greenwood *et al.* (2004) *Effective Professional Learning Communities*. Paper presented at ICSEI 2004 Conference Rotterdam, The Netherlands.

NCSL (2002) Networked Learning Communities: 'Like No Other Initiative'. Cranfield: National College for School Leadership: 3.

Papert, S. (1996) *The Connected Family: Bridging the digital generation gap.* Atlanta: Longstreet Press.

Rosenholtz, S.J. (1989) *Teachers' Workplace: The social organization of schools.* New York: Longman.

Schein, E. (1985) *Organisational Culture and Leadership*, San Francisco: Jossey-Bass.

Senge, P.M. (1990) *The Fifth Discipline: The art and practice of the learning organization.* London: Century Business.

Sergiovanni, T.J. (1992) *Moral Leadership: Getting to the heart of school improvement.* San Francisco: Jossey-Bass.

Sparks, D. and Hirsh, S. (1997) *A New Vision for Staff Development.* Alexandria VA: Association for Supervision and Curriculum Development and National Staff Development Council.

Stoll, L. (1999) Realising our potential: understanding and developing capacity for lasting improvement, *School Effectiveness and School Improvement*, 10(4): 503–32.

Stoll, L., Bolam, R. and Collarbone, P. (2002) Leadership for and of change: building capacity for learning, in K. Leithwood and P. Hallinger (eds) *The Second International Handbook of Research on Educational Leadership and Administration.* Dordrecht: Kluwer.

Stoll, L. and Fink, D. (1996) *Changing Our Schools: Linking school effectiveness and school improvement.* Buckingham: Open University Press.

Stoll, L., Fink, D. and Earl, L. (2003) *It's About Learning (And It's About Time).* London: Routledge Falmer.

Stoll, L., MacBeath, J., Smith, I. and Robertson, P. (2001) The Change Equation: capacity for improvement, in J. MacBeath and P. Mortimore (eds) *Improving School Effectiveness.* Buckingham: Open University Press.

Stoll, L., Wallace, M., Bolam, R. *et al.* (2003) *Creating and Sustaining Effective Professional Learning Communities: Questions arising from the literature and how they are being addressed in the project.* DfES Research Brief RBX12–03. Nottingham: DfES.

Watkins, C. (2003) *Learning: A sense-maker's guide.* London: Association of Teachers and Lecturers.

Wiley, S. (2001) Contextual effects of student achievement: school leadership and professional community, *Journal of Educational Change*, 2(1): 1–33.

five

Developing leaders for schools facing challenging circumstances

Gary M. Crow

Introduction

The phrase, 'schools facing challenging circumstances', may be unique to the UK context, but the conditions of downward spiralling student achievement, increased student mobility and high levels of economic and social deprivation are not unique and a great deal of attention in various countries is now being centred on these schools, their learning, teaching and leadership (Keys, Sharp, Greene and Grayson 2003). Moreover, there is a growing awareness that 'the way in which the characteristics of strong leadership and good management are applied in different circumstances is of fundamental importance' (Office for Standards in Education 2003: 3). Because leadership is contextual, we should expect this to be reflected in the preparation of leaders in schools facing challenging circumstances.

This chapter is based on an evaluation of a UK project to prepare aspiring leaders for challenging schools. The major purpose of this chapter, however, is to use this evaluation to identify lessons and recommendations for preparing innovative school leaders to work in schools facing challenging circumstances and to examine the pros and cons of one type of leader development mechanism, the internship. Before moving to this discussion, the chapter briefly describes the larger context in which leadership and leadership development for challenging schools occurs.

The context of challenging leadership

Leaders in schools facing challenging circumstances confront a changing context for leadership that is being shaped by the movement from an industrial to a post-industrial society and post-modern era. This movement has not been completed; some holdovers of the industrial model still exist in school leadership practice. Much of the folklore and traditional writing on school leadership assume a scientific management perspective taken largely from industrial psychology and managerial science (Callahan 1962). The practice of leadership in the industrial age, which was passed on to many current leaders, emphasized rationality and the goal of reducing the discretion of workers, e.g. teachers (Hage and Powers 1992). Standardizing curriculum, which remains an element of contemporary educational practice, emphasizing leadership as exercised by an individual in a formal role and reducing communication to a hierarchical system are all elements of this attempt to reduce ambiguity and discretion.

In post-industrial society, the focus is on leadership rather than management; and the work of leaders is characterized by complexity and uncertainty (Handy 1996). This complexity and uncertainty result from the changing demographics of schools, the explosion of technology and the rapid growth and change in knowledge that require individuals to live with ambiguity, consider multiple viewpoints, work flexibly and be creative. The ability to collect, analyze and apply relevant information in a rapid manner to understand complex learning environments, respond to changing problematic conditions, address a wider variety of student needs and inequities and sustain school improvement has become more important than strict adherence to policy manuals. Furthermore, facilitating the work of learning communities rather than separate teachers has become essential to increasing the learning and leadership capacity of schools (Bryk, Camburn and Louis 1999; Fullan, 2000; Hopkins 2001; Silins and Mulford 2002).

The understanding of leadership has changed from a focus exclusively on one person who alone turns schools around to an organizational quality distributed among numerous individuals (Elmore 2000; Spillane, Halverson and Diamond 2001; Silins and Mulford 2002). In this conception, headteachers become responsible for not only sharing leadership and delegating authority, but also increasing leadership capacity in the school.

Additional demanding forces magnify the unique complexity and uncertainty confronting leaders of schools facing challenging circumstances. Among these forces are:

> poor management, budget deficits, unsatisfactory buildings, staffing problems, low levels of pupil attainment on entry, behaviour management problems, high rates of pupil exclusion and unauthorized absence, low levels of parental involvement, falling rolls and high pupil turnover, and lack of public confidence in the school.
>
> (Keys *et al.* 2003: 2)

Preparation programmes based on industrial models of leadership and management that emphasize rationality, positional leadership and context-free leadership are inappropriate for developing innovative school leaders who can respond to the complexity, uncertainty and demands of their contexts and can facilitate the learning and leadership of others in schools facing challenging circumstances. Ofsted (2003) recently identified four key issues for the National College for School Leadership to consider in developing training for school leaders:

- distinguish between leadership and management;
- meet the needs of headteachers from different contexts;
- ensure coherence and progression; and
- evaluate the impact of training on school improvement and raising standards. These issues clearly reflect the needs of leadership and leadership preparation in a post-modern era.

Lessons and recommendations for preparing challenging leaders

In this section, the lessons and recommendations for preparing leaders for schools facing challenging circumstances in England will be identified and discussed. Before this discussion, the Trainee Head Scheme on which these lessons and recommendations are based will be described and the methods used to evaluate the scheme will be briefly discussed.

The Trainee Head Scheme and methods of evaluation

The Trainee Head Scheme was developed by the Department for Education and Skills in consultation with current headteachers in schools facing challenging circumstances and admitted the first cohort of 11 individuals in the autumn of 2001. The overall purpose of the scheme was to contribute to student attainment in these schools through leadership development. Primarily, the Trainee Head Scheme targeted the development of the knowledge, skills and dispositions important for headteachers in schools facing challenging circumstances. Secondly, the scheme sought to provide the schools that hosted these interns with additional leadership resources to enable each school to increase its learning capacity.

The scheme placed experienced deputies in secondary schools facing challenging circumstances for a period of one year to work alongside mentor headteachers credited with improving these types of schools. Because interns did not replace current deputies in the schools, they could experience more of the headship role without having substantial responsibilities that might diminish the learning opportunities for them. However, the scheme encouraged headteachers, together with the intern and the schools' deputies, to create a substantive role for the intern that enhanced the school's learning capacity.

Each intern met on a regular monthly basis with other interns and project administrators to gather information on best practices, to reflect on their experiences, and to develop supportive networking relationships. Furthermore, project administrators visited each internship school to monitor the experiences of interns, and to meet with mentor/heads and interns.

The lessons and recommendations identified later in this chapter are based on an evaluation of the Trainee Head Scheme described above. The evaluation used three sources of information. First, interviews with project administrators, mentors and interns and observations at school sites were conducted to determine the kinds of experiences and learning processes occurring in the project as well as participants' perceptions of the project's strengths and areas for improvement. Secondly, at the end of the programme after some interns were placed in schools, interviews and observations of interns and mentors were conducted. These data provide additional information on intern and mentor perceptions of how the project affected their knowledge and skills. Thirdly, documents provide evidence of the rationale for the project; the criteria and processes regarding intern, site and mentor selection and matching; and the learning processes used in the project.

The lessons and recommendations identified in this section are based on issues raised during the internship and immediately afterward and from literature on the preparation of school leaders. These recommendations are directed to policymakers, designers of preparation programmes, and mentors.

Programme goals. The preparation of leaders for schools facing challenging circumstances must focus on the specific context of these schools. As we mentioned previously in this paper, leadership in a post-modern era must acknowledge the contextual nature of leadership. Challenging schools, although similar in some respects to other schools, have their own demands and situational uniqueness that requires different skills.

Several participants in the Trainee Head Scheme stated that focusing leadership preparation on these schools helps to overcome the stereotypes sometimes encountered. Witnessing not only the challenges but also the opportunities of these schools helps to provide a more realistic, less stereotypical and hopefully more attractive image for aspiring leaders (Mulford 2003).

Moreover, the goal of the project to increase the learning capacity of the school is critical. In designing and implementing preparation programmes for leaders aspiring to take on schools facing challenging circumstances, designers and mentors should recognize that the rationale for leader development programmes in these schools is not simply to develop more leaders but to develop leaders of learning.

Design. The project's design involved several elements that pose questions and suggest recommendations. First, in light of our previous discussion of goals, how critical is it that aspiring leaders have socialization experiences within challenging schools? One could argue that leaders should be prepared in model schools where they can learn how things ought to be done. But in a post-modern world, these absolutist and non-contextual notions of leadership are problematic (Gronn 2002).

The literature identifies two types of work socialization: professional and organizational (Schein 1988). Professional socialization focuses on the initial preparation to an occupational role (e.g. the National Professional Qualification for Headship in England), while organizational socialization focuses on the specific context where the role is performed. The content of socialization for leaders includes three parts:

- skills to perform the role, e.g. how to conduct classroom observations;
- adjustment to the specific work environment, e.g. who to trust for information; and
- internalization of values, e.g. the importance of a professional learning organization (Feldman 1976).

This content, while having some generic components, clearly focuses on learning about the specific setting, e.g. challenging schools. The importance of placing those aspiring to take on challenging schools in these contexts as part of their training is attested to by the socialization literature as well as the perceptions of the participants in the Trainee Head Scheme.

Secondly, is there an optimal time limit for the intern's involvement in the preparation programme? The interns in the scheme entered with different degrees of management experience. Thus the length of time needed to develop skills to work in challenging schools differed for the interns. Leadership preparation programmes should consider whether, for some interns, a shorter pre-appointment training is sufficient, especially if followed by on-the-job mentoring and professional development. Intensive preparation programmes, such as the Trainee Head Scheme, are expensive. It is important to determine whether a long-term internship experience is necessary or simply a drain of valuable resources.

Thirdly, aspiring leaders do not walk into preparation programmes as blank tablets; they bring with them past experiences as deputies, teachers, etc. Contemporary socialization literature argues for a reciprocal notion of work socialization in which both the organization and the individual contribute to the role learning (Crow and Matthews 1998). Because of the intern's prior experience, there are likely to be different developmental stages of the interns' experiences. How should a preparation programme be designed to address the different types of learning outcomes at these stages? Several heads and interns spoke of changes in expectations and learning outcomes between the initial and later stages of the programme. Several writers have acknowledged the socialization and career stages that reflect different concerns, learning strategies and goals (Cordeiro and Smith-Sloan 1995; Mulford 2003; Weindling 1992). The design and implementation of a programme needs to reflect these stages in terms of expectations and learning outcomes. For example, the types of role assignments should change as interns move through the programme rather than holding to the initial negotiated role assignment.

Selection and matching processes. Matching interns with the right mentor and, in this case, the right challenging school is unfortunately for project designers and administrators not a science (Southworth 1995). Zey (1984) found that the most effective matches are those made by the mentors and interns themselves rather than some administrative matching process. But this informal matching process, if left to chance, may ignore some interns. In light of these issues, what are the lessons and recommendations about selection and matching that can be identified?

The developmental stage of the school should match the developmental stage of the intern. The Trainee Head Scheme ties the training of aspiring heads to enhancing the learning capacity of the host school. Although this increases the potential learning outcomes, it also raises at least three questions that have implications for selecting and matching. First, do some schools have conditions and needs that diminish the availability of mentoring, especially where the intern needs substantive attention from the mentor? Although all the schools in the Trainee Head Scheme were chosen because they had demonstrated that they were on an upward school improvement trajectory, several had circumstances that placed extensive demands on the mentor's time and on the school's resources for supporting headship preparation, e.g. recent dramatic changes in student and staff populations.

Secondly, is the intern learning to turn the school around or maintain a school that has already turned around? If interns are placed in schools that have already turned the corner on improvement, they may not have the learning opportunity to see how the head influenced the improvement. However, the mentors in these schools probably have more time available for mentoring. In contrast, if interns are placed in schools that have not yet begun to improve, they may have the opportunity to see how a headteacher can contribute to changing the school. However, mentors in these schools may not have sufficient time and resources to mentor.

Thirdly, is there an optimal match between the type and variety of deputy experience and the particular school context and challenges? Several mentors were clearly impressed with the way the intern's strengths matched the school's needs. Other heads did not see this close match. Prior leadership experience affects the learning of the intern, but it also affects the learning capacity of the school. The skills, sensitivity and values that interns bring can enrich the learning resources of the school or duplicate what is already there.

These questions suggest that both schools facing challenging circumstances and interns aspiring to headship may be at different developmental levels and needs that may complement or conflict with each other. Although there is no easy formula for answering these questions in order to make an effective match, the issues raised in these questions should be factored into selection and matching decisions.

Role assignments and experiences. In the Trainee Head Scheme, the interns described the broadening and enriching experiences they had as well as the confidence they gained from these experiences. But they also mentioned difficulties they encountered in negotiating these assignments. For instance, headteachers are sometimes reluctant to turn over responsibilities. The following questions suggest lessons and recommendations regarding how role assignments are made.

First, a difficult but important question for mentors involves the preferred title for interns, e.g. associate head or deputy. How interns are introduced to the school and mentored by heads depends upon the preferred title. In the Trainee Head Scheme, there was a range of mentor perceptions of the intern's role. Some mentors regarded the interns as equals with extensive previous experience and targeted their mentoring on headship preparation rather than additional deputy experience. In other instances, the interns were clearly additional deputies. Although there were no instances where the interns supplanted regular deputies, some role assignments emphasized the intern as an additional deputy rather than a headteacher in training. For example, some interns had significant pastoral responsibilities that would have suggested that the preparation focused more on developing deputy skills than headship skills.

Crow and Pounders (1996) found that the experiences of interns differed in other areas besides their title, e.g. how they were introduced to the staff and what kinds of special considerations they were given, e.g. building keys and an office. These considerations influenced, at least in the minds of the interns (and one would expect in the eyes of the staff), the effectiveness of the learning situation. Titles and assignments should serve to enrich the learning opportunities beyond the interns' prior administrative experiences.

Secondly, how do role assignments balance learning the direct leadership and the distributed leadership roles? One of the 'Ten School Leadership Propositions' of the NCSL's Leadership Development Framework is 'School leadership must be a function that is distributed throughout the school community' (National College for School Leadership 2001). Elmore (2000) found that distributed leadership is not simply a way to delegate authority but is a fundamental characteristic of effective learning communities. Mulford (2003) found that 'the leadership that makes a difference is both position based (principal) and distributive (administrative team and teachers) but both are only *indirectly* related to student outcomes'. Some types of mentoring run the risk of promoting a heroic image of the role focused only on the direct influence of the headteacher rather than a distributive image of how the head develops and encourages leadership capacity in the school.

Thirdly, what are effective ways to prepare aspiring heads to handle the increasing complexity of the role in a post-modern era (Hage and Powers 1992)? Typically leadership preparation programmes bombard the aspiring leader with the frequency, variety, fragmentation and complexity of job tasks. If aspiring leaders haven't been worn down through this method, they may respond to it by focusing on a limited set of approaches to problem solving in order to reduce uncertainty. The complexity required of post-modern leaders, especially in challenging schools, requires the ability to tolerate ambiguity and uncertainty while focusing on school improvement and student learning. Helping the intern deal with the ambiguity and uncertainty of leadership means acknowledging the limitations of the leader's knowledge, challenging the leader's assumptions of past practices and recognizing the power and value of multiple perspectives. This is not always a comfortable learning method. But if mentoring were all about supporting and not about challenging, there would be no development of critical, educative leaders.

Fourthly, how do the interns' role assignments and experiences balance the technical and cultural elements of the job? Greenfield (1985) identified these two elements necessary for the school leader: learning the technical skills to accomplish the tasks of the role and learning the values, e.g. innovation, experimentation and collegiality, that are necessary for changing the school. Many interns, due to their extensive management experience, may arrive with a good deal of technical learning. Cultural learning about the values and norms for changing schools facing challenging circumstances may be less developed for the interns and thus critical to include in leader preparation.

Making role assignments and designing experiences should prepare aspiring leaders to balance direct and distributed leadership, develop the ability to deal with complexity and ambiguity and develop cultural leadership skills. These elements are especially necessary in preparing aspiring leaders for challenging circumstances, where complexity, uncertainty and change are more problematic.

Mentoring opportunities. Mentoring traditionally has focused on knowledge-transfer as the primary means of learning a new role. But does such a method really have a place in preparing aspiring leaders to work in complex and challenging schools in a post-modern society? Gehrke (1988), instead, suggests viewing mentoring as 'gift giving' or 'awakening'. The mentor as

> door opener, information giver, supporter; [is] no doubt important . . .
> The greatest gift the mentor offers is a new and whole way of seeing
> things . . . It is a way of thinking and living that is given. (p. 192)

A more specific way to think about mentoring is by identifying the three functions of mentors: professional, career and psychosocial development (Crow and Matthews 1998; Kram and Isabella 1985). In fulfilling the professional development function, mentors help newcomers learn the knowledge, skills, behaviours and values of the leader's role. The career development function focuses on career satisfaction, career awareness and career advancement. The psychosocial development function focuses on personal and emotional well-being, as well as role expectations, conflict and clarification.

The literature on mentoring and the findings from the Trainee Head Scheme evaluation pose several questions for leadership development. How do mentor heads perform the professional, psychosocial and career functions of mentoring? In a leadership preparation programme, the most obvious type of mentoring involves helping the intern understand the unique knowledge, skills and dispositions of the role of headteacher in a school facing challenging circumstances. However, a more dynamic role for mentors and a more significant contribution for interns include all three functions, including helping interns deal with the personal-professional balances and role conflicts. Developers of internship programmes and mentors should consider whether there are gaps in the mentoring and what strategies, including training mentors to perform all three functions, should be used to bridge these gaps.

What are mentors who help prepare leaders of challenging schools trying to accomplish? Transferring knowledge and skills is important for helping aspiring leaders survive and manage challenging schools, especially in the beginning of the appointment. But this is clearly insufficient for enabling leaders to be change agents in these complex and constantly shifting environments. Awakening interns to the potential in these environments, as well as stimulating them to develop new ways to practice leadership, is likely to be more useful and valuable for preparing leaders for challenging schools.

Support and monitoring. Using the veteran to pass down the knowledge, values and skills of the role to the newcomer is a technique likely to produce custodial, non-innovative outcomes of socialization. Thus, one of the major issues for designers and administrators of preparation programmes for aspiring leaders of schools facing challenging circumstances is to develop mechanisms to diminish this custodial outcome and stimulate innovative orientations. Two methods that should be used in preparation programmes to avoid this outcome include mentor training and monitoring by external parties.

Walker and Stott (1993) found that mentor training was more important to the success of the mentoring relationship than mentor selection. Cohn and Sweeney (1992) found that the protégés of trained mentors rated the relationship with their mentors significantly higher. In the Trainee Head Scheme, both interns and mentors commented on the importance of mentor training not only initially but also as the mentoring relationship develops. As interns progress in their learning, as their relationship with the mentor and the senior management team changes and as the school adjusts to this new leader, mentors and interns need training that helps them interpret these changes and provides support in moving beyond custodial outcomes and goals.

Monitoring by a third party – be it project administrators, university consultants, LEA administrators, or training providers – can help to move the mentoring relationship beyond a custodial orientation. These individuals can use prompting, coaching and reflecting to awaken both interns and mentors to new ways of thinking about their relationship and the learning opportunities.

Pros and cons of internships for preparing challenging leaders

Internships are powerful learning tools for leaders of schools facing challenging circumstances. But they also have pitfalls that must be acknowledged. This final section identifies the pros and cons of internships by using literature and the comments from participants in the Trainee Head Scheme. These comments came during the internship as well as immediately following completion of the internship (Crow and Southworth 2003). The following section is organized in terms of the pros and cons for interns, mentors, and schools.

Interns. If designed well, internships can provide enriched opportunities for interns to learn about themselves – their learning styles, leadership styles and strengths and weaknesses. The interns in the Trainee Head Scheme described how the internship gave them an opportunity to use and develop their strengths and identify the areas they needed to improve. In addition, the internship can provide the opportunity for the intern to develop more reflective learning skills. Kanter (1977) suggests that mentoring opportunities, such as those found in internships, can increase the reflective power of the intern. In schools facing challenging circumstances, the complexity and uncertainty of the environment suggests the strong desirability of leaders with keen reflective abilities to understand the diverse needs of students and the shifting demands of the community.

Interns may also gain personal confidence from internship experiences. In the Trainee Head Scheme, this was among the most frequently cited outcome of the programme. Confidence is both a gift and a curse for aspiring leaders. It can result in cocky, self-assurance that ignores organizational landmines or perpetuates the use of previously successful formulas as if they are always effective for school improvement. However, confidence can be the stimulus that a new leader needs to take on difficult tasks and believe that change is possible in a challenging circumstance.

Effective internships provide an opportunity for the intern to broaden experiences that encourage new ideas and creativity. Torrance (1984) found a relationship between having a mentor and creative productivity. Interns in the Trainee Head Scheme described how the internship broadened their ideas by encouraging them to view the school in a new light.

Internships also can provide challenging opportunities to encourage risk taking. In an effective partnership between the mentor and intern, interns are challenged to move beyond their typical ways of seeing problems and arriving at solutions and are protected from damaging situations. This creates a delicate balancing act for the mentor who encourages risk-taking but is sensitive to how some failures may have career consequences.

Interns can also benefit by gaining networks, which provide visibility that is critical for later career appointments and promotions. Internships, such as the Trainee Head Scheme, which have cohort formats, also create networks of interns that can contribute to the knowledge repositories that new leaders need especially when they first become heads.

Internships have three major pitfalls for interns that must be acknowledged by project administrators and mentors. First, because of the important role that mentors play in the internship, there is a tendency for interns to develop a heroic image of the leader. Mentors for programmes such as the Trainee Head Scheme are chosen because they have demonstrated leadership competence in turning difficult schools around. If mentors do not sensitively and cautiously encourage interns to see the mentors' failures as well as successes, they run the risk of encouraging a heroic image of the role. Such an image is counterproductive to the research findings that effective leadership balances direct and distributive leadership (Mulford 2003).

The second pitfall involves the inherent nature of internships in which the veteran transmits knowledge and skills to the newcomer. This can result in perpetuating the status quo and creating a custodial, rather than innovative, view of the role. Because internships are such powerful learning tools, they can be used to promote role orthodoxies rather than role change.

Finally, internships can promote dysfunctional relationships between the mentor and the intern (Crow and Matthews 1998). These can include mentors who have personal interests and selfish concerns rather than the intern's learning in mind or mentors who create dependency relationships that cause the intern to become overly reliant on the mentor. Also, some mentors unintentionally create cloning (Hay 1995) when they promote a single image of the effective leader for a school facing challenging circumstances.

Mentors. Interns are not the only recipients of the benefits of internships. Several mentors in the Trainee Head Scheme described how their own personal learning increased by interns stimulating their thinking and by learning to critically evaluate their intuitive processes. Because leadership tends to be enacted in an on-the-run fashion, experienced leaders frequently do not take time to reflect critically on their decision-making, problem-solving and motivating styles. Having to reflect on these leadership behaviours with an intern can provide a learning opportunity for the mentor.

Mentors can also benefit from internships by gaining new organizational insights and skills. Several mentors described how the skills, e.g., in technology or assessment, brought by the intern contributed to their own development.

Internships have the added benefit for mentors of increasing their professional/career outcomes. For example, networking with other mentors and with project administrators can result in promotions. Also, the close relationship with an intern can result in a long-lasting professional friendship.

Just as poorly designed internships can have negative consequences for interns, mentors may also suffer. Being assigned an ineffective intern who refuses to be open to new learning or is insensitive to school culture can be a difficult drain on the psychological and time resources of the mentor. Furthermore, an unsuccessful internship experience can discourage the mentor from making a second attempt. For these reasons, monitoring, support and training are critical not only for the intern but for the mentor.

Schools and systems. Individual schools and larger educational systems also have a stake in the effectiveness of internships. In the Trainee Head Scheme one of the goals was to increase the learning capacity of schools. Mentors identified several ways in which the internship benefited the school's learning capacity, including additional resources for reforms, expertise on developing assessment, staff development and increased school status. In addition, if the internship is designed and promoted as a co-learning experience rather than simply transmitting management folklore, it can enhance an organizational learning environment.

In addition, internships can increase the leadership capacity of the school. This can occur by reinvigorating veteran school leaders as they participate in the mentoring process. If mentoring is seen as a school-wide process rather than simply a two-way relationship between the headteacher and the intern, the internship can increase the leadership capacity of the school. Also, if headteachers are sensitive and senior management team members are open, the opportunity may exist to provide these deputies and other school leaders with expanded leadership opportunities.

Internships can also benefit the larger system in at least two ways. First, effective internships can help respond to administrative shortages by creating a pool of qualified recruits for leadership positions in schools facing challenging circumstances. Secondly, mentors can enhance their mentoring skills in such a way that they can become consultants for other schools facing challenging circumstances. These 'consultant heads' multiply the effect of the internship beyond the single school.

Schools and systems, however, can also suffer from ineffective internships. Poorly designed internships and ineffective selection and matching processes can result in draining critical leadership resources from schools that can ill afford it. An intern who refuses to be open to learning or who does not bring the requisite skills can take away time and resources from more immediate and critical school needs.

Internships are expensive learning tools. They cost in terms of the salaries of interns and project administrators and of the time of mentors and senior management teams. In addition, they take what may be extremely qualified leaders out of other schools and create vacancies that may not easily be filled. In an earlier section, the question of the desirable length of the internship was raised. This question needs to be considered seriously in calculating the costs of an internship.

Conclusion

Leadership development for schools facing challenging circumstances is a dynamic and complex process. If leadership development policies and programmes are to respond to the complex and uncertain environments of postmodern schools, they must create ongoing learning opportunities that are dynamic. Rather than creating 'designer leadership' (Gronn 2002) programmes in which one-size-fits-all, we need to pay special attention to the uniqueness of schools facing challenging circumstances and the diversity of learning and leadership styles that are critical in a postmodern era.

Leadership development fundamentally must be viewed as contributing to student learning. We can no longer afford to create leadership learning opportunities that meet only the needs of leaders and the other adults in schools. The success of internships and mentoring opportunities must ultimately be assessed by the success of students in challenging schools. Challenging leadership is empty without challenging learning.

Bibliography

Bryk, A., Camburn, E. and Louis, K.S. (1999) Professional community in Chicago elementary schools: Facilitating factors and organizational consequences, *Educational Administration Quarterly*, 35 (Supplemental), 751–81.

Callahan, R.E. (1962) *Education and the Cult of Efficiency: A study of the social forces that have shaped the administration of public schools*. Chicago: The University of Chicago Press.

Cohn, K.C. and Sweeney, R.C. (1992) *Principal Mentoring Programmes: Are school districts providing the leadership?* Paper presented at the American Educational Research Association, San Francisco CA.

Cordeiro, P.A. and Smith-Sloan, E. (1995, April) *Apprenticeships for Administrative Interns: Learning to talk like a principal*. Paper presented at the American Educational Research Association, San Francisco CA.

Crow, G.M. and Matthews, L.J. (1998) *Finding One's Way. How mentoring can lead to dynamic leadership*. Thousand Oaks CA: Corwin Press, Inc.

Crow, G.M. and Pounders, M.L. (1996, April) *The Administrative Internship: 'Learning the ropes' of an occupational culture*. Paper presented at the American Educational Research Association, New York City.

Crow, G.M. and Southworth, G. (2003) *Administrative Internships: Learning outcomes for new administrator*. Paper presented at the University Council for Educational Administration, Portland OR.

Elmore, R. (2000) *Building a New Structure for School Leadership*. Washington: The Albert Shanker Institute.

Feldman, D.C. (1976) A contingency theory of socialization, *Administrative Science Quarterly*, 21, 433–52.

Fullan, M. (2000) The return of large scale reform, *The Journal of Educational Change*, 1(1), 5–28.

Gehrke, N. (1988) Toward a definition of mentoring, *Theory into Practice*, 27(3), 190–4.

Greenfield, W.D. (1985) The moral socialization of school administrators: Informal role learning outcomes, *Educational Administration Quarterly*, 21(4), 99–119.

Gronn, P. (2002) Leader formation, in K. Leithwood, P. Hallinger, K. Seashore-Louis, G. Furman-Brown, P. Gronn, B. Mulford and K. Riley (eds.), *Second International Handbook of Educational Leadership and administration*. Dordrecht: Kluwer.

Hage, J. and Powers, C.H. (1992) *Post-Industrial Lives. Roles and relationships in the 21st Century*. Newbury Park CA: Sage.

Handy, C. (1996) *Beyond Certainty. The changing world of organizations*. Boston MA: Harvard Business School Press.

Hay, J. (1995) *Transformational Mentoring: Creating developmental alliances for changing organizational cultures*. London: McGraw-Hill.

Hopkins, D. (2001) *Meeting the Challenge: An improvement guide for schools facing challenging circumstances*. London: Department for Education and Employment.

Kanter, R. (1977) *Men and Women of the Corporation*. New York: Basic Books.

Keys, W., Sharp, C., Greene, K. and Grayson, H. (2003) *Successful Leadership of Schools in Urban and Challenging Contexts*. Nottingham, England: National College for School Leadership.

Kram, K.E. and Isabella, L. (1985) Mentoring alternatives: The role of peer relationships in career development, *Academy of Management Journal*, 28(1), 110–32.

Mulford, B. (2003) *School Leaders: Changing roles and impact on teacher and school effectiveness*. Education and Training Policy Division, OECD.

National College for School Leadership (2001) *Leadership Development Framework*. Nottingham, England: National College for School Leadership.

Office for Standards in Education (2003) *Leadership and Management. What inspection tells us*. London: Office for Standards in Education.

Schein, E. (1988) Organizational socialization and the profession of management, *Sloan Management Review*, 53–65.

Silins, H. and Mulford, B. (2002) Organizational learning and school change, *Educational Administration Quarterly*, 38(5), 613–42.

Southworth, G. (1995) Reflections on mentoring for new school leaders, *Journal of Educational Administration*, 33(5), 17–28.

Spillane, J.P., Halverson, R. and Diamond, J.B. (2001). Investigating school leadership practice: A distributed perspective, *Educational Researcher*, 30(3), 23–8.

Torrance, E.P. (1984) *Mentor Relationships: How they aid creative achievement, endure, change, and die*. Buffalo NY: Bearly.

Walker, A. and Stott, K. (1993) Preparing for leadership in schools: The mentoring contribution, in B.J. Caldwell and E.M.A. Carter (eds.), *The Return of the Mentor: Strategies for workplace learning*. London: Falmer.

Weindling, D. (1992) New heads for old: Beginning principals in the United Kingdom, in F.W. Parkay and G.E. Hall (eds.), *Becoming a Principal: The challenges of beginning leadership*. Needham Heights MA: Allyn and Bacon.

Zey, M.G. (1984). *The Mentor Connection*. Homewood IL: Dow-Jones Irwin.

NB: The author wishes to thank Geoff Southworth and Dick Weindling for many insightful conversations about leadership development, which enriched this chapter. Although their ideas are interwoven throughout this paper, the author retains the responsibility for how these ideas have been articulated.

six

Developing leadership in context

Allan Walker and Clive Dimmock

Introduction

For a number of years we have worked closely with principals on ways to improve school leadership through the design and implementation of contextually grounded, needs-based approaches to professional development aimed at improving schools and student learning outcomes. This direction was determined largely by a concern for the scant attention paid to context by many leadership training programmes with which we were familiar, and a general dissatisfaction with some of the existing values and structures bounding principal preparation and ongoing learning. Our motivation for involving principals drew, and indeed continues to so do, on a belief that the neglect of context in development programmes is unavoidably linked to the lack of meaningful involvement of principals in their own and their peers' learning. Accordingly, one of our major aims has been that principals take greater control of their own professional agendas through deeper levels of peer cooperation, support and connection in areas ranging from learning design to sustainability. However, as we worked more closely with principals, our initial expectations concerning control and involvement became somewhat more tempered. We realized that total or unfettered professional control carries hazards similar to those associated with excessive control by others outside the profession, that is, a general disregard for the complexity and divergence of the different contexts within which school leaders work. Accordingly, our belief is that principal's professional development not only needs to involve principals more actively, but should be framed by consideration for contextual specificity and marked by intentionality, strategic thinking and formal design.

In this chapter we present a three-stage argument for greater principal involvement in their professional development. The first stage holds that development programmes for school leaders have often excluded experienced practitioners from authentic involvement in their own and their colleagues' professional learning and growth. Increased principal involvement can add immense value to principal development programmes and hence to the quality of school leadership and, ultimately, student learning. Too often in the past, principal involvement has been confined to instrumental or political roles. While the involvement of principals has been underplayed, conversely, that of higher education providers has been allowed undue influence. The second stage of the argument is that while greater principal involvement is generally beneficial, it needs qualification. We believe that principal involvement should coincide with greater recognition given to leadership in context. If both these arguments informed professional development programmes for principals then this would overcome the reproduction of inappropriate skills and practices, the lack of a practitioner tradition in theoretical grounding and problems of transferability. The third and final stage of our argument suggests that the value of principal involvement is magnified when it is intentionally designed to target more contextually specific school and community situations. This suggestion holds, for example, that a principal aspiring to lead a multicultural school in an urban setting would intentionally and strategically engage, at least as part of a wider agenda, in a formally designed, personalized professional development programme with leaders and others known to be successful in such schools. Engagement in such a programme would aim to have its definitive impact in the life and work of the school and its classrooms when the new principal took up duty.

Increasing principal control of professional development and preparation

The value of increased principal input to the development of their professional preparation has been acknowledged recently by the National College for School Leadership (NCSL) in the UK, and the Hong Kong Centre for the Development of Educational Leadership (Walker, Cheung, Chan, Chan, Wong and Dimmock 2002). It has also been recognized through the rebirth of various forms of mentoring programmes, such as that described by Gary Crow in Chapter Five. Genuine involvement, however, remains, at best, underplayed. Calls for the enlarged and more meaningful involvement of principals are made on a number of grounds (see for example Crow 2001; Littky and Schen 2003). The most commanding of these is that despite considerable rhetoric and even some purposeful action, principal professional development and preparation (PPDP) too often lacks *bona fide* connections between theory and practice. This is most commonly apparent in neglect of the context within which leaders lead and learn, especially that beyond simplistic divisions such as the primary and secondary divide. The greater involvement of school leaders in their own and their peers' learning has the potential to contribute appreciably to the contextual relevance and usefulness of many PPDP programmes.

A persistent lack of relevance in leadership development programmes stems from a failure to connect theory and practice. The problem of 'disconnection' appears to have intellectual, political and instrumental elements, which combine to lessen the contextual relevance of the professional development, and actively prevent principals from addressing the problem. In other words, a lack of connection between theory and practice is synonymous with disregard for context, a phenomenon that can be usefully addressed through greater principal involvement in their own, and their peers', PPDP. We now explain what we mean by the three elements of 'disconnection'.

From a broad perspective, *intellectual disconnection* stems from the generally weak knowledge base underpinning the field of educational administration and leadership (Dimmock and Walker 1998). Despite the continued proliferation of literature on educational leadership, the knowledge base used to guide the development and preparation of principals is largely normatively and prescriptively based, lacking a solid empirical school-focused foundation. Indeed, leadership research often employs decontextualized paradigms and is presented in ways that make it inaccessible to practitioners. Research used to guide principal development and which, at the same time, lacks contextual specificity and relevance, is problematic within national boundaries and perhaps even more so when carelessly transported across national and cultural borders. For example, PPDP systems in many Asian systems draw almost reverently on theories, frameworks, ideas and presenters from elsewhere, particularly the UK and the USA (Walker and Dimmock 2000). This over reliance on Anglo-American theory, values and beliefs stretches from policy makers to all sectors of higher education and schools. In PPDP terms, naive adoption distorts the meaning of the programme content for participants and influences its design, structure and even presentation (Walker and Dimmock 2002). Although cross-fertilization of ideas and approaches is generally beneficial, there are dangers in failing to recognize that theory, practice and imported expertise may not readily transplant across geo-cultural boundaries.

Intellectual disconnection also refers to the common approach to principal professional development taken by providers, such as universities and other institutes of higher education. PPDP providers tend to locate the content of their formal and informal leadership 'preparation' and in-service programmes within the normative domain and then to communicate the ideas as (decontextualized) exemplars for practice. This is exacerbated by academics sometimes determining the content and pedagogies of programmes in line with their own particular 'specialisms' or areas of claimed expertise – which may or may not hold relevance for school leaders, or for current policy, and rarely if ever do so for specific school contexts. One particularly sombre side of intellectual disconnection is that much PPDP continues to ignore knowledge needed by leaders in terms of curriculum, pedagogy and research into student learning – areas craved by practitioners, but too often neglected by 'leadership and management' specialists.

In short, many leadership development programmes run by universities and other higher education institutions appear unsound in terms of the efficacy or legitimacy of their knowledge base. Such programmes are often reflective of the personal interests and expertise of those conducting them, rather than of the needs of the principal clientele, and their physical location remote from their intended point of influence is symbolic of a lack of contextual relevance. Lacking contextual relevance and application, and a professional input from those they intend to 'develop', it is hardly surprising that they draw only fleetingly on the realities of practice. While such a 'disconnection' can be labelled as intellectual, it also touches on the political.

Political disconnection can lead to reluctance to involve principals in their own development, which has both a macro and a micro aspect. From a macro perspective, we define it as a chasm between the claims of politicians, policy makers and central bureaucrats and the realities of schools – as interpreted by principals. While politically motivated PPDP can introduce a future-oriented perspective towards change, which may be seen as desirable, development opportunities grounded too exclusively within possibly tenuous political agendas may lack practical relevance and meaning for schools and their leaders. Involving principals more at policy-making and system implementation levels may help address such issues. From a micro perspective, political disconnection involves the allocation of resources for PPDP on micro-political rather than on quality criteria. In some systems, for example, historically grounded traditions of 'sharing' the provision of PPDP among all of the relevant higher education institutions and/or other providers – regardless of quality of provision – has taken precedence. Such practices inevitably run counter to the successful implementation of comprehensive, coherent principal development policies. Although unstated, politically driven allocation traditions can be reflective of the power of institutes of higher learning over PPDP in some systems. Such practices are antithetical to quality PPDP and emphasize political rather than content/delivery concerns. Jealousies and overt competition between providers, when combined with a lack of principal involvement, entail 'disconnection', because they upset the intent, relevance and implementation of high quality principal professional development.

Instrumental disconnection can be thought of as the reverse side of intellectual disconnection. It denies principals' control of their own learning through oversimplifying and equating their development with generalized knowledge or simple sets of skills. Although resembling political disconnection, this form of development assumes that PPDP is linked neither to theoretical/intellectual knowledge nor to overt political agendas but, rather, to generic management knowledge and skills deemed necessary for the smooth bureaucratic functioning of a school. This type of professional development often conforms to system policy and is conducted by mid-level bureaucrats themselves, or by co-opted 'system approved' principals. As such, it tends to be based almost completely on practitioner experience, or an in-depth knowledge of rules and regulations. Although such professional development fulfils a purpose of sorts, it also overlooks the importance of specificity of leadership context, and tends to restrict principal involvement in the development of their present and future peers to that of detached instructor – one who is concerned more with mechanical operation than future improvement. Reducing leadership development to such a level fails to recognize the complexity of its nature.

The three types of disconnection are simultaneously the result of limited or superficial principal involvement and a powerful stimulus for this to continue. At a basic level, principals need to be more involved in PPDP in order to connect its content, conduct and aims more closely with the realities of their school contexts. Increased involvement may engage principals at a number of levels and in a number of forms. It is not simply a matter of providing principals with increased visibility in formalized programmes. While such visibility is important, it may lead to bland symbolism, where principals are, in effect, used as little more than (very capable) 'mouthpieces' for academics or other providers whose main aim is to demonstrate the 'practical legitimacy' of a programme. In these instances, principals rarely have input into the substance, relevance or pedagogy of such programmes.

While it is not our purpose here to detail the ways principals can or should be involved, we hold that genuine principal involvement needs to address the three elements of disconnection discussed. For example, at the 'big picture' level, principals could be more involved in research groups commenting on and vetting the direction and relevance of research and knowledge construction. They can also be more involved at various levels of the policy-making process as it influences their school development and learning, perhaps through moderating overly ambitious political change agendas. It is at a practical level, however, where they could play a major part – in both formal and informal ways.

In formal course development, principal involvement can play a key role in partnership with academics and others. Such partnerships can promote relevance by conceptualizing purposes and frameworks, as well as teaching and facilitating and communicating. The Singapore programme described in Chapter Seven is one illustration of this. Such input is as important for award bearing courses as it is for shorter more professionally oriented programmes. For example, case studies and Problem Based Learning can be shaped for relevance by principals. Principals can also play a greater role through (either structured formal, or unstructured informal) mentoring and coaching, through providing opportunities for shadowing and peer observation, establishing and running focus groups and personal and professional support/learning networks. They can also work across different levels of leadership; for example, experienced principals can provide new principals with invaluable insight and information. They can also help aspiring or emerging leaders, and each other on an ongoing basis. The reciprocal benefits which can result from such configurations inevitably rely on the contextualization of values, knowledge and skills, a point of great importance in our argument.

In this section we have argued that principals should be more intimately involved in their own and their peers' PPDP. An appropriate starting point to achieve this is to target the 'disconnection' which pervades PPDP and prevents it from adequately addressing issues of context, and from bridging the divide between theory and practice. Our advocacy for professional involvement, however, needs to be qualified by a number of factors; among these is the reality that unless such involvement is appropriately structured, it may still downplay the importance of context within which principals operate. The following section elaborates this and a number of other qualifications.

Qualifying principal involvement in their professional development and preparation

Despite the attraction of principal involvement in their professional development, a number of qualifications are necessary in order to maximize the benefits that can flow.

The first qualification relates to the gap between practice and theory. Just as an over-dependence on theory as a component of PPDP is undesirable, so is an over-concentration on personal experience and practice. Experience alone does not automatically indicate that the person has the prerequisite expertise or ability to shape the professional development of their peers, or that they are capable of transferring this to others. Experience is no guarantee that a principal has actually been successful in their school, nor is it necessarily equated with honed expertise. If care is not taken about *what* experience is worth sharing, principal involvement can run the risk of degenerating into 'ignorance breeds ignorance'. Indeed, Walker and Stott (1993) warned of this in relation to Principalship mentoring in Singapore in the 1990s when they discovered that 'politically correct' rather than educationally sound practice governed some formal mentoring relations between principals.

To take the quality of expertise argument further, even if a principal has been successful in a particular setting at a particular time, this does not guarantee that what has worked for them – their experience – will necessarily work for others. Likewise, a willingness to be heavily involved in working closely with fellow principals, or being 'politically connected' (or wanting to be) may also be false indicators of what a principal can actually contribute to the development of their peers, whether they be aspiring, newly appointed or experienced.

A second related qualification is that experience may not be transferable across school contexts. For example, one could justly ask how qualified is a principal who is currently leading a comprehensive high school in a pre-dominantly white upper-middle class suburb to teach, mentor or coach a principal taking over an urban secondary school with 80 per cent of the student population Afro-Caribbean or Somali? Likewise, the efficacy of a principal of a 'famous' high-achieving English Medium school on Hong Kong Island attempting to 'teach' a newly appointed colleague at a Chinese Medium School with a large Mainland student population, may be equally questionable. We return to this issue later in the chapter, but it is interesting to note that concern for contextual relevance runs just as strongly through arguments against overplaying principal involvement in PPDP, as it does through those calling for it to be strengthened.

A third qualification is that not all principals have the skills to communicate their ideas and experientially based knowledge, even when such knowledge is worth sharing. Being a good principal does not necessarily equate to being a good teacher, mentor, coach or programme designer. And even if principals are good communicators, their effectiveness as developers may be limited, again, by their limited experience of school and leadership context, and also by the varying learning styles and needs of fellow principals. Hence, decisions about which principals to select for involvement in PPDP become quite complex, and need to take into account, *inter alia*, experience of particular school contexts in relation to the training and development needs, as well as a complex mix of personal characteristics and other factors.

A final qualification may be particularly relevant to the level and scope of involvement of principals in their own PPDP. Given the often fragmented nature of their jobs, principals may not have developed the conceptual abilities necessary to frame meaningful professional development and preparation. For example, principals may not have clarified or articulated why they do what they do in the way they do it. Many are not fully cognisant of the values and reasons behind their policies, actions and behaviours. While there is general agreement that good leaders have the ability to conceptualize and to see the bigger picture of what they are doing in schools, not all principals have this ability. An inability to conceptualize can lead to subsequent professional learning being trivialized and piecemeal, focused on superficial, narrowly based skills, knowledge and values. Relevant experience needs to be closely integrated with conceptual ability, and assuming this to be the case, mutually respectful partnerships between practitioners and academics, and purposeful identification of principals who posses the necessary conceptual ability, seem an appropriate way forward.

While our stance remains strongly one of increasing principal involvement in their professional development, this does not mean that only principals should be involved or that such control should be total. As we explain in the next section, we believe that involvement must be framed by the context of the schools that principals head. As well as continued, if more guided, contributions by academics and system officials, other groups with school interest should also be involved. For example, parents have rarely been involved in principal development, and in many if not all contexts may present a largely untapped resource. One of these, for example, would be in multi-ethnic, multi-cultural school settings where parents can contribute immensely through helping principals understand the needs of the students and values of the broader community. Likewise, policy makers, curriculum professionals, psychologists and other paraprofessionals could together form a comprehensive yet integrated perspective on principal professional development and preparation.

Each of the above caveats indicates the need for a considered, judicious approach to principal involvement in their own professional development. At worse, such involvement can lead to the mutual sharing of ignorance or practice devoid of theoretical and conceptual understanding that provides explanation. Even when principal involvement is well-intentioned, with relevant experiential, practice-based knowledge passed on using good communication skills, there is still the danger of a misplaced focus on helping future leaders lead today's rather than tomorrow's schools. The salient point is that principal involvement with their own and their peers' professional development requires careful scrutiny to ensure that what is being transferred is indeed worthwhile.

To summarize, our argument is that while we strongly support the greater involvement of principals in designing and sustaining their own professionalism and professional development, such involvement needs qualification. For principal involvement in initial and ongoing learning to be worthwhile, it is not simply a case of assembling principals together in classrooms, forming mentoring relationships, networking or clustering, and then expecting them to learn. Equally, it is increasingly clear that for principals to abdicate control of the content and delivery of their preparation and development to academics, central agencies and others, is inadequate, indefensible and possibly unprofessional. A key issue underpinning the qualification to principal involvement is context of leadership. The crucial factor commonly missing from principal professional development is the relating of practice to context. It is this more than any other factor, we contend, which should shape leadership preparation and development in future. School contexts are becoming ever more complex, divergent and difficult to manage. In the following section we argue that PPDP would be more meaningful if it is deliberately framed and designed to address issues of context.

Framing principal involvement in professional development and preparation with concern for context

Our argument is that PPDP needs to be framed by the context within which leaders lead and/or wish to lead and that this may be usefully done through involving practicing school leaders in a range of ways. We believe that such framing holds the potential to match principals' own callings, interests and abilities with specific school contexts. A close match or fit between the principal and school context is more likely to enhance the leader's capacity to meaningfully influence student lives and learning. In other words, we are not arguing for the increased involvement of principals and consideration of context simply as ways to provide a more fulfilling experience for those involved. Rather, we believe that such learning is likely to have its ultimate impact on the quality of the new leaders' schools.

Considered reference to context remains absent from many leadership development endeavours as does the meaningful involvement of leaders themselves. School principals should play a greater role in shaping and driving their own development, but to gain maximum benefit, their involvement should be located within a framework of intentionality, strategic thinking and formal design – all connected by context. Greater recognition of the influence of contextual forms and their link to student outcomes has been flagged recently by organizations such as the NCSL in the United Kingdom and current Hong Kong principal development policy. These have mainly focused on the level of schooling or stages of the Principalship. For example, Hong Kong policy bases PPDP around aspiring, newly appointed and serving principals; NCSL identifies an even greater number of divisions. Such moves are to be applauded. Our suggestion is that the differentiation be taken a step further by intentionally building more specific aspects of organization, learning and cultural context into Principalship preparation and further development, and that this be more heavily supported by appropriate principal control and involvement.

Intentionality in this instance asks aspiring and future principals to identify the type of school context within which they would like to work, or have been working. A declaration of intent then places a responsibility on principals and systems to consider more carefully the specific circumstances within which leadership will be exercised and to connect consciously PPDP to this context. At present, defining more precisely the contexts in which particular principals work, or intend to work, is rarely undertaken, and consequently such considerations fail to enter professional development agendas. The fact is that this neglect normally continues after appointment, when context is still not used meaningfully to shape leadership learning. In cases where the context is unknown until shortly before commencement of appointment, principals and appointing authorities could work on improving their selection procedures in advance. At the same time, greater differentiation in focus and design of appropriate professional development strategies to match as closely as practicable the contexts to which principals will be appointed involves a form of strategic thinking and planning by both the individual and the supporting system.

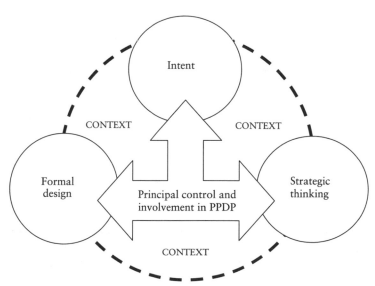

Figure 6.1 A contextually sensitive approach to PPDP

Strategic thinking takes cognizance of the social-cultural context within which leaders intend to lead. It is predicated on an intimate understanding and reflection of the cultural and contextual conditions of schools and the communities they serve. A particular and increasingly important manifestation of this, for example, is the nature and profile of schools in inner city areas that reflect the multi-ethnic composition of their localities and intakes. Strategic thinking when applied to contextually relevant PPDP encompasses a personal and an instrumental side. In personal terms, strategic thinking requires the nominating principal (whether they be aspiring or experienced) to clarify and articulate their values – that is, the 'why' they want to lead such a school and what they believe they can achieve as principal. Self-reflection should challenge them as to how their values and beliefs may integrate with those of the school, what they see as the strengths and weaknesses of the context, and whether they feel a sense of identity with that type of environment. Such reflection may best be done with peers and colleagues working in similar contexts. The purpose of strategic thinking at this personal level is that it challenges the principal to make explicit the context within which they anticipate leading, and where they believe they can best make a positive contribution to school improvement.

In instrumental terms, strategic thinking has two parts – professional background of the principal, and the features of school context. In regard to the first part, namely, consideration of the professional background from which the principal comes, the areas of relevant concern include their past and present position, years on the job and type of workplace context. This aspect focuses on what the new leader will bring with them to the school in terms of formal background. This is of vital importance when designing a worthwhile professional development agenda in preparation for a particular context. A list of at least some of the possibly relevant contextual features is shown in Table 6.1. The second aspect of instrumental strategic thinking attempts the identification of the key contextual features of the type of school the principal or aspirant has in mind to lead. These features are important in that they promote an understanding of the new context, and also serve as a frame for the design of a learning agenda. Contextual features for this instrumental dimension may include, *inter alia*, those presented in Table 6.2 (this is not intended as finite list). Such features may also be used to guide strategic thinking along the first instrumental dimension. As with the more personal or values-based aspects of strategic thinking, the instrumental sides may best be processed with peers.

Formal Design refers to a purposeful, context specific leadership learning agenda designed and operationalized by the nominating principal/s in collaboration with suitable peers, as well as the employing authority and professional development providers. A design purports to be a coherent mix of values, vision, research and experiential-driven knowledge and

Table 6.1: Coming From (Present Personal Professional Background)

Level
  Kindergarten
  Primary
  Secondary (comprehensive/senior College)
  Higher Education
  Business
  Public Service
Position
  Principal
  Deputy-Principal
  Head of Department
  Teacher
  Non-Education
  Other
Experience
  Years
  Number of schools
Principal Experience
  Newly appointed
  Mid-career
  Experienced
  Retired
Appointment
  Applied
  Appointed (agreed, forced)

intuition that enables school leaders to work closely with colleagues to construct appropriate professional development pathways. Formal design of an agenda involves building a realistic and coherent approach to professional development which draws predominantly on principals and others, including community leaders and parents from diverse social and cultural contexts, which are at least similar to those environments the principals may find themselves working in. The design is formal in that it needs to be planned and carefully constructed with the involvement of others who are knowledgeable about the nominated context. The design focuses on ways to best prepare for improving student outcomes and overall quality in the 'target' school. Formality need not imply that the professional development activities within the design are drawn exclusively from formal offerings. In fact, given that the design is driven by the context, development strategies could be eclectic and draw on a number of formal and informal sources.

Table 6.2: Going To (Future Organizational/Community Context)

Age
Relocation
Student/Staff numbers
Location
  Urban
  Suburban
  Rural
  City, village, etc.
Student/community culture
Student demographics
Anticipated demographic shifts
Student/community ethnicity
Student/community SES
Status of school (Tradition)
Staff (ethnic) profile
Staff/student gender profile
Recent history
Previous principal
Curriculum
Learning profile

Although it may not be necessary to have strict conventions for the design strategy, the aim is to match the level of development, experience and knowledge of the (future) principal with peers and others who can provide relevant development and/or preparation. Such arrangements should be based on reciprocal advantage, where those providing the knowledge or experience can also benefit from their involvement, perhaps by having their own views challenged or refreshed. The design strategy should rest quite heavily on involving principals currently working in similar contexts, but it can also include more formal elements of knowledge, which may be communicated by scholar-practitioners or more formally by academics with relevant expertise. We appreciate that identifying and matching contexts and relevant peer support will not be an exact science, and may not always be possible or successful, but it could be considered and promoted more than at present, and may even be built into development, recruitment and selection policies.

Conclusion

We realize that the ideas we have sketched are not without considerable conceptual and practical difficulties, particularly in terms of resource constraints, manageability, the entrenched nature of existing knowledge and conventional ways of conducting professional development. We certainly do not claim that the proposed model will cure the ills of PPDP, or that it adequately replaces the range of valuable opportunities currently available. Equally, the promotion of context-based PPDP as a pre-eminent guide for principal development does not deny the considerable value of existing cross-contextual exchange and learning, the necessity of theoretical input provided through more structured programmes, nor other approaches to individual and collective learning. There are clearly many useful ways to promote principal professional development; and while acknowledging these, we continue to argue for context-based PPDP, when possible and desirable, to be given an important place within them. We do, however, suggest that the structured and meaningful involvement of principals in their own PPDP may be a useful way of improving leadership for learning at the only level that really counts – that of the school.

The ultimate test for any form of PPDP must be its potential to make a difference in schools; or to create better schools of tomorrow. Better schools are defined as places where student lives and learning are improved regardless of their economic, social, ethnic or religious background. We suggest that the closer principal training and development is located to the context within which principals lead, the greater the chance that their leadership will have a positive influence on learning and teaching. For example, a principal moving to work in a multi-ethnic school and who has followed a programme designed intentionally to learn more about the cultural intricacies that define the school community should be better prepared to make a difference to students and the broader community. We also hold that an intentionally designed and focused programme which takes account of the context within which student learning takes place requires the meaningful involvement of school leaders with 'front line' experience. As stressed throughout the chapter, principal involvement in PPDP makes most sense when it is relevant; such relevance is best provided by partnerships involving leaders with successful track records in a variety of school communities and contexts.

In this chapter we have suggested that much PPDP, as it presently stands, is not as effective as it could be, and that this can be traced back to two inseparable factors. The first is the disconnection between practice and theory, and the second, the undervalued status of principal involvement in the design and delivery of leadership learning and development. The disconnection between theory and practice invariably results in a gap between what principals are offered as learning experiences, and what they need. In the interests of more meaningful, contextually relevant leadership development and preparation, this gap should not go unchallenged. A lack of relevant understanding and provision is a result of insufficient principal involvement in their own professional development and preparation. Consequently, a considerable store of knowledge and expertise is left untapped. On the other hand, unfettered increases in principal involvement – even control – of their own professional development, carries a number of flaws. Simply 'handing over' total discretion to the profession appears inadvisable. Problems associated with either too much or too little professional participation appear strongly related to a lack of consideration of the different contexts and contextual specificity within which principal preparation, development and leadership take place.

Our contention is that the future path for meaningful principal professional development and preparation lies in the following direction. Principals (and employers) should be more heavily and purposefully involved in identifying and clarifying their existing and future leadership contexts. As a consequence, relevant programmes of professional development can then be strategically designed in reworked partnerships with appropriate colleagues and other members of the educational and school community. When leadership preparation and development reaches this stage of development, we can rightfully claim a degree of sophistication.

Bibliography

Crow, G. (2001) School leader preparation: A short review of the knowledge base. National College of School Leadership. (http://www.ncsl.org.uk/mediastore/image2/randd-gary-crow-paper.pdf)

Dimmock, C. and Walker, A. (1998) Comparative educational administration: Developing a cross-cultural conceptual framework. *Educational Administration Quarterly*, 34(4): 558–95.

Dimmock, C. and Walker, A. (in press) Strategic school leadership – toward better learning and teaching. *School Leadership and Management*.

Littky, D. and Schen, M. (2003) Developing school leaders: one principal at a time, in P. Hallinger (ed.) *Reshaping the Landscape of School Leadership Development*. Lisse, Netherlands: Swets and Zeitlinger.

Walker, A. and Dimmock, C. (2000) One size fits all? Teacher appraisal in a Chinese culture. *Journal of Personnel Evaluation in Education*, 14(2): 155–78.

Walker, A. and Dimmock, C. (2002) Moving school leadership beyond its narrow boundaries: developing a cross-cultural approach, in K. Leithwood and P. Hallinger (eds.), *Second International Handbook of Educational Leadership and Administration* (167–204). Netherlands: Kluwer Press.

Walker, A., and Stott, K. (1993) Preparing for leadership in schools: The mentoring contribution, in B. Caldwell and E. Carter (eds.) *The Return of the Mentor*. England: Falmer Press.

Walker, A., Chan, A., Cheung, R,. Chan, D., Wong, C. and Dimmock, C. (2002) *Principals Developing Principals: Principal professional development in Hong Kong*. Paper presented at National College of School Leadership 1st Invitational International Conference, October 16–18, Nottingham, UK.

seven

Developing innovative leadership

Kenneth Stott and Lee Sing Kong

Introduction

The previous chapter in this book by Allan Walker and Clive Dimmock asks for a 'degree of sophistication' in headteacher/principal training. In Singapore the spirit of what we are doing in terms of fusing theory and practice, and involving principals in their own learning agendas suggests that our thoughts have much in common with Walker and Dimmock.

We have been preparing educators for Principalship at the National Institute of Education since the mid-1980s. In the year 2000, though, we began to question whether we were training them for a context of education that no longer existed. Previously, the focus had been on a set of skills – ten to be precise – that were seen as central to the principal's role, and this was backed up by a mentoring attachment to an experienced and highly regarded principal. It worked quite well. These people became reasonably skilful and they were able to emulate the qualities of their mentors. But was that what we really needed? We were producing competent school principals, but were we turning out 'extraordinary' leaders?

So one of the first questions we asked was: do we want to imitate best practice or do we want to move beyond best practice? For us, imitating the good principals had the potential for reproducing what already existed. That can be very useful, because it helps to keep the good things in the system. However, by definition, it does not take you any further than you are at present. We knew things were changing and we had grave doubts about whether the old leadership – as effective as it had been – was capable of leading the changes necessary.

In terms of our learning as we reflected on the above issues and started to put together the new programme, we developed several learning points. For example, the language of best practice and benchmarking had become part of the accepted vocabulary. We had to challenge such terms. So the questions – around one collective theme – that yielded our first learning point were:

• Do we accept uncritically the rhetoric that has emerged from a main-stream management literature that has more to do with stability and linearity than with conditions we have not experienced before? Are we really satisfied with chasing the best? Why not let others chase us?

The Singapore system: rapid change

At this point, let us explain something about the education system in Singapore and what was happening in the last few years of the decade that was provoking these questions. We have nearly four hundred schools, staffed by some 25,000 teachers. The schools are large by international comparison. The largest primary schools, for example, have over 3,000 pupils. It is easy to see how the principal's role has moved him or her well away from the classroom and into the chief executive's office.

There has always been an emphasis on academic achievement, and Singapore has excelled in international comparative tests, particularly in science and mathematics. In 2003, a study reported that Singapore students were on a par with English speaking countries like New Zealand and Scotland in terms of reading skills, even though there are four official native languages in Singapore (Straits Times 2003). Singaporean mathematics text books are used in the USA and Scandinavia, and we receive frequent visits from educators from many parts of the world, all searching for the secret academic success.

Towards the end of the 1990s, there was a feeling beginning to emerge amongst those of us involved in training school leaders that things would have to change. The educational landscape in Singapore was giving rise to new and escalating challenges. The Prime Minister announced a vision for the education system: *Thinking Schools, Learning Nation* (Business Asia 1999); there was a series of landmark initiatives such as 'Ability Driven Education' (Crawford 2002) and increasing levels of autonomy were being planned for schools. These were coupled with calls for quality improvements, wider accountability and raised levels of achievement. They all pointed to the fact that we had to rethink how we prepared selected educators for the role of school leadership.

Although things had been going well in Singapore, it was recognized that the old forms of success would not do well in a global, competitive environment. Sheer hard work, discipline and the ability to prepare for examinations would not be enough. In the new environment, the ability to innovate and to think creatively through the emerging complex problems and issues would become more prominent on the agenda.

It was never going to be easy. Students had been steeped in a tradition of absorbing all information thrown at them without question. Conformity and compliance were the order of the day. Teachers were required to set test after test, and for many parents, the quality of education was judged by the amount of homework, and the child's success by the proximity to measurable perfection.

On the plus side, though, parental support for their children is very strong, and in a highly competitive society, children are encouraged to concentrate on their studies and are usually given the support of private tutors. Even the poorest families often find the resources to pay for tutoring.

Innovation and creating new knowledge

Let us return, though, to the changing scene. As we recognized that new skills and new ways of thinking would be needed, we also knew that leaders themselves would have to be different. We needed extraordinary, not ordinary, leaders. That led us to rethink our whole approach of preparing leaders for schools of the future, and thus we introduced the Leaders in Education Programme (LEP) in 2001 to replace the previous programme. The Ministry of Education each year goes through an exhaustive process of selecting educators to prepare for Principalship, and then sends them (about 25–35 per year) to the National Institute of Education for a six-months-full-time programme. Generally, these educators have been identified early as talented individuals and have been given a range of duties to test their capability. That means that, once they have been selected for the LEP, they are likely to be offered posts as principals on completion of the programme. The need for change has been reinforced by the government, which has laid emphasis on innovation as the driver for a fast improving economy. Innovation has become a central concept in future leadership. The creation of new knowledge is seen as crucial. We indeed recognized the need – in an environment of innovation and competitive advantage – to move *beyond* best practice. Fullan (1999) remarks that knowledge creation 'is not the acquisition of best practices as products. It is the ability to generate and learn new ideas'.

For us, the building of new insights, new knowledge and new practices has become a central theme in our preparation of school leaders.

> The practice of extraordinary management . . . is above all else concerned with the creation of new knowledge, largely of a qualitative kind

– it is only through new knowledge that an organisation can innovate and develop new strategic directions.

(Stacey 1993: 365)

This led to a second learning point:

• We must concern ourselves with new knowledge creation, which is a complex and necessary process. Codified knowledge is readily accessible.

The critical issues

Creating new knowledge is problematic, however, from a mainstream management perspective. Several issues emerge:

1   When you concern yourself with creating new knowledge, you can't have 'intended outcomes' and 'learning objectives' because you don't know what will be learned!
2   In a knowledge creation environment, there are no experts: only co-learners. Thus, the power relations and dynamics are affected.
3   Sufficient challenging experiences have to be provided that will give the depth, range and diversity of input needed to provoke the development of new knowledge.

Of course, it is not easy explaining all this in conditions that are constrained by objectives and outcomes, because the programme architecture, instead of being one that is dictated by deliverable ends, is one of creating the conditions in which new knowledge might emerge. This means that the *content* of leadership programmes is far less important than the nature of the diverse experiences that provoke new and powerful learning.

From this perspective, classroom sessions are no longer central; they are present only as learning support. The main learning forum, instead, is the syndicate meeting. It is during this meeting (involving about six or seven participants with a university tutor) that participants present their experiences of leading innovation. Through the critical questioning and comment of others, they develop new perspectives and insights. Also discussed are topical issues, policy matters and learning from the range of experiences offered. These experiences include a two-weeks overseas visit (USA, UK, Australia, Sweden, Denmark and Canada have been visited so far), an industrial attachment, visits to organizations both within and outside education, 'dinings' at the Academy of Principals and special sessions led by people both from overseas and Singapore.

Yet another challenge for us was to move people's thinking beyond competencies, skills, codified knowledge and the imperatives of pervasive conceptual approaches, all claiming to be the panacea for the world's leadership ills. This, indeed, represents one of the major ongoing issues we face, and although there may be practices in the system that appear to be incompatible with our approach, we have found a way of working together in what one might call 'conditions of paradox'. This is not necessarily a bad thing.

Designing a programme for a changing world: innovation

In designing the new programme, we looked at various models of leadership training, many of which seemed to help their trainees to acquire knowledge and skills for the present situation, based on an assumption of stability. These programmes may have little to do with a turbulent future or with innovation. In other words, the focus is on a set of skills and tasks required to operate the current stable system better. But this does not bring about a different system, which is pivotal to our concern for meeting the needs of a fast changing environment (Portsmouth, Stott and Walker 2000).

We saw many training strategies that were based on deficit models, where the intention was to diagnose leadership deficiencies and then attempt to bring the performance up to some predetermined standard. We label this standard 'the line of mediocrity'. In a sense, this probably works well in a stable environment, because extraordinary performance is not required. However, in an uncertain context, a different level of capability is needed, and that may be achieved – we would argue – by building on strength. From this perspective, innovative schools must capitalize on what they are good at, and lessen the emphasis on weaknesses.

A focus on the future was intensified by being conspicuous on the government agenda, and gave rise to our next learning point:

- Our development of leaders must be more for the future, and not so much for the present. We have to provide not specific skills or competencies, but a broad spectrum of capability that will enable them to thrive in the future.

We must be careful, though, not to give the impression that capability is simply about 'reacting' to a changing future; it is also about exerting some influence over the shape that future will take. At the same time, we realize that the future is unknowable and the outcomes of our efforts are always uncertain. This yielded another, fourth, crucial learning point for us:

- It is the things we 'do' today that have an impact on what happens tomorrow.

While that may seem perfectly obvious, it is often missed. We are not talking about plans, though. Rather, if we experiment with new ideas, try different pedagogical approaches on a small scale, start talking to people more and listening to what they say: all these will, we believe, change tomorrow in some advantageous way. This is what happens when we send our principals-in-training into schools to lead innovation. They try out ideas in the real world; and they learn about intended and unintended outcomes, about the impact on people and about the need to account for contingencies.

The host schools for these innovation experiences must have principals who are confident enough to 'risk' innovation. While it has become obvious over the last two years that these innovation projects reap rich benefits for the schools concerned, they can also present uncomfortable experiences for those at the helm. This is because the projects are *real*. They are not simulations. However, they are not 'add-on' extras. To be successful, innovation projects must be built into the normal routine working of the school.

The process we went through at the university in developing the programme was also an interesting learning experience and taught us much about how things happen in the real world rather than the world of strategic planning committees and the like. We recall that several committee meetings had taken place to examine how to fine tune the former programme, but nothing had changed, apart from the introduction of a new module. We are all probably familiar with that scenario. When we took over responsibility for leading this and other programmes, we spent much time in casual – sometimes crazy – conversations over coffee with a range of people. Many of these conversations led to nothing, apart from the opportunity to air views and grievances. One day, though, a colleague talked about the notion of 'competitive advantage' and how schools need to create new knowledge if they are to gain such advantage. From there, the discussion generated a stream of thought that enabled us to challenge our existing assumptions, which were strongly grounded in mainstream management and prior experience. For us, this was a crucial breakthrough. It also supported the view that creative breakthroughs in organizations are likely to emerge from informal social interactions amongst enthusiastic individuals who gather round an issue (Stacey 1993).

Let us summarize some of the points that formed a new frame of reference (Stacey 1993) for us and that guided our thinking about the development of principals for a changing world:

Current thinking	A new frame
We know roughly what will happen and can plan things in a linear way	The future is largely unknowable
Visions, missions and plans are important, including shared vision across the school	We need learning teams of professionals, surfacing conflict and engaging continuously in conversations
Decision making should be logical and analytical, based on facts and figures	Decision making needs to be more exploratory and experimental
We should decide what to do in the school as a result of careful planning	What we choose to do (strategy) should stem from challenge and contradiction, from learning and politics
Top management should control strategic direction	Top management should create good conditions for people to generate new directions and ideas
We should control the long term by measuring our progress against plans and by using indicators	Development is an open-ended process, with opportunities to change and learn.

It would be misleading to suggest that we could actually derive prescriptions from this new frame of reference, but we were able to identify several pointers that would guide our thinking. Essentially, we were asking: how can we create the conditions in which innovation and new strategic direction can emerge? Obviously, when our participants become principals, they must apply the same questions and challenge the existing ways of viewing control and predictability, which, logically, lead to the imitation of innovations by others. The pointers were:

1 The notion of control would have to be challenged. Learning teams would assume more importance, which meant that we would have to let go and allow things to happen. That was not easy in an environment where control has been pervasive.
2 The use of power by force leads to conformity, submission or rebellion. In order to search for new perspectives, the dynamics need to be changed. We need to alternate between conflict and consensus, and between confusion and clarity. Thus, we have to withdraw sometimes and allow things to happen; sometimes intervene with ideas; and sometimes exert authority. This calls for an acceptance of individual expression, astutely illustrated in the work of Crowther, Hann and McMaster (2001), who advocate the legitimacy of strong individualism, and question collegial consensus and teamwork being open to managerial manipulation.

3   We must allow groups of people to gather round issues that interest them and take them forward. If we form groups, it is best to give them ambiguous challenges and open up the opportunity for creative ideas we may not have thought of.

4   We should provoke different cultures. Allowing dominant cultures of managers with the same philosophy to dominate does not provoke new perspectives. One way is to change people's responsibilities and to bring people from other organizations into the team.

5   Just because the future is problematic and unknowable does not mean we should do nothing. Rather, we must take the risk of exposing ourselves to considerable challenges. Innovation invariably carries with it a degree of risk

6   We must give attention to how we encounter existing mindsets and beliefs. We need to constantly question deeply held beliefs and points of view. One way we do this on our programme – apart from frequent conversations – is to require participants to read contrasting perspectives every time they are presented with one conceptual viewpoint. Another idea – a practical one for school leaders – is given in a chapter by Stott and Zhang (2000), where they explain how the principal, in wishing to introduce a significant change to a professional development scheme, legitimized the opposition to her proposals by asking members of the management team to identify the flaws.

7   Fullan (1999) tells us that 'a flow of new and better knowledge and ideas is the lifeblood of continuous improvement'. Yet, knowledge creation is not about a 'thing' called knowledge, but a process. When teachers engage in conversation, the interaction itself is the essence of knowledge. Our programme is, therefore, an attempt to ascribe value to 'the ordinary, observable communicative interactions between people in local situations in the living present' (Stacey 2001).

The learning experiences

Earlier, we talked about the need to provide diverse learning experiences for extraordinary management development. It may be helpful to explain a little more about these experiences. The architecture we designed relegates the importance of 'content' to a supporting role and elevates the significance of learning 'in the job' and in an intellectually stimulating support environment.

There is a basic content agenda, which lends support to the learning, and participants may draw on this agenda as they see fit. That agenda includes topics such as 'schools as competitive learning organizations', 'marketing and strategic choice', 'the new technology in learning', 'policy' and 'contemporary issues in teaching and learning'.

The international visit lasts for two weeks. Participants travel in syndicates to one location or area. They visit schools, education offices and other places of learning. Generally, the visits involve an intensive period of up to three days in one institution in order to gain insights into what is happening and how it is happening. The purpose is not to import good practice, but to use observations and conversations as a basis for challenging the thinking and ideas of oneself and others. Most evenings, a debriefing session takes place, and on returning to Singapore, a reflective report is prepared for dissemination to fellow educators. This process is supported by sessions with groups of principals and vice-principals to tease out some of the more challenging issues emerging from the visits.

The industrial attachment is again an opportunity to inspire different ways of thinking about leadership issues. Generally, the participants go out in small groups to multi-national corporations and meet with senior personnel. The learning points are then discussed in syndicate meetings and recorded in journals.

The learning journal is an important document. It is one of the elements of the course that has had a noticeable impact on participants, revealed by their comments in the journals. Keeping a journal, of course, is a well-known learning methodology, but unlike some other programmes, we choose not to have a framework, but rather to allow participants to find their own ways of developing their learning through recording.

We expose the participants to a range of experiences and views. For example, we organize seminars by educators from overseas. In 2002, for instance, we invited, separately, two experienced leaders from Canada, one of whom runs a school with no classrooms and teachers who don't teach – in the conventional sense! We did this in order to provoke different ways of thinking about the physical configuration of schools, the deployment of teachers and a host of related issues. We also had visits from the Minister for Education, the Senior Minister of State for Trade and Industry and for Education, and the Permanent Secretary (Education). These interactive sessions gave the participants the opportunity to understand how key policy issues are conceptualized at political and top administrative levels.

Yet another learning experience is the reading participants are required to undertake. While much of the reading material may be selected by them, we also introduce set texts, partly to open up contrasting viewpoints. For example, while one text may explore the merits of the 'learning organization', another text is highly critical of the concept. We see this as an important part of the process of creating new insights into how we and the system in which we operate might work effectively.

Finally, an innovation in the 2003 programme was the introduction of an assignment called *The Future School*. In teams, participants had to produce a publishable book on the shape a future school in Singapore might take, based on all the stimuli they had experienced in their visits, readings and discussions.

The story so far

After only a few years of running this programme, it would be foolish of us to claim total success. At the same time, we have to make rapid judgements about what needs changing, because the programme has to be as dynamic as the environment in which it operates.

We also recognize the need to reach coherent conclusions about whether the programme is having the size of impact that matches the resource investment. We felt unable to do this through the usual end-of-course survey, so we initiated a funded research project that was designed to evaluate training impact over time. This longitudinal study is a challenge, because the Leaders in Education Programme is about insight, challenge and mindset change. How does a researcher ask someone how they would have behaved had they not gone through a process of challenge to their thinking? This is the sort of issue that the research team is grappling with.

It is a mainly happy story so far. We have encountered now several cohorts of 'confused' educators! They come to us quite uncertain about what they are in for, because they are used to being told what to do and how to do it. By the end of the programme, though, many recognize the transformational process they have been through and are ready to approach impending Principalship with new eyes.

One of the important things we discovered early was that we must use our diverse strengths. To intensify learning, we operate with small groups, each led by a university tutor. What we tried to do initially was to standardize the way these groups operated and to provide a common agenda. We have found a better way. Our university staff members are very different, with different conceptual positions and different *modi operandi*. We have moved beyond a common agenda and allowed each group to develop its own learning agenda, which will generate excitement that can be shared with the full cohort. This means the various groups are discussing different issues, reading different materials and drawing on different resources. They are deeply engaged in what they are doing and choosing to go way beyond our expectations of them. Thus, a learning point here draws on something we said earlier in relation to innovation:

- It is more powerful to capitalize on strength than to focus on weakness. It is a question of where you locate your attention.

Finally . . .

It may seem strange to admit that we, as the Leaders in Education Programme designers, are just beginning to find out what is really happening in the programme. After just a few years of experience, our conversations and encounters – some of them less volatile than others – are helping us to see and feel the effects of the programme. Participants themselves report significant change in the way they think, and they tell us – several months into their first Principalship – how they believe the experience has served them. Some of the stories we hear are quite unpredictable and convince us that individuals take away substantially different learning gains.

We are also starting to understand the way in which the programme is being felt by others in the system. For many, there are regrets that they have not been through this programme, and they explain that they can see the difference in present graduates. Those at the top of the profession speak warmly about the programme's achievements and believe that it is meeting a deep need for fundamental change. Not everyone necessarily shares that view. But this is the real world, and working in new ways carries risks as well as rewards. Our participants experience this and so do we.

In developing a greater understanding of how the programme works and impacts upon the lives of participants, certain key words seem to be coming to the fore. We have mentioned already the word 'challenge'. This is something that permeates everything we do in each learning experience. We present contrasting points of view, different ways of doing the same things, new ways of achieving new ends, and the belief that whenever someone claims something cannot be done, someone will do it! Challenge has indeed been a key feature. As one participant wrote in his journal: 'Always challenge assumptions. Recognising where the assumptions are is important. Being willing to challenge even wrought-iron assumptions is also important. Challenge them for the fun of challenging them. Challenge them just to see if there is anything to challenge.'

Another key word has been that of 'breakthrough'. There have been many fine examples of breakthroughs in the innovation projects. These successes have taken the schools concerned to new levels. But breakthroughs go beyond the projects: they are equally important in changing people's thinking.

No doubt other words will arise as the months go by. Some things may become more prominent on the agenda, while others may slip quietly away. This is a phenomenon we have to contend with if our programme is going to ride the waves of change and provide the extraordinary leaders that are needed to keep Singapore education as a key player on the world scene.

We have mentioned the notion of 'extraordinariness' several times in this chapter without explaining what it means. Perhaps that is because we don't truly know. What we do know, though, is that 'ordinary' leadership is not good enough for what our system is trying to achieve in schools. In probably our favourite paper of the 1990s – *Leadership for the New Millennium* by Hedley Beare, which was delivered as the William Walker Oration in 1998 in Australia – the enigmatic nature of great leadership is discussed. For example, Hedley Beare says:

> This wisdom of sensing what is right or opportune is a quality which memorable leaders often have. Gifted leaders seem to experience conjunctions of unlikely events which work together almost miraculously.

Beare also talks about artistry, symbolism, meaning, cultural creativity and transcendence. He talks about the supra-rationality of leaders, the spirit and the soul. He explains: 'Leading from the soul means that they understand themselves at deep levels; and leading from spirit means that they position their own efforts in a much wider scheme of things.' That may point the direction to extraordinariness.

Amidst all this rhetoric about 'extraordinariness', we have not lost sight of the day-to-day realities of life as a principal. Indeed, our thinking has been based on challenges to the unreal and idealistic. For example, there is persuasive evidence that much of the effort we put into planning is probably wasted in today's turbulent times. We are, therefore, as much concerned with the realities of management as is Fullan (1999), who talks about lofty ideals when facing your worst class on a Friday afternoon.

The trouble with the 'realities', though, is that they are a pervasive distraction, and they stand in the way of innovation if you let them. We argue that our way has the good of students in mind, for leaders prepared to think in new ways stand a chance of engendering new thinking in teachers, and this may lead to better practices in our classrooms, better relationships with parents and better administration from the principal's office. The true test of innovation, as we are frequently reminded, is in student achievement gains and an overall enhanced experience of education (Varghese 2001.)

We finish this chapter with a question. It is a question that may have come to your mind as you read this, because it has practical consequences for principals in schools. It is also a question that should generate some research interest amongst academics. The question was provoked by something Stacey (1995) wrote and we thought about what it meant for school leaders. It is this: It is almost part of conventional wisdom that leaders must be visionary and must set the direction for their schools. But what does extraordinary leadership mean when powerful leaders select, plan and control certain courses of action, but cannot select, plan or control the outcomes of those courses of action?

Bibliography

Beare, H. (1998) Leadership for a New Millennium. Paper presented as the William Walker Oration at the ACEA Conference, Gold Coast, Queensland, Australia.

Business Asia. (1999) Thinking schools, learning nation: A smart move, *Business Asia*, Singapore, 15 March.

Crawford, L. (2002) Towards an ability-driven education system in Singapore: Problems and opportunities. *REACT*, National Institute of Education, Vol. 21, No. 1, 1–12.

Crowther, F., Hann, L. and McMaster, J. (2001) Parallel leadership: A new strategy for successful school reform, *The Practising Administrator*, 4, 12–14.

Fullan, M. (1999) *Change Forces: The sequel*. London: Falmer.

Portsmouth, F., Stott, K. and Walker, A. (2000) School Management Teams: Partners in a new story for a new future, in K. Stott and V. Trafford (eds.) *Partnerships: Shaping the Future of Education*. London: Middlesex University Press.

Stacey, R. (1993) Strategy as order emerging from chaos, *Long Range Planning*, 26(1): 10–17.

Stacey, R. (1995) The science of complexity: An alternative perspective for strategic change processes, *Strategic Management Journal*, 16: 477–95.

Stacey, R. (2001) *Complex Responsive Processes in Organizations: Learning and knowledge creation*. London: Routledge.

Stott, K. and Zhang, Y. (2000) Team Leadership: Reflections on theory and practice, in C. Dimmock and A. Walker (eds) *Future School Administration: Western and Asian perspectives*. Hong Kong: The Chinese University Press.

Straits Times, (2003) Singapore pupils hold their own in reading skills test, 9 April.

Varghese, J. (2001) 'IDEAS project builds on success', *Education Views*, Education Queensland, 10(3), 16, February, http://education.qld.gov.au/marketing/publication/edviews/html/art-2001-03-02.html

eight

Developing beginning leadership

Fred Paterson and John West-Burnham

Introduction

Becoming a new headteacher is, arguably, the greatest step-change in the career of a school leader. The research literature shows that new headteachers commonly feel isolated in their new role and swamped by the multiple demands made of them. It is a time of enormous challenge. In many education systems, however, much less emphasis is placed on support for the early stage of a leaders' career than is offered to pre-headship preparation and in-service development.

This chapter explores one particular programme for newly appointed headteachers – the National College for School Leadership's (NCSL's) New Visions programme in England – and its contribution to our understanding of leadership learning for new headteachers who will be creating the schools of tomorrow. New Visions aims to address the learning needs of new headteachers via a mix of active, collaborative and dialogic approaches. Implicit in this is the aspiration to develop career-long learning 'habits', such that analysis, reflection, conceptualization, enquiry, collaboration, networking and futures thinking become integral to the professional practice of school leaders.

The programme sets out to achieve this by providing, amongst other things, three rare commodities in the hectic arena of early headship. Firstly, it offers dedicated time for analysis and reflection. Secondly, it places an emphasis upon dialogue with peers as the basis for meaning-making and problem-solving – an approach that clearly helps reduces heads' sense of isolation. The third key commodity is the support and advice of more experienced consultant heads.

Substantial time and funding has been devoted to the research and evaluation of the programme. This in itself makes the programme unusual, as public evaluation outputs from national scale leadership development programmes are rare. However, the positive outcomes described in the independent evaluation of New Visions (Bush, Briggs *et al.* 2003), both in terms of participants' experiences of the programme and its impact upon schools, suggest that the programme can offer some useful lessons to providers and consumers of leadership development.

An emerging knowledge base for early leadership development

The literature on leadership development is awash with unsubstantiated claims about what leaders should learn (Bush and Glover 2004). There is, in fact, a dearth of empirical evidence about what learning is effective, and even less is written about HOW leadership learning works (Bennett and Marr 2002; Weindling 2004). Research into the New Visions programme (Bush, Briggs *et al.* 2003; Paterson and Coleman 2003), therefore, makes a useful contribution to the knowledge base about 'what works' in leadership development for new leaders – although much of what follows may also apply to leadership development more generally.

NCSL's commitment to build from what is known about leadership and leadership learning stimulated a wide range of study visits, evaluations, research studies and literature reviews, which have both informed the development of New Visions and enhanced our developing understanding of the programme.

One review of research into the needs and problems of new headship shows that although school contexts and personal histories vary, getting to grips with finance, staffing, site management and government initiatives are familiar challenges for new headteachers (Hobson, Brown *et al.* 2003). However, the multiple demands, ambiguity, and complexity of the role often leave new headteachers feeling overwhelmed and isolated (Bright and Ware 2003; Hobson, Brown *et al.* 2003).

It seems that in the UK and internationally, new headteachers get to grips with the job the hard way – 'by learning from their mistakes' (Bright and Ware 2003). One investigation shows that only 17 per cent of new headteachers in England thought they were 'very prepared' for headship, with nearly one in ten indicating that they were 'not prepared at all' (Earley, Evans *et al.* 2002). The study by Bright and Ware (2003) also describes how new heads felt ill prepared by previous educational experiences for their new role and that those who believed they were ready for the job attributed this to prior experience as opposed to training. These studies suggest that provision for new heads in England was somewhat inconsistent prior to the launch of NCSL in November 2000. Although experience is a powerful stimulus for learning, not all experience stimulates learning, and leaving new headteachers to learn solely from their mistakes is clearly unsatisfactory.

In designing its programmes, the College asked 'what does the international knowledge base tell us about effective provision for new headteachers and principals?'. NCSL's international study visits suggested that leadership development programmes were shifting away from prescribed, standardized, theoretical courses, to more practical, school-focused programmes that are customized to meet the specific needs of individuals. Chapters Six and Seven, for instance describe programmes such as this operating in Hong Kong and Singapore. Such programmes are participatory and interactive, and offer ongoing support over time rather than being standalone presentations. The visits demonstrated the value of involving successful practising school leaders, targeting 'steep steps' in leadership learning, the importance of developing communities of learning and practice, and signalling the challenges of developing system-wide innovation.

A review of 43 international programmes for new headteachers and principals suggests that mandatory provision is as common as voluntary provision (Weindling 2004). Unlike New Visions, the content of early headship programmes is commonly based on 'national standards', especially in the USA where the Interstate School Leaders Licensure Consortium (ISLLC) standards are increasingly used as a basis for mandatory state-wide provision. Most schemes focus on instructional leadership; school improvement; effective leadership and the management of change; as well as specific current national initiatives such as the 'No Child Left Behind' initiative in the USA. Modules on basic management skills such as finance and educational law are also prevalent. Indeed, there appears to be a growing international consensus about the content of leadership development programmes (Bush and Jackson 2002; Gronn 2002; West and Jackson 2002; Bush and Glover 2004).

Although the majority of leadership development internationally remains content rich, a study by Daresh and Male (2000) casts doubts on the relevance of content-based training. The content is often rooted in beliefs about what leaders should know, rather than evidence about what works. Bush, Briggs *et al.* (2003) argue that 'a predominantly process-based approach, anchored in participants' schools, may be more effective in promoting leadership learning than content-based courses'.

A widening range of approaches to leadership learning are being offered internationally. These include many used within the New Visions programme:

- Mentoring
- Coaching
- Diagnostic self-assessment
- Portfolios

- Enquiry visits
- Problem-based learning
- Case studies

- Learning groups
- Action learning
- E-learning

A review of American programmes by Leithwood (1995) concluded that there was 'unequivocal' evidence that preparation programmes that stress reflection, collaboration and active problem solving make a significant difference to leaders' success. There is little evidence in the research literature more widely, however, that explores the effectiveness of support strategies and development methods for early school leadership, or crucially how they influence this leadership.

Many writers recognize that each leader's context and lived experience needs to be both the focus of learning and provide the vehicle for that learning (Leithwood and Steinbach 1992; Lambert 1998; Barnett 2001; Creasy, Cotton *et al.* 2004). Although the study by Hobson, Brown *et al.* (2003) showed that headteachers tend to go through a similar process of professional and organizational socialization and experience similar kinds of problems, it also noted that headteachers have individual needs at different stages of development. This means that support strategies are not necessarily applicable or effective for all new heads and that support should be flexible, individualized and negotiable.

The strongest empirical evidence is for the efficacy of mentoring and peer support networks (Hobson 2003; Hobson, Brown *et al.* 2003). Earley (2003) found that nine out of ten heads felt that other school leaders were a source of inspiration to them – greater than any other influence. A survey of one hundred New Visions participants reinforces this outcome; these heads were asked about their previous professional development for headship. The three types of support considered to be of most help were: networking with experienced heads, critical friendships and personal discussions with other leaders. This preference for peer interaction was mirrored in a post-programme survey; where both structured and informal contact with colleagues were rated as the most helpful aspects of the programme (Bush, Briggs *et al.* 2003).

Clearly, interactional approaches offer the potential to address the personal challenges described above (i.e. feeling overwhelmed and isolated) as well as new headteachers' technical needs (such as finance, personnel and legal issues). However, is leadership development as simple as putting a group of heads together in a room and giving them time to talk?

An overview of the New Visions programme

Since the introduction to the Headteachers' Leadership and Management Programme (HEADLAMP) in 1995, new headteachers in England and

Wales have been provided with funds to spend on leadership and management development of their choice. Until recently, various programmes of induction and support were provided by Local Education Authorities (LEAs), by some universities and by private consultancies who all competed for a share of headteachers' HEADLAMP funding. Since September 2003, the HEADLAMP Programme, now called HIP (Headteachers' Induction Programme), has been delivered across England by 20 regional providers (consortia of LEAs, universities and private consultancies) to leaders in their first three years of headship.

New Visions is one element of HIP and is delivered by NCSL on a national basis. Each year the programme recruits new heads across England who attend a two-day residential followed by eight single-day sessions. There are approximately 20 cross-phase cohort groups of 12–15 participants. Each regional group is led by a facilitator and supported by an experienced and successful consultant headteacher. New Visions provides opportunities for new heads to work together in a challenging learning community to reflect and analyse personal leadership practice, and engage in enquiry, problem solving and peer support.

The programme literature articulates a number of principles for learning. New Visions aspires to give participants the opportunity to:

- work in a learning community;
- address real issues from their own context and relate practical and theoretical knowledge;
- access the best national and international research and practice;
- develop key leadership skills;
- focus upon generating powerful pupil learning and achievement;
- engage in mutual support, reflection and analysis of personal leadership practice;
- develop enquiry approaches to learning and leadership that will have direct impact on their school;
- develop powerful lifelong professional learning habits.

The programme focuses on leadership rather management, in the belief that it is intuition, creativity, wisdom and futures thinking that support healthy organizations in a hectic, complex and unpredictable world (Claxton 1997; Eraut 1999). It is this singular focus upon leadership and leadership learning processes that makes New Visions distinctive.

The design team also believe that a strong sense of moral leadership, clarity of values, shared leadership and an emphasis upon leadership for learning are fundamental to the pursuit of excellence in education in the 21st century. This is a point, of course, emphasized by James Spillane and Dean Fink in other chapters in this book. The validity of these beliefs are strengthened by the 'remarkably' positive outcomes from two studies of the programme (Bush, Briggs *et al.* 2003; Paterson and Coleman 2003). Not only is there strong evidence of participant satisfaction and personal learning,

> there is significant evidence of school effects arising from participants' involvement in the programme
>
> (Bush, Briggs *et al.* 2003)

Bush, Briggs *et al.* state that participating in the programme has stimulated a clearer vision and sense of purpose, a greater focus on pupil learning, more shared leadership, changes to professional development processes, increased innovation and improvement in standards. Perhaps even more crucial to New Vision's long-term impact upon schools are the habits of leadership learning engendered by the protocols used within the programme. The internal enquiry identifies the development of a range of learning habits, such as increased and improved reflection; more self analysis; greater self awareness; more incisive analysis; deeper thinking; enhanced listening skills; and more engagement with research.

Innovative aspects of the programme

Earlier chapters have highlighted the challenges of preparing innovative school leaders who are equipped to address the increasing demands of our post-industrial context and the knowledge society. The positive evaluation outcomes from New Visions offer evidence of effective leadership development provision that makes an impact in schools; and intelligence emerging from the New Visions programme helps address a number of the aforementioned challenges. Below, we explore three fundamental issues that reflect the innovative nature of the programme and which respond to key themes addressed throughout this book. We discuss the significance of:

- articulating and enacting an explicit theory of learning;
- practical, dialogic and issues-based learning protocols;
- framing participants, consultant heads, facilitators and programme staff as a community of learners.

In different ways, each of these build learning that is sustainable beyond the life of the programme for participants, their schools and the wider educational system.

Articulating and enacting an explicit theory of learning

Although it is uncommon for the theory of professional learning underpinning leadership programmes to be made explicit, our work in New

Visions has highlighted the importance of the programme being explicitly learning centred. By this we mean that a clear theory of professional learning is articulated and that facilitators bring attention to participants' own learning as they experience the programme processes and protocols.

At the heart of the New Visions programme is a model of professional learning that structures all learning activity. The model frames learning as a social process rooted in: the learners' individual contexts; three fields of knowledge; and the move from 'shallow, to deep, and profound' learning. The model contends that by utilizing all three fields of knowledge in collaborative and practical endeavour, professional learning shifts from shallow to deep learning; and offers the potential for profound learning. The New Visions programme has shown that articulating and enacting this theory of learning has provided participants with a vocabulary and understanding that helps build their capacity to lead learning in school more effectively.

'Three fields of knowledge'

Although New Visions is structured by four guiding themes (values and context, learning and teaching, shared leadership and facing the future), it differs from many programmes in that its aim is not simply to impart knowledge; rather, it is to interrogate theory through the lens of practical experience and so create new shared knowledge. The interaction of academic and personal knowledge becomes the source of reflection, collaborative learning, re-framing values and practice. This principle conveys the importance of externally validated or academic knowledge without diminishing the utility of headteachers' practical knowledge. It shows how practice can be enhanced by careful consideration of the knowledge that already exists; as well as highlighting how new knowledge can be generated from a synthesis of theory and practitioners' perspectives. It is through this process that deep learning emerges; learning that has the potential to enhance practice in school. In this way, the programme seeks to alter the cognitive landscape of educational leadership in that it brings theory into the service of practice.

New Visions provides participants with a conceptual model of leadership knowledge that is used to structure learning activity within each of the four leadership themes addressed by the programme (see Fig. 8.1). The three fields of knowledge reflect the sources through which learning enters the programme, these being:

- headteachers' personal knowledge;
- public knowledge in the form of theory, research and other knowledge in the public domain;

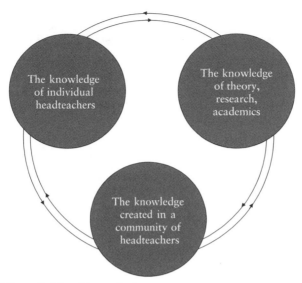

Figure 8.1 Three fields of knowledge

- new knowledge, created though the collaborative processes offered on the programme.

The learning activities utilized in the programme are designed to extend, deepen and connect these three fields of knowledge. Respect for the knowledge and experience that individual headteachers bring is reflected in the time offered for dialogue about heads' personal leadership challenges. The use of paired and group dialogue provides a vehicle through which personal knowledge can be articulated and ultimately developed into shared knowledge. Dialogue also supports the celebration of successful practice.

Participants indicate that the *three fields of knowledge* model is highly accessible and easy to understand. The fact that individuals' own knowledge and experience were placed on an equal footing with more formal inputs sends a powerful message about the extent to which they are valued as professionals:

> The three fields of knowledge articulated the expectation that everyone would contribute and that everyone's contribution was important. I've used this in school too to draw all into the meeting.
> (New Visions participant – Paterson and Coleman 2003)

Many participants also appreciated the fact that this gave them clear ownership of the process, providing them with the opportunity to review specific issues and concerns and ensuring that the programme remained 'grounded' in their day-to-day contextual reality.

An explicit model of professional learning

A 'shallow, deep and profound' learning model (Fig. 8.2) was developed as a synthesis of various theories of learning.

Shallow learning can be very important in many areas of work-related development. However, the model asserts that leadership learning programmes should be designed with a focus on *deep* and *profound* learning, as these lead to knowledge that can subsequently be transformed into leadership action. This is achieved principally using enquiry processes, focused dialogue and reflection:

> Leaders need opportunities to engage in reflective practices, enquiry approaches and protocols which enable them to reach deeper understandings about themselves and others in ways which impact on their behaviour.
>
> (Creasy 2002)

The dual models of knowledge and learning presented by the programme offer a vocabulary that participants use more and more as the programme progresses. New Visions participants also find the concepts of *shallow, deep* and *profound* to be very powerful and provide a real stimulus for reflection upon wider learning in their school:

> The shallow deep profound model informs what we do with the children as well. You can look at any piece of learning and think: 'At what level have I really learnt this and has it really become part of me?'
>
> (New Visions participant – Paterson and Coleman 2003)

	SHALLOW	DEEP	PROFOUND
Means	Memorisation	Reflection	Intuition
Outcomes	Information	Knowledge	Wisdom
Evidence	Replication	Understanding	Meaning
Motivation	Extrinsic	Intrinsic	Moral
Attitudes	Compliance	Interpretation	Challenge
Relationships	Dependence	Independence	Interdependence

Figure 8.2 Shallow, deep, profound learning model

Dedicated time for reflection

The importance of reflection for professional practice is well established (Schon 1987; Day 1993; Hatton and Smith 1995). Providing dedicated time for thinking, contemplation and quiet reflection is an essential element of the New Visions model of learning. Opportunity is provided in sessions for quiet reflection, to write in a learning journal, and for silent reading of texts. Given the overwhelming demands of new headship, it is perhaps unsurprising that the space, time and opportunity provided for reflection by the programme was considered the main benefit to personal professional development (Bush, Briggs *et al.* 2003). The internal enquiry into New Visions (Paterson and Coleman 2003) suggests that reflection, critique and analysis are supported by structured activity and explicit attention to reflection.

> Quality time away from school to reflect is a benefit well known, but I feel for me it is the fact that New Visions is actively involving me in techniques to sustain that reflection, e.g. Action Learning Sets, mentoring with partners, a leadership journal etc. which is making the difference, as it is giving me tools with which to work.
>
> (New Visions participant – Paterson and Coleman 2003)

Practical, dialogic and issues-based learning protocols

Although it is hoped that the knowledge and understanding derived from the programme will influence these new headteachers and impact upon their schools in the medium and long term, early influences upon their schools are largely derived from the protocols, methods and approaches modelled within the programme.

The review by Weindling (2004) has shown that active, work and problem-based learning are becoming more prevalent in leadership development programmes. By placing an emphasis upon 'live issues', practical challenges and organizational needs, learning becomes relevant to participants and their schools. The New Visions programme utilizes a range of learning protocols that address live issues and school interests, whilst at the same time deepening a range of learning habits. This is achieved by various approaches: action learning sets, narrative as text, clinical review, questioning for understanding, case studies and school enquiry visits. This portfolio of strategies offers a flexible approach to practice focused learning through dialogue, listening, questioning, analysis and reflection.

Action learning sets (ALS), which are valued in a range of professional settings (Isaac 2001), are arguably the single most popular aspect of the programme and considered to be 'extremely powerful' by the independent evaluators (Bush, Briggs *et al.* 2003). Comment after comment from participants across the country offer testimony to the utility and power of the method:

> ALS brilliant – It's having an appreciation of each other's context without being judgemental. It is having that trust to learn together, rather than talking for the sake of it and asking questions because you feel you should do. We really got quite involved after we had had a couple of practices. When it was first introduced and we were asked to do a task, I thought it would take five minutes, but after three-quarters of an hour we were still going, because it takes time if you're going to do it properly.
>
> (New Visions participant – Paterson and Coleman 2003)

Based on the work of Revans (1983), the ALS protocol encourages non-judgmental probing of an individual's key issues that helps participants to organize their thoughts and lead them towards solutions and actions. In this method the listener/supporter(s) are given clear protocols that define their role; for instance, to listen only; to respond only with questions that clarify; to offer challenging questions to push their peers' thinking further, or to debate the presenter's perspective. This means that each listener/supporter is developing their own listening, questioning and analytical skills whilst the narrator is reflecting on their own problem or issue. There are a number of key influences on the success of these approaches: the clarity of explanation of the protocols; the rigor applied to the protocols – keeping participants on task; and the skills of facilitators and consultant heads in promoting the aforementioned dialogic skills.

The programme also emphasizes the importance of school-based enquiry and activity between sessions. School enquiry visits highlight the value of evidence-informed practice for school improvement, whilst at the same time encouraging participants to embed new learning in school-based activity that draws upon their experience of the programme and the perspectives of their New Visions colleagues. School enquiry visits are structured and focused visits by members of a regional group to each other's schools. The visits have a clear agenda for enquiry and are supported by protocols that structure the investigation. Critically they are based upon the principle of reciprocity and a mutual obligation amongst participants to develop and share knowledge. The programme evaluations (Paterson and Coleman 2003; Bush, Briggs et al. 2003) indicate that participants who completed school enquiry visits were universally positive about the experience. Not only did the process provide valuable insight for the hosts; it also gave visitors a better understanding of their colleagues' contexts, and resulted in a range of learning outcomes, including specific approaches to organizational development, learning and teaching, and wider shifts in perceptions and attitudes.

Headteachers define their leadership in what they say and do. The New Visions programme believes that empowering the dialogue of new leaders is at the heart leadership learning.

> Leading conversations . . . is a role of active involvement through which leaders insist on the conventions of conversations, facilitate the reciprocal processes, and connect participants to the visions, values and established norms of the group
>
> (Lambert 2002)

The key to the success of the programme's processes is that they provide clear protocols by which issues can be interrogated, analysed and solutions framed, thus supporting focused and thoughtful articulation of practice issues. Activities such as questioning for understanding, action learning sets, narrative as text, clinical review and problem-based learning are designed to develop the skills of listening, questioning, analysis, critique and conceptualization of leadership issues. The aim is that these learning habits become part of participants' professional repertoire – and that these habits spread amongst their staff. Creasy (2003) notes how the New Visions programme has

> . . . developed a range of approaches to engage heads in conversations to challenge their thinking, support their reflective skills and deepen their understandings by relating their own practice to the wider knowledge base. Such conversations themselves influence the way heads practise their leadership within their own schools and build learning relationships across a community of peers which offer the potential for ongoing networking

New Visions participants indicate that these protocols are readily transferable to their school contexts; and have been used to:

- support personal leadership practice; such as allocating time for quiet reflection;
- enhance collaborative approaches with staff; such as using action learning sets in senior team meetings;
- promote enquiry amongst staff; such as using the school enquiry protocol for school self evaluation;
- promote engagement with research amongst staff; by using Thinkpieces as a stimulus for analysis and critique of public knowledge and its application to their own school context and needs.

By being explicit about learning habits, the programme sets out to address 'higher order' leadership learning skills and hence build capacity for leadership learning that is sustained beyond the life of the programme and which spreads within the educational system more widely. Consultant heads, for instance, have used learning set, study group and enquiry protocols in their work in LEAs.

A community of learners

A key aspiration of the programme is that participants develop *communities of practice*; professional networks that share a commitment to action learning and school improvement. Participants on the New Visions programme valued the local knowledge of peers that supported common and contextualized understanding of issues. We found that communities of *support* develop quickly as participants listen to their peers, question one another and offer support for the problems and issues that are raised; thus addressing the sense of isolation often felt by new headteachers. Heads also preferred to work together in small groups that are local but avoid involving nearby colleagues. Where headteachers from neighbouring schools were members of the same regional group, participants report feeling constrained and less inclined to raise thorny professional issues. *Communities of learning* emerge from these communities of support – sometimes encompassing the whole group; sometimes encompassing a subset. These communities embrace individual and collaborative learning that exists within the confines of the programme.

The collaborative processes used in the programme support the development of such communities in several ways.

1   Such approaches support sharing knowledge, collaborative thinking and targeted action.
2   The use of formal protocols that structure group activity promotes learning about how to participate within a learning community.
3   By providing a basis for constructing meaning from individual and collective experiences, the group develops an identity.

It is interesting to note that it took many participants until the second or third theme before they understood the importance of learning about learning and assimilated the notion of learning collaboratively. For some the concept of 'learning on behalf of others' was not embedded at all.

Where *communities of practice* developed this was often as a response to school enquiry visits. These communities rely on heads investing time in between sessions to work together on leadership practice in context. Due to this time commitment, the emergence of communities of practice has been less prevalent. Although many participants express a desire to continue their collaborations beyond New Visions, communities that are sustained beyond the life of the programme are uncommon.

The fact that New Visions draws so heavily upon the experiences, values and attitudes of the participant heads means that individuals need to feel secure and empowered if they are to contribute fully and provide the personal real-life perspectives that are such a critical aspect of the collaborative learning process. The importance of establishing a climate within which mutual learning can occur is central to the success of the programme and supported by groups agreeing learning contracts early in the programme. As Peterson notes:

> Some of the most successful professional development programs for principals develop a strong, positive culture among participants with a clear set of symbols and ceremonies. A strong culture in a professional development program is likely to build commitment and identification with the program and its mission.
>
> (Peterson 2002)

The consultant heads play a key role in the New Visions community of learners. They bring an experienced perspective to the problems and issues of the new heads, help raise important issues, exemplify leadership attributes and act as a source of validation and celebration. They 'bring credibility to the programme', ground facilitation in the needs of new leaders, and their presence is highly valued by both participants and facilitators (Paterson and Coleman 2003). New heads also find it reassuring to hear that their experienced colleagues still grapple with difficult issues, have anxieties and concerns and, that they too, are sometimes overwhelmed by their task.

Consultant heads need to develop additional skills to operate as co-facilitators, process supporters, critical friends, coaches and mentors, as well as developing the insight to know when each of these roles is appropriate. In doing this, consultant heads derive as much learning from the experience as participants – both in terms of content and process knowledge. As such, these consultant heads feed the wider development of the educational system, not only in the benefits to their own schools, but in the leadership knowledge and facilitation skills they employ beyond their schools.

The programme frames consultant heads, facilitators, programme staff and participants as co-learners; and research into the programme shows that there has been as much, if not more, learning for the consultant heads, facilitators and NCSL staff, as for the participants. Indeed New Visions has sought to exemplify a learning-rich system in which learning for each of these stakeholder groups is made available to the others. In addition to the use of formal quality assurance and evaluation intelligence for reflection during facilitator training sessions; interim reports from the evaluation and enquiry processes are offered to the facilitation teams and summaries posted on the online community; facilitators and consultant heads pose problems and share ideas on a dedicated online community; the lead facilitators reflect on their learning publicly in preparation sessions; and facilitation teams provide personal session reviews to the design team. The development of this community of learning is undoubtedly a key element in the functioning of the programme.

The principles and approaches used in New Visions require facilitators to display high-order skills – in modelling and drawing attention to learning, meta-cognition and inter-personal dynamics. In order for a national programme of this size and philosophy to offer coherent and quality provision to scale, significant attention must be given to recruitment, preparation and support for facilitators. The collaborative and interactive activities used in the New Visions' recruitment processes model the principles and processes of the programme; and candidates are selected based on their aptitude and readiness to engage in these processes. The programme also offers significant preparation for facilitators and consultant heads which has been deemed invaluable in embedding the principles of the programme. As new facilitators enter the programme the preparation days 'socialize' them into the principles of the programme. Experienced facilitators and consultant heads continue to attend preparation and support sessions in order to: share their own learning about facilitating the programme; learn from their colleagues; and inform their work in the wider educational system. In this way, New Visions supports a sustained learning community for the benefit of all those engaged in the programme.

In conclusion

In founding NCSL in 2001, the Secretary of State challenged the College to become a driving force for world-class leadership in our schools; a provider and promoter of excellence; a major resource for schools; and a catalyst for innovation. New Visions is one of the earliest projects inspired by this remit – so it is timely to review its success in pursuing these aims.

Early headship provides both a 'steep step' in leadership learning and a great opportunity to influence the socialization and learning habits of leadership. New Visions is founded on the notion that 'it is only by engaging at a deep level that leadership learning is likely to be sustained' (Creasy 2003). Thus, the programme aspires to make the habits of enquiry, analysis, critique, reflection, collaboration and networking integral to the professional socialization for new headteachers.

The enduring high levels of satisfaction of participants and the international interest in the programme are early indicators that the programme is offering excellent, and perhaps world-class, leadership development for new headteachers in England. Beyond the personal and professional development of participants, the intention is that these learning habits will impact upon participants' schools and endure beyond the programme. Although it is too early for the evidence to be authoritative, it is encouraging that, based on the approaches to learning offered by the programme, participants witness a range of impacts upon their schools. In addition to this, the considerable impact upon consultant heads and facilitators offers the prospect of further gains for the educational system more widely.

Although there are encouraging indicators of success the research into the programme leaves some questions unanswered. We do not know, for instance, how the quality and depth of thinking, meta-cognition, reflection and analysis have been affected. Nor do we know whether the programme will remain as powerful as it increases in scale. We are also under no illusions that creating a more learning-centred cadre of school leaders is simple. In a provocative thinkpiece for NCSL Williams and Jackson (2002) ask, 'If principals are not directly involved in learning about learning, then what is their core purpose?' Whilst school leaders are experienced in analysing the learning of their pupils, one surprising outcome of our enquiry into the programme is how challenging participants found reflecting upon their own learning. In addition, many participants continued to see learning as an individual process and engaged in only very limited ways with activities designed to capture knowledge for sharing more widely. The notion that 'learning on behalf of others' is part of headteachers' role appears to be poorly embedded across the profession and remains a challenge to the programme's aspiration to enhance the cognitive landscape of early headship preparation.

It is clear, however, that the strong conceptual framework and learning-centred processes employed by the programme are central to its success. The programme's approaches are the seeds by which sustainable learning habits are propagated. Maintaining the integrity of these processes will be crucial as the programme grows and as these processes are used more widely in schools. Creasy, Cotton *et al.* (2004) argue that it is:

> the links between learning experiences and leadership behaviours which seem to offer the prospect of a 'new cadre of school leaders' ... If leaders can construct for themselves learning communities which apply robust theoretical frames and employ powerful learning processes ... there is potential for widespread impact. The evidence of the evaluation studies of New Visions, however, suggests that such collaborative leadership learning groups require facilitation and that facilitators (ideally practitioners themselves) are most able to support the group's learning if they have the opportunity to experience the learning processes for themselves and develop their own frames and learning habits
>
> (2004: 23–4)

Developing shared understanding of learning processes is integral to the culture of learning-centred schools (West-Burnham 2004). In a similar fashion, the study of New Visions suggests that developing shared understanding of the learning processes within leadership development is central to its impact upon pupil learning. Modelling learning-centred principles within programmes therefore mimics the culture of learning-centred schools. This requires facilitators to demonstrate learning-centred skills; which in turn requires high-quality ongoing facilitator preparation, that provides a template and fundamental stimulus in a chain that links programme designers with facilitators, participants and their schools. We have learned that 'trainers' experienced in delivering modules from training manuals sometimes need considerable support to move into learning-centred facilitation modes.

Emerging from our work on New Visions is the prospect that if we wish to enhance radically the learning opportunities for pupils in our classrooms we must also re-conceptualize the way we learn as professionals and as school leaders. If we are to become more learning-centred we must develop shared understandings about learning – and be clear that it is just as important to reflect upon our own learning, as it is to reflect on the learning of our pupils. If pupils are to become more sophisticated learners, then so must school leaders – and in a society awash with information, surely school leaders must learn to learn on behalf of others? If we want pupils to become increasingly self directed as learners – what place is there for mandatory professional learning? If schools are to become learning organizations that respond flexibly to pressing real-time issues – what place is there for rigidly-defined curricula for leadership development? And if pupils and schools are to learn more collaboratively then surely, so must school leaders?

Bibliography

Barnett, B.G. (2001) Preparing to face the challenges of principalship: The Prism model, *Monograph No. 3*, Australian Principals Centre.

Bennett, N. and Marr, A. (2002) *Leadership Development and School Middle Management: Problems in judging its impact on practice*. Annual Conference of the Canadian Society for the Study of Educational Administration, 24–28 May, Toronto.

Bright, T. and Ware, N. (2003) Were you prepared? Findings from a national survey of headteachers, *NCSL Research Associate Reports*. Nottingham: NCSL.

Bush, T., Briggs, A. *et al.* (2003) *External Evaluation of the New Visions Induction to Headship Pilot Programme*: Cohort One. Nottingham: NCSL.

Bush, T. and Glover, D. (2004) *Leadership development: Evidence and beliefs.* Nottingham: NCSL.

Bush, T. and Jackson, D. (2002) 'A preparation for school leadership', *Educational Management and Administration* 30(4): 417–29.

Claxton, G. (1997) *Hare Brain Tortoise Mind: Why intelligence increases when you think less*. London: Fourth Estate.

Creasy, J. (2002) *Principles for leadership learning design: A discussion paper for the NCSL leadership team.* Nottingham: NCSL.

Creasy, J. (2003) *Early Principles in Action: NCSL's New Visions programme.* Nottingham: NCSL.

Creasy, J., Cotton, C. *et al.* (2004) *Meaningful Leadership Learning: Reflections and evidence from external and internal evaluations.* The International Congress for School Effectiveness and Improvement, Rotterdam, 6–9 January.

Day, C. (1993). Reflection: A necessary but not sufficient condition for professional development, *British Education Research Journal*, 19(1).

Earley, P., Evans, J. *et al.* (2002) Establishing the current state of school leadership in England, *DfES Research Report 336.* London: DfES.

Eraut, M., T. Bush, L. Bell, R. Bolam, R. Glatter and P. Ribbens (1999) Headteachers' knowledge, practice and mode of cognition, in *Educational Management: Refining theory, policy and practice.* London: Paul Chapman.

Gronn, P. (2002) Designer leadership: the emerging global adoption of preparation standards, *Journal of School Leadership* 12: 552–78.

Hatton, N. and Smith, D. (1995). Facilitating Reflection: Issues and Research, *Forum of Education* 50(1): 49–65.

Hobson, A. (2003) Mentoring and Coaching for New Leaders, *Literature Reviews.* Nottingham: NCSL.

Hobson, A., Brown, E. *et al.* (2003) *Issues for early headship: Problems and support strategies.* Nottingham: NCSL.

Isaac, J. (2001) *Can 100 Gas, Electricity, Telecom and Ports Managers Help?* BELMAS Annual Conference.

Lambert, L. (1998) *Building Leadership Capacity in Schools*, ASCD.

Lambert, L. (ed.) (2002). *The Constructivist Leader.* University of Columbia, Teachers College Press.

Leithwood, K. (1995) 'Preparing school leaders: What works?' *Connections* 3(3, Spring): 1–8.

Leithwood, K.A. and Steinbach, R. (1992) Improving the problem-solving expertise of school administrators, *Education and Urban Society* 24(3): 317–45.

Paterson, A.S.F. and Coleman, A. (2003) New Visions for Early Headship Pilot Programme – Cohort One: Internal Enquiry Final Report. Nottingham: NCSL.

Peterson, K. (2002) The professional development of principals: Innovations and opportunities. National Commission for the Advancement of Educational Leadership Preparation.

Revans, R.W. (1983) Action learning: Its terms and character, *Management Decision* 21(2): 39–50.

Schon, D. (1987) *Educating the Reflective Practitioner.* San Fransisco: Jossey-Bass.

Watkins, C. (2003) Learning about learning enhances performance, *NSIN Research Matters.* London Institute of Education.

Weindling, D. (2004a) *Innovation in headteacher induction.* Nottingham: NCSL.

Weindling, D. (2004) *Leadership development in practice: Trends and innovations Nottingham*: NCSL.

West, M. and Jackson, D. (2002) *Developing School Leaders: A comparative study of leader preparation programmes.* Paper prepared for American Educational Research Association Annual Conference, New Orleans.

West-Burnham, J. (2004) *A secondary perspective: A study of leadership in 21 schools*. Nottingham: NCSL.
Williams, C. and Jackson, D. (2002) Leaders learning together. *NCSL Thinkpiece*. Nottingham.

nine

Developing leadership for e-confident schools

Tony Richardson

Introduction

In 1978, in my third year of teaching, I was working in a primary school in Coventry and held a post for language development and drama. As a teacher of nine-year-olds, with a interest in developing children's literacy, thinking skills and abilities to work cooperatively in groups, I was for ever experimenting with new ways of involving the children in their learning and encouraging them to systematically review and reflect upon their learning and progress. I was interested in the ways in which children worked on tasks together, how they constructed, set and negotiated 'rules' and how they tackled problem-solving tasks.

Around that time, I attended a course at which I saw a demonstration of a micro-computer – a 'Commodore 8K PET'. The friendly sounding PET brand, actually stood for the less catchy – 'personal electronics transactor'.

It had a monochrome integrated screen and keyboard and a cassette tape 'drive'. It came with two pieces of software; Commodore Basic (a simple programming language) and 'paddle battle' – an extremely rudimentary tennis-style game. The Local Education Authority had two such machines. I persuaded the maths adviser to let me borrow the machine for a term, found out how to write a times table tester program and placed it in my classroom. I was fascinated how the machine seemed to immediately engage the children. Girls and boys equally took to the task of working out how to beat the machine at paddle battle and to practice the 132 times table! The focus on the machine itself seemed to engage the children. They focused on the task, talked constantly, laughed, cooperated, experimented, tried to find out how it worked, tried to explore its limitations ... and

Figure 9.1 A Personal Electronic Transactor

they concentrated. I thought this was just the novelty of a new toy but I was wrong.

During the next couple of years, other machines appeared with more and more interesting and relevant software. Early word processors, simulations, logo, adventure games and databases started to provide a set of unique resources and tools for extending and enhancing learning in the classroom. I observed similar kinds of high motivation in learning when children interacted with the technology and with each other. I began to think that the technology had something very special to offer learning and teaching. Detailed thinking and rationalization of just what it was that the technology offered was, however, poorly articulated by teachers and academics of the time. In some senses, the use of ICT in schools in the early 1980s was very much an enthusiastic act of faith that it would bring positive benefits to learning and teaching.

Emerging evidence of impact

About every six months since those early experiences, I have believed that we are on the cusp of something very important for learning and teaching by the use of the technology. Every six months, I have been proved wrong! During the last 20 years, the use of new technology within schools has remained largely peripheral to the core business of teaching and learning.

There is no doubt that huge progress has been made in establishing the infrastructure necessary to make learning and teaching using new technologies a practical reality in all schools. Computer to pupil ratios have improved dramatically, but in England, during the past five years, whilst we have seen a massive expansion in the levels of hardware available to support learning in every school in the country, ICT is effectively and well used to extend and enhance learning and teaching in only about 20–25 per cent of schools (DfES 2003).

Recent research by the British Education and Communications Technology agency, (Harrison 2003) has shown that where ICT is used effectively in well-led schools with good levels of ICT infrastructure there is a measurable and significant impact on standards. Their overall findings are the clearest evidence so far of the importance and significance of the impact of ICT on attainment. The research clearly demonstrates that the effective use of ICT in learning and teaching leads to improved standards, measured by national tests.

Since the systematic spread of the information technologies within schools commenced in the early 1980s, information technology has been presented and promoted mainly as an aid or tool of learning. ICT has in some senses been described as just another classroom tool – like the pencil, pen or book – and a good deal of the current use of ICT within schools reflects this view. A good deal of the practice observed in schools has shown that since 1990, a disproportionate emphasis has been placed upon the use of word processors for writing and composing text or narrative. Areas such as measurement and control, modelling and to an extent even information handling receive very much less attention. It is these areas that have the greatest potential for exploiting the learners' capacity to develop power and control over their own learning processes.

This situation is not surprising, given the orthodoxy that describes ICT as just another, although 'powerful', classroom tool. Essentially, our current practice in schools has 'implanted' the technology on the existing curricular and learning organization without any real attempt to transform the nature of the conventional classroom and school organizational and pedagogical processes. Moreover, recent school-building design itself maintains this position, reflecting assumptions about learning style, grounded upon the pre-technology curriculum. The design normally accepts as given, that pupil groups of between 15–32 will work in a single area or room, with one teacher, for defined blocks of time on either skills-based 'vocational' activity or academically based study.

The emergence of ICT within the curriculum (and within school organization and management) during the past 20 years or so has begun to raise a series of important questions about the relative roles of the teacher and learner; the nature, definition and status of knowledge; the learners' access to knowledge; the learners' control of the curriculum; and where and when 'education' should occur. These issues include:

- the relevance and appropriateness of current school organization, learning methodology and the teachers' role given the widespread availability of IT and other new technologies at home, at school at work and in other settings;
- the drive towards learning improvement supported through the new technologies
- improving 'access' to further, continuing and higher education and the role of the information technologies;
- the implications for teaching, learning and leadership development in schools.

As has been suggested earlier, ICT conventionally operates at a tangent to the core experience of most pupils and teachers, in the great majority of schools. The full potential that ICT has for enabling learners to understand and have control of their own learning is likely to remain rhetoric unless ways can be found to structure the new technologies into the heart of the processes of learning and teaching. ICT systems can no longer be perceived as 'additionality' or as 'enhancement' – to be added to the concept of the curriculum or the physical school design at the requirements stage. Rather, the learning and curriculum demand and requirements should define both the pedagogical and organizational design of the school – and ICT systems as an essential element, should be structured into the design brief at the outset.

Learning to lead the e-enabled curriculum: the radical shift to come

The use of ICT as a normal part of the learning context is raising a set of new issues for teaching, learning, its organization and location and crucially, its leadership. A key element of much observed activity involving ICT is the ways in which language, thinking and particularly decision-making skills can be promoted. This is particularly so in relation to the use of content-free software modelling tools such as databases and spreadsheets, but is becoming increasingly the case with content-rich software now available through the internet, mixed and multimedia applications and both synchronous and asynchronous communication, simulation and interaction. This has important implications for the professional development of teachers and school leaders and for the design of learning programmes geared to pupils' personalized needs.

Developments in these areas are already beginning to raise questions about the traditionally linear patterns of learning organization and design that current curricular arrangements imply for many pupils and students. The importance of such language and thinking-based competencies is likely to increase, as the demand for creative, innovative and sophisticated individuals able to work cooperatively in teams to work on solving problems increases. It is not just a highly skilled, ICT literate population that will be required in the future but individuals who are able to use technology to extend and enhance creativity in order to produce effective solutions and outcomes to complex industrial, social or political problems. The impact of the new technologies means that people will increasingly need to know how to access, retrieve, handle and evaluate a diverse range of information, in a myriad of forms. They will need to possess a repertoire of interactive communication skills in order that sense and use can be made of such knowledge. Such a shift in emphasis from the acquisition of knowledge to its manipulation has profound implications for the teacher's traditional role and the setting in which 'formal' education takes place (Richardson 1988).

In this new context, learners will need to become self-reliant to a much greater extent and teachers will need to recognize that their task will be to promote and develop their learners' personal skills, qualities of self-reliance, interdependence, self-organization and self-assessment. Learning, using ICT systems, is increasingly taking place in a variety of settings including the home and this factor alone is raising important issues for the education system, particularly in terms of the accreditation of learning. The ICT systems used by individuals are becoming more 'intelligent' and able to customize and match content and learning activities as the learners interact with the systems. Managed learning environments working in the background of applications are steadily increasing in their sophistication and are now near to the capacity to accurately assess the learners' need and performance and to 'customize' and personalize the applications, learning programmes and content appropriately, effectively helping to manage the learners' route through the learning programmes in dynamic and sophisticated ways.

In England, the National College for School Leadership's (NCSL) 'Learning Gateway' demonstrates this in practice. The Learning Gateway is an online learning system that will give participants in the College's programmes the power to personalize their learning as never before. The system allows users to create their own learning pathway to fit around their individual circumstances. It means that they can access learning in their own time, choose activities and content to suit their own learning styles, specific needs and experiences, as well as track and evaluate their progress. The Learning Gateway includes access to e-learning activities and content, a Learning Management System, needs analysis and evaluation tools and access to tutors and fellow programme participants through the College's *talk2learn* online community. The Gateway not only provides a powerful practical tool for extending the College's reach and access but is also giving school leaders first-hand experience of what it is like to be an online learner, themselves. Other developments accelerating the spread of ICT within school education are similarly poised to present the school education system with a major and radical challenge to orthodoxy. As Checkland and Holwell (1998) have noted, 'because of the kind of thinking it entails, ICT is not simply a new tool with which to do traditional tasks. It stirs things up, introduces uncertainties, gets people perceiving their world in a new way.'

In January 2003, the Secretary of State for Education and Skills in England launched the government's education resource and learning portal 'Curriculum Online'. In time, this portal will potentially provide a rich set of online national curriculum content and media-rich learning tools available to pupils whether they are at school, at home or elsewhere. Pupils will increasingly be able to access and learn with these materials 'virtually' alongside their peers, parents/carers, independently or 'face-to-face' in school.

How will the school take steps to lead and manage this concurrent and distributed learning? How will the school act to minimize the social class differences between the groups of students and compensate for those who are not well supported for independent learning in their home contexts? This scenario is already developing very quickly and is becoming a reality in a number of schools. All of this will have major implications for the organization of the curriculum in school and the assessment of pupils' learning and must be urgently addressed by school leaders, teachers, parents and policy makers.

In the new digital curriculum world, schools will need to take account of the learning that pupils will have undertaken – which may well have been assessed and accredited outside of the school – when planning teaching and learning. One of the most difficult aspects of teaching and learning has always been ensuring that learners' needs are carefully and accurately assessed and that the curriculum and learning experiences provided through the curriculum are accurately matched to the learners' needs. The accountability that schools have to meet individual needs and to promote a personalized approach to learning, progress and achievement will be very much sharpened by the introduction of a digital curriculum. The school will need to demonstrate with greater clarity than now, precisely how it is adding value to the prior learning that pupils may well be undertaking and gaining credit for, outside of the school.

The leadership lag: developing e-confidence

All these developments have major implications for school leadership. Despite investment in ICT infrastructure, content and teacher professional development in schools during the last 15 years – many schools remain relatively untouched. ICT equipment levels have increased dramatically but the promise of ICT having a major impact on improved learning process and outcomes has failed to be delivered.

One of the main obstacles to developing the effective use of ICT within the curriculum in many schools (and also within the organization and management of the school) has been the lack of engagement and confidence of senior school leaders in actively and strategically leading ICT development. Many Heads left the classroom before ICT really began to bite within the delivery of curriculum. Many in senior leadership roles lack the practical knowledge and understanding of how ICT can transform teaching and learning and are therefore in a weak position in terms of their strategic leadership responsibilities in the area. Given the pivotal role of the school leadership group and especially the headteacher in securing continual school improvement, it is not surprising that ICT has failed to deliver its promise. In some senses, the confidence of our school leaders lags behind both the pupils and new entrants to teaching.

Building 'e-confidence' amongst the whole of the school workforce in order to create 'e-confident schools', where pupils and teachers can use and apply new technology wherever and whenever it is appropriate, is an attainable and vitally important goal.

The good news is that we now know from BECTa's Impact 2 report (Harrison 2003) that ICT helps to raise achievement and we also know that personalizing the learning experience for the learner and matching the learning much more precisely to their needs and their learning styles will increase motivation, enjoyment and impact upon both their level achievement and motivation to learn. Given the major advances in the availability of new technology in the school and in the home, the moment is now right for the school to exploit the opportunities the new technologies present for engaging all learners and for minimizing both the social and digital divide. This will mean the school seeing its role as leading and orchestrating learning beyond the bounds of the traditional timetable, and traditional structure of the school day. It will mean developing and deploying both teaching and teaching support staff in different and creative ways – enabling them to support pupils and students in face-to-face lessons within the school – in independent study and as virtual or online learners – working both individually and in learning communities within their home and family settings.

For these ambitions to be translated into practical action, schools need support to develop their use of ICT across all areas of teaching, learning and organization – wherever and whenever the application of ICT improves, extends and enhances both the quality of children's learning and outcomes. To be in a secure position to be able to do this, schools need to develop their e-confidence in ten key dimensions. These are:

- ensuring coherent professional training and support to develop high levels of staff confidence, competence and leadership;
- actions to transform teaching, learning and assessment, integrating effective use of ICT;
- the active leadership and management of distributed and concurrent learning, within and beyond the bounds of the traditional school timetable;
- effective application of ICT within organizational and management processes;
- a guarantee of coherent personal learning development, support and access – for all leaders, teaching and non-teaching staff;
- professional dialogue and action to secure, informed professional judgement;
- plans and actions to ensure that there is appropriate resource allocation to ensure sustainable development;
- making sure that the schools' ICT is available, operating effectively, accessible to pupils and staff and technically supported;
- structuring ICT within teaching, learning and planning to ensure that pupils/students develop and can show high ICT capability;
- developing the school as the lead community learning and information hub.

In taking this work forward, we need to develop much greater under-standing and clarity about what we mean by 'e-learning' as it is applied to both professional development for teachers and leaders and to learning and teaching within the curriculum. The National College for School Leadership has developed an approach to leadership learning which not only provides leaders with opportunities to learn, share and collaborate with other colleagues in face-to-face encounters, but also through *talk-2learn*, an online collaborative learning environment. The College has developed these learning tools, opportunities and programmes to create a 'blended learning' experience, combining the best of face-to-face learning with individual reflection and study and with online learning and collaboration.

There is increasingly strong research evidence that getting the blend right is key to the effectiveness of the learning experience and that the integration of online dialogue and communication actually helps learners to get to higher levels of thinking and reflection. As McBain (2001) suggests in his discussion of the current use and application of e-learning, mainly within the commercial sector, there is now solid evidence that blended approaches using asynchronous dialogue really do enhance learning and potentially increase engagement and participation. He outlines the relative strengths and weaknesses, arguing for a 'blended' approach which plays to the advantages of both virtual and face-to-face learning. He cites Weingartner's (2000) review of asynchronous distance learning which discusses the current research on classroom learning versus e-learning, which concludes:

> there is no significant difference between classroom courses and asynchronous courses ... asynchronous courses are at least as good at achieving learning objectives. A blended approach may be even more effective.

In Weingartner's review, whilst face-to-face learning provides much richer opportunities for immediate feedback from tutors, web-based learning seems to provide other significant advantages. Greater opportunities exist for more student oriented learning and the web-based learning environment helped learners to take more responsibility for their own views and opinions. Indeed, once the formalities and conventions of face-to-face interaction are effectively modified in the virtual learning environment, the research suggests that the higher education students involved in the study were more prepared to offer views, engage in open debate and to justify their thinking at a deep level. This has important implications for leadership development. One of the key purposes of the online communities is not only to provide a means of sharing practice, but the critical interrogation and reflective discussion of ideas and concepts pertinent to leadership and school improvement.

We need to identify the most useful and effective forms of teacher intervention, questioning and feedback to pupils, when the learning is taking place at a distance synchronously and asynchronously. We also need to identify clearly what kinds of online tutoring, facilitation and intervention are most effective in the leadership development activities of online communities and networks. Salmon (2000), in her work on e-learning, argues that a systematic approach to encouraging online participation and collaboration is required if learning within new virtual environments is to be maximized.

The success to date of the online community and e-learning offered by NCSL for school leaders has resulted from a combination of the approaches advocated by Salmon, combined with supportive facilitation, access to equipment, proactive encouragement and most importantly, the provision of a mechanism of developing thinking about school leadership issues. The key features of the online provision being that of sharing opinion, exchanging ideas, having access to policy makers and experts, enjoying a stimulating discourse in an interesting environment which helps to generate new ideas and new knowledge. In many ways, this combination of structure, content, pressure and support is not too far removed from the more familiar face-to-face encounters of traditional approaches to in-service training and CPD. As Lally and Wallington (2002) have commented:

Developing these aspects of teaching and learning so that e-learning is a success involves a mixture of course design issues and pedagogical issues. The two go together, just as they do in face-to-face teaching. Successful e-learning will involve a combination of group activities, structure, stimuli cajoling by tutors and peers, and giving people a purpose or a reason to go online.

Next steps

Our next steps should involve moving to a clearer definition and set of purposes for our online communities and e-learning to offer for professional development and exchange. Simultaneously we need to provide advice for school leaders as they lead the debate and developments in their schools, as they build the new online distributed and concurrent learning environments for pupils' learning, which will soon be commonplace as the digital curriculum becomes a reality.

In summary then, the evidence of NCSL practice to date is indicating a number of advantages in the use of e-learning for leadership development which have broader implications for the school curriculum, as schools increasingly adopt and integrate the use of new technology within pedagogical approaches and move to ICT being 'mission critical' to them. These include the potential for:

- deeper levels of engagement – in the online environment there is greater opportunity for pause and reflection before responding than can sometimes be the case in a conventional face-to-face conversation or conventional 'discussion';
- a broader range of views of opinion to be reported and represented than is sometimes the case in conventional conferences/seminars or, indeed, classroom encounters where it is likely that the more interpersonally self-confident individuals are more likely to speak up;
- learners to have more direct control over their learning or discussion in that they choose to participate in an increasing choice over their learning pathways.
- the potential for access to vast arrays of information and learning beyond that defined through the national curriculum;
- a greater range of feedback from co-learners, as well as teachers/tutors.

The advantage of involvement in e-learning is that the time for involvement in learning can be at the point most conducive to the learner – contrasted with a conventional timetabled activity within schools and face-to-face continuous and professional development.

We have a good chance during the next five years to integrate the use of ICT within teaching and learning in powerful ways that will transform the quality and nature of learning and teaching. We have the best and most highly skilled school workforce we have ever had; the ICT infrastructure across schools and communities has vastly improved, home use has substantially increased and school leaders understand that it is their key leadership role to ensure that the use of ICT in teaching and learning really does extend, enhance and improve the learning. We have the best chance we ever had to find ways of making the use of ICT 'mission critical' to the school and learning in radical ways which will change the organization of learning – transform where, when and how learning take place and vastly increase pupils' access to and engagement to learning inside and outside of the traditional structures and organization of the school. Just as in the 21st-century hospital, it would now be impossible to undertake the new and radical surgical and medical practices devised in the last decade without the use, integration and transformational potential of new technology, so e-confident schools as part of an e-confident system of education will become radically different institutions where high-quality, personalized learning, integrating new technologies as a part of their 'blended learning' offer will expand range and opportunities, guaranteeing that every pupil has a tailored approach to learning matched to their needs, enabling them to fulfil their learning potential. In these e-confident schools, the school workforce will also have potential access to the whole of the profession and be in a position to benchmark their practices, share ideas, critique and build new knowledge and professional practice through their routine engagement in online collaboration. If the new technology in the operating theatre was removed overnight, many of the advances in medical practice of the last decade would be lost – the hospital would not be able to function and deliver quality health care. We need to make the use of ICT in schools similarly vital to its role in ensuring high standards for all.

Our next challenge must therefore be to identify the impact of online learning upon leadership development and ultimately find ways of evaluating whether or not engagement online hinders or helps school leaders in their role of ensuring that every child can succeed and achieve their potential. Similarly, as schools develop online environments for pupils, we need to gather evidence of impact and outcomes on pupil learning. This is important for two reasons. Firstly, to create the optimum 'blend' that is right for the nature of the learning experience itself and the blend that is right for the individual – tailoring and matching the opportunities to learn to the needs of the individual and personalizing the experience. Secondly, to create a model for personalized online and face-to-face learning which can give leaders the experience of being 'online learners' themselves – as we believe that having a deep understanding, insight and awareness of this will help teachers and leaders in their roles as designers and creators of online and blended learning for their pupils.

This will be crucially important as teachers develop and implement a 21st-century curriculum that fully exploits new technology for learning – a distributed curriculum which enables and encourages concurrent and distributed learning. For this to happen, it will be essential that teachers and leaders come to clearer views about how the use of new technology and online learning can improve, extend, enhance and in some areas change the nature of the learning experience. Similarly, just as we have developed clear views about what works best in conventional approaches to teaching and learning in the classroom, we need to come to a clearer understanding of how pedagogy and learning supported by ICT will change the role of the teacher and the student as learning continues to occur in face-to-face encounters but also in virtual learning worlds, if we are to develop truly, e-confident pupils, e-confident teachers in e-confident schools and communities.

Bibliography

Checkland, P. and Holwell, S. (1998) *Information, Systems and Information Systems: Making sense of the field*. London: Wiley.

Department for Education and Skills (2003) *Survey of Information and Communication Technology in Schools 2003*. London: DfES (www.dfes.gov.uk/rsgateway/DB/SBU/b000421/release.shtm).

Harrison, C. *et al.* (2003) *ImpaCT2: The Impact of Information and Communication Technologies on Pupil Learning and Attainment*. Coventry: Becta (www.becta.org/research/reports/impact2).

Lally, V. and Wallington, J. (2002) Enticing Learning, *TES Online* (8 February 2002).

McBain, R. (2001) E-learning: towards a blended approach, *Manager Update* (19 November 2001). Henley: Henley Management College.

Richardson, T. (1988) Education for personal development: a whole school approach, in Lang, P. (ed.) *Thinking about Personal and Social Education in the Primary School*. Oxford: Blackwell.

Salmon, G. (2000) *E-moderating: The key to teaching and learning online*. London: Kogan Page.

Weingartner, H.M. (2002) *Quality of E-Learning: Report on computer mediated distributed asynchronous instruction*. American Graduate School of Management.

ten

Developing leadership for organizational learning

Bill Mulford and Halia Silins

Introduction

Reforms for schools, no matter how well conceptualized, powerfully sponsored, brilliantly structured or closely audited are likely to fail in the face of cultural resistance from those in schools. By their actions, or inaction, students, teachers, middle managers and headteachers help determine the fate of what happens in schools, including attempts at reform.

Sometimes this is not a bad thing, for many a school has been badly disillusioned by the galloping hoof-beats of the itinerant peddlers behind the new movements who ride in and out again extorting their latest elixirs. On the other hand, there are reforms that may have great potential for school improvement. To have these advances fall to the same fate as the latest gimmickry or short-term political opportunism benefits no one, especially those in schools, for they are the people most responsible for the long-term improvement of schools and the children in them.

Where do school leaders start sorting the wheat from the chaff, exchanging the quick-fixes and short-term opportunism for genuine growth and long-term improvement? The current and growing emphasis on evidence-informed policy and practice is as good a place as any. However, if one is seeking to establish a useful evidence base for organizing leadership to create the schools of tomorrow then one also needs to establish the value of the evidence that is presented. The old computer adage 'garbage in, garbage out' remains as relevant today as it has always been.

In this chapter we present some quality evidence for those considering organizing leadership for school reform. We believe it is quality evidence because it has integrity and predictive validity as well as clearly defining its variables. The evidence has integrity in the sense that it is complex enough to come closer to the reality faced by schools than much of previous research in the area, has been gathered from other than headteachers – who tend to overestimate the effectiveness of reforms when compared with their teachers (McCall *et al.* 2001) – and has been collected by other than those involved in the design or implementation of the reform. It has predictive validity because it attempts to link leadership with organizational learning and student outcomes. The link to student outcomes is a rare event indeed in the research literature on educational leadership and school improvement (EPPI-Centre 2001).

The directions suggested by this quality research evidence on leadership development to create the schools of tomorrow include the importance of distributive leadership, development, the context and broad measures of student outcomes.

The LOLSO research project

The Leadership for Organisational Learning and Student Outcomes (LOLSO) research project addresses the need to extend present understandings of school reform initiatives that aim to change school practices with the intention of supporting enhanced student learning. In what follows, we will briefly outline the nature of the LOLSO research design and results before turning to what we believe are some of the major implications of this research for organizing leadership for school reform. For this chapter we will restrict ourselves to the results of the quantitative survey responses from teachers and pupils (Silins and Mulford 2002; Mulford and Silins 2003).

LOLSO's research design required four phases of data collection and analysis conducted over four years:

- In Phase 1, surveys of 3,500 Year 10 students and 2,500 of their teachers and headteachers were conducted in half the secondary schools in South Australia and all the secondary schools in Tasmania (a total of 96 schools).
- In the second phase of the study, case studies of best practice were collected from four schools selected from the sample to triangulate and enrich the information generated by the survey data.
- In the third phase, South Australian Year 12 students, teachers and headteachers were resurveyed.
- The fourth phase saw the results from the quantitative and qualitative data used to develop and trial professional development interventions for school leaders (Mulford, Silins and Leithwood 2004).

In brief, the project's research design allowed for iterative cycles of theory development and testing, using multiple forms of evidence.

Results from LOLSO's teacher surveys ('teacher voice') and student surveys ('pupil voice') can be organized around six of the project's major research questions. In what follows, a diagramme summarizing the answer to the question precedes the written explanation.

- How is the concept of organizational learning (OL) defined in Australian secondary schools?
- What leadership practices promote OL in schools?
- What are some outcomes of schooling other than academic achievement?
- What are the relationships between the non-academic and academic outcomes of schooling?
- Do school leadership and/or organizational learning contribute to student outcomes?
- What other factors contribute to student outcomes?

How is the concept of organizational learning (OL) defined in Australian secondary schools?

OL was found to involve, *sequentially*:

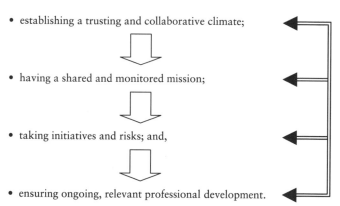

- establishing a trusting and collaborative climate;
- having a shared and monitored mission;
- taking initiatives and risks; and,
- ensuring ongoing, relevant professional development.

Figure 10.1 Sequential aspects of organizational learning

What leadership practices promote OL in schools?

The LOLSO research demonstrated clearly that the predominant conditions accounting for variations in OL between secondary schools were a headteacher skilled in transformational leadership and administrators and teachers who are actively involved in the core work of the school.

In brief, leadership which is transformational and distributive promotes a school which has a community focus, staff who feel valued and OL. Having a community focus means that the teachers perceive the school as having

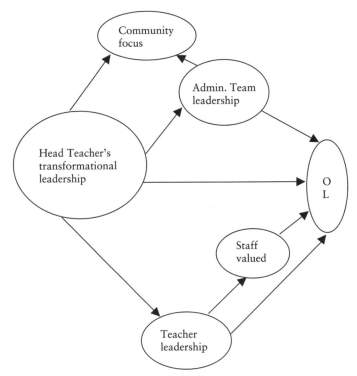

Figure 10.2 Effects of transformational leadership

productive working relations with the community and that the school's leaders are sensitive to the community, work with community representatives and incorporate community values in the school.

The headteacher who is transformational focuses on:

- *Individual Support* – providing moral support, showing appreciation for the work of individual staff and taking their opinion into account when making decisions.
- *Culture* – promoting an atmosphere of caring and trust among staff, setting a respectful tone for interaction with students and demonstrating a willingness to change his or her practices in the light of new understandings.
- *Structure* – establishing a school structure that promotes participative decision making, supporting delegation and distributive leadership and encouraging teacher autonomy for making decisions.
- *Vision and Goals* – working toward whole staff consensus in establishing school priorities and communicating these priorities and goals to students and staff, giving a sense of overall purpose.

- *Performance Expectation* – having high expectations for teachers and for students and expecting staff to be effective and innovative.
- *Intellectual Stimulation* – encouraging staff to reflect on what they are trying to achieve with students and how they are doing it; facilitating opportunities for staff to learn from each other and modelling continual learning in his or her own practice.

What is important is that staff are actively and collectively participating in the school and feel that their contributions are valued.

We also found that the headteacher's gender, or teachers' years of experience or gender or age, were not factors promoting OL, but school size was. The larger metropolitan schools of over 900 students, staffed by experienced and ageing teachers, did not provide the environment most conducive for transformational leadership or teacher distributive leadership. Perhaps surprisingly, having a community focus was not found to be related to promoting OL.

What are some outcomes of schooling other than academic achievement?

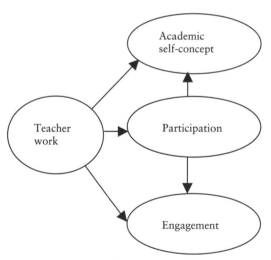

Figure 10.3 Other outcomes of schooling

There have been consistent and growing calls for broader measures of school success beyond academic achievement (for example, Elliott and Voss 1974; McGraw 1992; DfES 2001). Alienation of pupils from school can be a critical step leading to failure to complete schooling and is especially important for middle and senior high school students. Pupils who experience acceptance, or belongingness, are more highly motivated and engaged in learning and more committed to school. Engagement and commitment are closely linked to student performance, and more importantly, to the quality of student learning (Osterman 2000).

The LOLSO Research Project took such calls on board and included surveys of Year 10 and Year 12 pupil views of their schooling. The following factors emerged from the statistical analysis of their responses. In schools where there was a high degree of organizational learning, a number of positive factors were evident:

- *Teacher Work* – pupils
  - like the way the teachers teach,
  - see a variety of activities, constant challenge and good organization in class, and
  - believe teachers discuss their work with them and expect them to do their best work.
- *Academic Self-Concept* – pupils are
  - confident of success and graduating,
  - satisfied with marks now and at the end of the year, and
  - satisfied with the extent of their learning and ability to understand material.
- *Participation* – pupils
  - respond to questions and enjoy giving their opinion,
  - set goals,
  - participate in extracurricular activity, and
  - have low number of days where they were late and/or skipped classes.
- *Engagement* – pupils
  - are satisfied with student-teacher and student-student relationships,
  - identify with their school, and
  - see the usefulness of schoolwork for future life.

The findings on the relationships among these four non-academic achievement student outcomes reinforce the importance of the teachers' work for academic self-concept, participation and engagement. They also highlight the central role participation, that is the active, behavioural dimension, has for the attitudinal dimensions of academic self-concept and engagement.

What are the relationships between the non-academic and academic outcomes of schooling in schools with high organizational learning?

The LOLSO Research Project gathered data from over half of its student sample on whether or not they continued on from Year 10 to Year 12 (Retention) and their five subject aggregate Tertiary Entrance score from

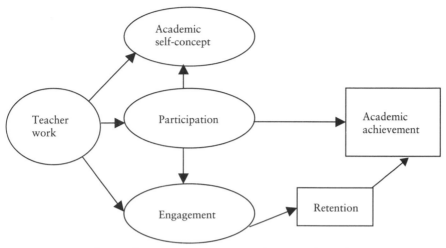

Figure 10.4 Relationships between non-academic and academic outcomes

the Secondary Assessment Board of South Australia's formal assessment procedure (Academic Assessment).

We found that students who stay in school and complete Year 12 and who participate in school are most likely to achieve academically. Retention is more likely when students are engaged with school. In other words, engagement is a direct predictor of retention but only indirectly influences achievement (through retention). The contra-intuitive result that academic self-concept is not a predictor of engagement, retention or achievement should be noted. We will return to this finding in our discussion of the implications of our research.

Other results indicated that the size and socio-economic status (SES) of the school and the pupil's perception of their home educational environment also influenced non-academic and academic student outcomes. Home educational environment involves having a space and aids for study as well as having discussions about and help with school work and conversations about world events.

Larger schools were more likely to have students with higher academic self-concept but to have lower student participation. Schools of higher SES were more likely to have students with higher academic self-concept, retention and academic achievement but lower perceptions of teachers' work. There was a very strong positive relationship between home educational environment and teachers' work and participation and a less strong but still positive relationship between home educational environment and academic self-concept.

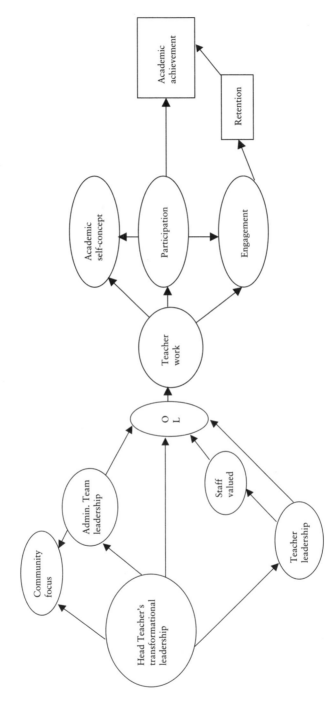

Figure 10.5 Effects of contributions from school leadership and/or organizational learning

Do school leadership and/or organizational learning contribute to student outcomes?

Both positional (headteacher) and distributive (leadership team and teacher leaders) leadership are only *indirectly* related to student outcomes. OL, or a 'collective teacher efficacy', is the important intervening variable between leadership and teacher work and then student outcomes. Said another way; leadership contributes to organizational learning which in turn influences what happens in the core business of the school; the teaching and learning. It influences the way teachers organize and conduct their instruction, their educational interactions with students, and the challenges and expectations teachers place on their pupils. The higher the teachers' ratings of the school on the four sequential dimensions defining organizational learning, the more positively teachers' work is perceived in classrooms by their pupils. Pupils' positive perception of teachers' work directly promotes participation in school, academic self-concept and engagement with school. Pupil participation is directly and pupil engagement indirectly, through retention, related to academic achievement.

What other factors contribute to student outcomes?

To repeat earlier findings, larger schools were not only less likely to promote transformational or teacher distributive leadership but were also more likely to have students with higher academic self-concept and lower student participation. In addition, schools of higher SES were more likely to have students with higher academic self-concept, retention and academic achievement but lower perceptions of teachers' work. Higher SES was related to having a positive home educational environment. Also, there were very strong positive relationships between home educational environment (pupil provided with study space and aids) and teachers' work and participation, and a less strong but still positive relationship between home educational environment and academic self-concept.

Student participation and engagement in school were either directly or indirectly related to retention and academic achievement. What was important was that pupils, just like teachers, are actively participating in the school and feel that their contributions are valued. However, neither pupil academic self-concept nor the school having a community focus was directly or indirectly related to any of the other student outcomes.

Implications: distributive leadership, development/learning, context, and broadening student outcome measures

Distributive leadership

The first of four implications of the LOLSO research is that leadership that makes a difference in secondary schools is both position based (headteacher) and distributive (administrative team and teacher) and that the effects of this leadership on student outcomes is indirect (through OL and teacher work). The positional/headteacher leadership we are talking about is what we termed 'transformational'. What is important is the collective efficacy of the staff, their ability to engage in organizational learning. How the teachers are treated is reflected in how the students perceive the teachers' work, which, in turn, is related to the outcomes of their schooling.

This first implication is consistent with the findings of a recent review of the research literature that identified three major and aligned elements in successful school reform (Silins and Mulford 2002). The first element relates to how people are treated. Success is more likely where people act rather than are always reacting; are empowered, involved in decision-making through a transparent, facilitative and supportive structure; and are trusted, respected and encouraged. The second element concerns a professional community. A professional community involves shared norms and values including valuing differences and diversity; a focus on continuous enhancement of learning for all students; and de-privatization of practice, collaboration, and critical reflective dialogue, especially that based on performance data. The final element relates to the presence of a capacity for learning. This capacity is most readily identified in an ongoing, optimistic, caring, nurturing professional development programme.

The importance of distributive leadership is consistent with the UK Government's White Paper on education (DfES 2001) and some of the directions espoused by the National College for School Leadership in England (NCSL 2001). The White Paper, for example, states that 'Only if we can build on the commitment and enthusiasm of all those who work in schools will we succeed in implementing a truly diverse secondary system'. It talks about 'Education with character' and the importance of the school's ethos for successfully achieving such character. The NCSL's documentation points out that their work is founded on four beliefs including that 'Our most successful schools are self-improving' and that 'Leadership in such schools tends to be shared'. Elsewhere NCSL gives priority to concepts such as 'capacity', 'dispersed leadership' and 'learning communities'.

The rejection in our findings of 'the great man or woman' theory of leadership should be noted. Faith in one person, 'the leader', as the instrument for successful implementation of the Government's educational policy, let alone broader and longer term educational outcomes, might bring initial albeit temporary success but the dependency relationship that it establishes will eventually ensure mediocrity if not failure. There is a clear difference here between the LOLSO research and the Hay-McBer model of excellence for school leaders (Hay-McBer, no date). In contrast to the Hay-McBer 'model', the LOLSO 'model' has no emphasis on the leader showing initiative by acting decisively, having impact by persuasion, calculation and influencing, or creating the vision through, for example, strategic thinking. Nowhere is the difference clearer than in our different interpretations of the concept 'transformational leadership'. The Hay McBer emphasis on the 'drive and the ability to take the role of leader, provide clear direction, and enthuse and motivate others' is a mile away from LOLSO's stress on support, care, trust, participation, facilitation and whole staff consensus.

Development/learning

The second implication is that successful school reform is all about development and, therefore, learning. Hersey and Blanchard (1988) made this point some time ago in respect of a leader's use of a task and/or relationship emphasis depending on the maturity of the group he or she was leading:

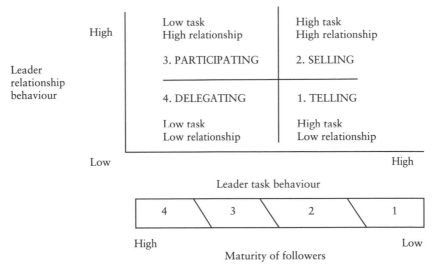

Figure 10.6 Leader's use of task and/or relationships emphasis

A group low in maturity would need a 'telling' style of leadership (high task, low relationship). At the next level of group maturity the leader would need a 'selling' style (high task, high relationship), then 'participating' style (low task, high relationship) and finally with a group high in maturity a 'delegating' style (low task, low relationship). The weakness of this model, however, is that it is not really about development. For example, if a leader keeps 'telling' or 'selling' an 'immature' group then the group is never going to become more mature. Of course, this assumes one wants mature groups, that is groups (a school staff) that have the ability (skill, knowledge, experience) and willingness (motivated, committed, self-confident) to take responsibility for directing their own behaviour!

In other words, one needs first to get the personal/interpersonal, distributive leadership, collective teacher efficacy or trusting and collaborative climate 'right'. Once the personal/interpersonal is 'right' then it can be used to focus on the educational/instructional, including having a shared and monitored mission. Once the educational/instructional is 'right' and there is confidence in what the school is doing and why it is doing it, then the leaders and school can move to development/learning/change, including working with others schools in a 'nested' model.

Development implies another important principle – one needs stability for change, one needs to constantly move ahead but without losing one's roots. Put another way, one needs a base or agreed position from which to develop; one needs to stand for something, to first be 'grounded'.

The context for leadership

The third implication of the LOSO research is that the context for leadership and school reform must be taken more into account. Variables such as socio-economic status, home educational environment and school size have a clear interactive effect on leadership, the school and student outcomes. Recent research by Harris and Chapman (2001) examining leadership in schools facing challenging contexts has shown that effective leadership in these schools is tight on values, purposes and direction but loose on involving others in leadership activity. The result of such leadership is clear direction and widespread involvement. But given our first implication on the importance of distributive leadership for significant and long-term school reform, we need to be careful here. As Barnett *et al.* (2001) have found, a visionary head teacher can actually distract teachers from concentrating on teaching and learning, let alone have ownership of the vision!

Our results help to revive the school size debate and add weight to the research drawing attention to the advantages of smaller schools (Lee and Loeb 2000). This issue has been recognized in some parts of USA with large schools now dividing themselves into sub-schools in order to provide the web of support necessary for student and teacher identification and involvement with the school and improved learning outcomes (Hodges 2000).

The lack of a link between the school having a community focus and organizational learning or student outcomes is potentially problematic. On the basis of our results, and if a choice needs to be made between working with and being sensitive to the community, and improving home educational environments, then the latter will have more direct and immediate 'payoff' for student outcomes. The success of the Excellence in Cities education mentors programme is a case in point (Radice 2001). Of course, having a strong community focus may be important for other reasons such as for the development of social capital in the community, especially in poor inner-city and rural communities.

Broadening of student outcome measures

The fourth implication is the need to broaden what counts for effective education beyond academic achievement. Self-concept is a case in point. Even though we, along with others (e.g. Silins and Murray-Harvey 2000), found that academic self-concept did not link to other student outcomes, including academic achievement, it does not follow that academic self-concept is not an important student outcome. For example, pupil self-concept has been shown to be related to later life successes such as employment and earnings (Feinstein 2000). Data from this British cohort study followed all children born in UK in the first week of April 1970 and surveyed them again in 1975, 1980, 1986, 1991 and 1996. At aged 10 in 1980 over 12,000 children were tested for mathematics and reading ability and the psychological attributes of self-esteem and locus of control. The children's teachers were questioned about their behavioural attributes of conduct disorder, peer relations, attentiveness and extraversion. In 1996, at age 26, information was then collected on highest qualification attained, earnings and periods of unemployment. The author, an economist, summarizes his findings as follows:

> . . . attentiveness in school has been shown to be a key aspect of human capital production, also influencing female wages, even conditioning on qualifications. Boys with high levels of conduct disorder are much more likely to experience unemployment but higher self-esteem will both reduce the likelihood of that unemployment lasting more than a year and, for all males, increase wages. The locus of control measure . . . is an important predictor of female wages . . . Good peer relations are important in the labour market, particularly for girls, reducing the probability of unemployment and increasing female wages. (p. 22)

> [These results] suggest strongly that more attention might be paid to the non-academic behaviour and development of children as a means of identifying future difficulties and labour market opportunities. It also suggests that schooling ought not to be assessed solely on the basis of the production of reading and maths ability. (p. 20)

Findings such as this, as well as those from the LOLSO Research Project, add weight to those expressing concerns about the sole reliance on academic achievement as the measure of a school's success.

The UK Government's White Paper (DfES 2001) gives hope that this argument may be being accepted when it states that, 'Critical though effective academic education is to children's life chances, it is not the only important part of schooling' and that 'we want schools to play their part in developing rounded individuals who are prepared well for adult life'. LOLSO's emphasis on children's active participation in their education is also given priority in the Government's support for schools to 'Encourage children's active participation in decisions that affect them', the introduction of citizenship into the National Curriculum promoting not just political literacy but also 'social and moral responsibility and community involvement' and extending 'opportunities for children to be involved in out-of-school activities'.

Another interesting development in the White Paper is the interest in 'pupil voice' with proposals not only for greater involvement but also adding pupil voice to the requirements for school inspection. This development may be timely for research is now 'beginning to encounter students expressing doubts about the genuineness of their school's interest in their progress and well-being as persons, as distinct from their contributions to their school's league table position. [The result is that] contract replaces community as the bond of human association' (Fielding 1999). Another recent study based on interviews with 195 Year 10 and 11 pupils found their attitudes towards school to be uniformly negative. Most worrying, however, was that teachers were beginning to be seen by their students as only representing other people's wills as they seek out the best means to adapt to the requirements of academic achievement results and inspection – 'every effort that a teacher makes to cajole the pupils into more work is interpreted as a sign of the teacher's selfish insecurity . . . all appears to be done for the sake of the external powers' (Cullingford 2001).

Despite research such as the LOLSO Project pointing to the importance of not just pupil but teacher voice for successful school reform, the continued ignoring of teacher voice in some education systems is extremely baffling.

Conclusion: building in canvas?

We are pleased to find that the results of the LOLSO Research Project and the implications for positive school reform that arise from these results are consistent with other contemporary research in the area. For example, in the USA both Goddard and Heck (Goddard 2000; Heck 2000) have found close links between school environments and improved student learning. Goddard *et al.* found that 'collective teacher efficacy is a significant predictor of student achievement . . . [and] is greater in magnitude than any one of the demographic controls [including socio-economic status]'. These researchers conclude, 'a one unit increase in collective teacher efficacy is associated with an increase of more than 40% of a standard deviation in student achievement.' Heck found that not only was higher socio-economic status directly related to greater student improvement, and larger schools produced smaller student gains, but also that schools where the headteacher leadership was rated as more supportive and directed towards instructional excellence and school improvement and the school climate was seen in positive terms 'produced greater-than-expected improvements in student learning over time'.

One detailed case study (Maden 2001) following up on eleven effective schools in disadvantaged areas some five years after the initial investigation has found that the levers of change and improvement included:

- distributive leadership – 'It is tempting to dwell solely on the head teacher as a kind of miracle worker, but these heads know that, above all else, securing improvement comes through the hearts and minds of teachers', and '. . . extra mental and emotional energy seems to be triggered off by a shared sense of achievement, particularly when this is the result of the real efforts of staff and pupils';
- organizational learning – 'It is probable that "school capacity" is the single most important matter in trying to identify how and why some schools maintain and sustain improvement' and,
- pupil participation and engagement – 'Effective headship seems always to include the nurturing of leadership opportunities for teachers, but also . . . for pupils.'

In their chapter bringing together the lessons from a book of international research on leadership for change and school reform, Riley and Louis (2000) focus on leadership that is more than role-based, that is leadership as an organic activity involving the formation of a network of values-driven relationships. Integral to the success of such dispersed leadership are both pupil and teacher voice. Finally, an OECD nine-country study on innovative initiatives in school management also concludes that 'Changes designed with little involvement of those destined to use them are rarely effective . . . In that sense every teacher is a school leader . . . It is striking . . . how frequently team-working is cited as a key ingredient to the success of new approached to school management.' The study points out that, 'In such learning organisations, individuals and teams become reflective practitioners and are able to review their own situations and deal with problems or challenges as they arise' (OECD 2001).

It will be noted that LOLSO, as well as this other contemporary research, places much less emphasis on the organizational, managerial or strategic than has previously been the case. This should not be surprising when it is realized that there is very little evidence to link such an emphasis to either OL or student outcomes. Elsewhere we have discussed such 'transactional' leadership as too readily having the potential for 'facades of orderly pur-posefulness', 'doing things right rather than doing the right thing', 'building in canvas', or 'procedural illusions of effectiveness' (Mulford 2000).

Sizer (1984) has talked about 'Horace's Compromise', which is working toward a facade of orderly purposefulness, exchanging minimums in pursuit of the least hassle for everyone. Sometimes this compromise can be likened to 'doing things right' rather than 'doing the right thing'. As Sergiovanni noted (2000), it has the same purpose as the latest military technology of 'building in canvas', that is, folding canvas tanks and canvas missile launch-ers designed to serve as decoys and to create an illusion of strength. Thus the purpose for education is to provide the right public face thus gaining the freedom for the Government to interpret, decide and function in ways that make short-term political but not necessarily long-term educational sense.

Meyer and Rowan (1978) point out that procedural illusions can be employed to maintain the myth of education and function to legitimize it to the outside world. In the absence of clear-cut output measures we turn to processes as outputs. For example, there are precise rules to classify types of headteachers, types of teachers, types of students and sets of topics. All these rules and regulations, competency lists, strategic plans, examinations and so on give confidence to the outside (and to many of those inside) that the education system and its schools know what they are doing.

The structure of the system or school is the functioning myth of the organ-ization that operates not necessarily to regulate intra-organizational activity, but to explain it, account for it, and to legitimate it to the members outside the organization and to the wider society. The transactions in educational organizations are concerned with legitimacy. Structures are offered that are congruent with the social expectations and understandings about what edu-cation should be doing, e.g. process goals explicitly stated by an education department to help maintain or develop this legitimacy may influence the use of certain 'approved' consultants, the creation of organizational sub-units such as an audit section or office of review, the setting up of national examination boards and training institutions and so on. While such actions may have little proven positive effect on what goes on in schools, classroom or with pupils, they do, at the time of their creation, demonstrate congru-ence with the goals and expectations of the wider society as perceived by the department or authority.

Here we are talking about high visibility and the *impression* of decisive-ness of action. Such goal displacement does, of course, raise important moral questions, especially if you believe, as we do, that deception has no place in education and its leadership or administration.

Galton makes the point well in terms of teachers:

By making certain techniques mandatory you run the danger of turning teachers into technicians who concentrate on the method and cease to concern themselves with ways that methods must be modified to take account of the needs of individual pupils. As we face the demands of a new century, creating a teaching profession which while technically competent was imaginatively sterile would be a recipe for disaster.

(Galton, 2000)

As it is for teachers, so it is for organizing leadership for school reform.

Bibliography

Barnett, K., McCormick, T. and Conners, R. (2001) Transformational leadership in schools, *Journal of Educational Administration*, 39(1): 24–46.

Bishop, P. and Mulford, B. (1996) Empowerment in four primary schools: They don't really care, *International Journal of Educational Reform*, 5(2): 193–204.

Bishop, P. and Mulford, B. (1999) When will they ever learn? Another failure of centrally-imposed change, *School Leadership and Management*, 19(2): 179–87.

Cullingford, C. (2001, July) Pupil attitudes to schools, Paper presented at The Learning Conference, Spetses, Greece.

DFES. (2001) *Schools – achieving success*. http://www.dfes.gov.uk/achievingsuccess/

Elliott, D. and Voss, H. (1974) *Delinquency and Dropout*. Lexington MA: Lexington Books.

EPPI-Centre (2001) *Core Keywording Strategy: Data Collection for a Register of Educational Research Version 0.9.4*. London: EPPI-Centre, Social Science Research Unit.

Fielding, M. (1999) Target setting, policy pathology and student perspectives: Learning to labour in new times, *Cambridge Journal of Education*, 29(2): 277–87.

Feinstein, L. (2000) *The Relative Economic Importance of Academic, Psychological and Behavioural Attributes Developed in Childhood*. London: Centre for Economic Performance, London School of Economics and Political Science.

Galton, M. (2000) Big change questions: Should pedagogical change be mandated? Dumbing down on classroom standards: The perils of a technician's approach to pedagogy. *Journal of Educational Change*, 1(2): 199–204.

Goddard, R., Hoy, W. and Hoy, A. (2000) Collective teacher efficacy: its meaning, measure, and impact on student achievement, *American Educational Research Journal*, 37(2): 479–507.

Harris, A. and Chapman, C. (2001, September) Leadership in schools in challenging contexts. Paper presented at British Educational Research Association conference, Lancaster.

Hay-McBer (no date) *Models of Excellence for School Leaders*. http://www.ncsl.org.uk/index.cfm?pageid=hayhome2

Heck, R. (2000) Examining the impact of school quality on school outcomes and improvement: a value-added approach, *Educational Administration Quarterly*, 36(4): 513–52.

Hersey, P. and Blanchard, K. (1988) *Management of Organizational Behaviour: Utilizing human resources*. Englewood Cliffs NJ: Prentice-Hall.

Hodges, A. (2000, April) Web of support for personalised, academic foundation Paper presented at the annual meeting of the American Educational Research Association, New Orlean LA.

Lee, V. and Loeb, S. (2000) School size in Chicago elementary schools: Effects on teachers' attitudes and student achievement, *American Educational Research Journal*, 37(1): 3–31.

Maden, M. (ed.) (2001) *Success Against the Odds – Five Years On: Revisiting effective schools in disadvantaged areas*. London: Routledge Falmer.

McCall, J., Smith, I., Stoll, L. *et al.* (2001) Views of pupils, parents and teachers: vital indicators of effectiveness and for improvement, in J. MacBeath and P. Mortimore (eds) (2001) *Improving School Effectiveness*. Buckingham: Open University Press.

McGaw, B., Piper, K., Banks, D. and Evans, B. (1992) *Making Schools More Effective*. Report of the Australian Effective Schools Project. Hawthorn VIC: Australian Council for Educational Research.

Meyer, J. and Rowan, B. (1978) Notes on the structure of educational organisations: revised version, Paper prepared for the Annual Meeting of the American Sociological Association. Reported in J. Hannaway, Administrative structures why do they grow? *Teachers College Record*, 79(3): 416–17.

Mulford, B. (1998) Organisational learning and educational change, in A. Hargreaves, A. Lieberman, M.Fullan and D. Hopkins. (eds) *International Handbook of Educational Change*. Norwell MA: Kluwer;

Mulford, B. (2000) The global challenge: a matter of balance, William Walker Oration. ACEA/NZIEA/PNGCEA/CCEAM International Conference, Hobart, September. http://www.cdesign.com.au/acea2000/pages/con03.htm

Mulford, B. and Silins, H. (2003) Leadership for organisational learning and improved student outcomes, *Cambridge Journal of Education*, 33(2): 175–95.

Mulford, B., Silins, H. and Leithwood, K. (2004) *Leadership for Organisational Learning and Improved Student Outcome*. Dordrecht: Kluwer.

NCSL (2001) First Corporate Plan: Launch Year 2001–2. Nottingham: National College for School Leadership; NCSL. Leading by a head. www.ncsl.org.uk

OECD (2001) *New School Management Approaches*. Paris: OECD, Centre for Educational Research and Innovation's 'What Works in Education' series.

Osterman, K. (2000) Students' need for belonging in the school community, *Review of Educational Research*, 70(3): 323–67.

Radice, S. (Tuesday July 31, 2001) Our adult friend. *Guardian Education*, pp. 2–3; Mentors in School Network. http://www.dfes.gov.uk/thelearninggateway/mentoring/index.htm

Coughlan, S. (2001) How mentors make a difference, BBC News EDUCATION. http://newssearch.bbc.co.uk/hi/eng . . . ucation/newsid_1132000/1132928.stm

Reynolds, D. (no date) *Effective School Leadership: The contribution of school effectiveness research*. http://www.ncsl.org.uk/index.cfm?pageid=ev.auth_reynolds

Riley, K. and Louis, K.S. (eds) (2000) *Leadership for Change and School Reform: International perspectives*. London: Routledge Falmer.

Sergiovanni, T. (2000) *The Lifeworld of Leadership*. San Francisco: Jossey-Bass.

Silins, H. and Mulford, B. (2002) Leadership and school results, in K. Leithwood and P. Hallinger (eds). *Second International Handbook of Educational Leadership and Administration*. Dordrecht: Kluwer,

Silins, H. and Murray-Harvey, R. (2000) Students as the central concern, *Journal of Educational Administration*, 28(3); 230–46.

Sizer, T. (1984) *Horace's Compromise*. Boston: Houghton-Mifflin.

Overview and conclusions

Geoff Southworth

This chapter aims to offer an overview of the emerging themes and issues raised in the previous chapters. Therefore, what this chapter seeks to do is three things. First, identify the emerging themes. Second, discuss them and begin to examine what they mean for both practitioners and researchers. Third, link them to the work of the National College for School Leadership in England and show how those of us at the College are addressing them.

In very broad terms there are two themes which run across all the chapters:

- Leadership development;
- Creating schools for tomorrow.

It is no surprise that these are the two major themes given the title of this book. However, it is also clear from many of the chapters that the two themes together create a third one:

- Developing leaders for tomorrow's schools.

This third theme is sometimes explicit, sometimes implicit in the writing. In some school systems, most notably Singapore, there is a clear commitment to preparing leaders for tomorrow's schools. Elsewhere educators are not so bold and are not nearly as candid in setting out where they see leadership going. Yet if we are to prepare leaders for their present and future roles we should have some clarity about what they need to do and the skills they will be expected to have.

In the following three sections these themes will be discussed in turn. Each will be explored in some detail, either by identifying the range of ideas which the writers here have focused on, or by thinking about the issues they have highlighted.

Leadership development

Much is said about leadership development in the previous ten chapters. All the writers are themselves involved in school leadership development and preparation and each has ideas about the nature and the focus of this activity. The theme of leadership development covers a number of important ideas and issues. Five stand out most prominently across the chapters. They are:

1 the importance of context;
2 distributed leadership;
3 leading learning communities;
4 leadership succession and sustainability;
5 leadership development processes.

The importance of context

The idea that context matters is simply an expression of contingency theory. What leaders do is largely contingent upon the circumstances and situations they find themselves in. Contingency thinking assumes that:

> What is important is how leaders respond to the unique organisational circumstances or problems that they face as a consequence, for example, of the nature and preferences of co-workers, conditions of work and tasks to be undertaken. This approach to leadership assumes, as well, that there are wide variations in the contexts for leadership and that, to be effective, these contexts require different leadership responses. Also assumed by this approach to leadership is that individuals providing leadership, typically those in formal positions of authority, are capable of mastering a large repertoire of leadership practices.
>
> (Leithwood *et al.* 1999: 15)

Earlier in the same text Leithwood and his colleagues state that there can be no final word on good leadership because, whilst we can now understand the 'basic skills' of leadership, 'outstanding leadership is exquisitely sensitive to the context in which it is exercised' (1999: 4).

This is a powerful theory, and one which underscores all the chapters in this book. For some, context is taken to mean the school as an organizational setting for leaders and leadership (e.g. Hargreaves, Spillane, Stoll and Bolam, Crow, and Mulford). For others, culture is taken to be the context (e.g. Stott and King Song). Whatever the interpretation of context it is strongly present in the chapters of this book. In other words, it appears that contingency theory steers current thinking about school leadership.

In my own work contingency theory plays a large part. For example, I have recently studied how different school sizes impact on the work and roles of leaders (Southworth 2004). Moreover, I have always been careful to emphasize the way in which school phases and sectors influence leadership – which is why I always stress my interest in primary (elementary) school leadership. I know that leading a secondary school is not entirely the same as leading any other type of school.

Given this belief in the importance of context two things follow. First, there is the issue of how much leadership development should be context specific and how much can be generic. Much leadership development tends to be more generic than specific. There is some sense in this, although sometimes it happens because it is easier for providers to work in this way. Whilst we could make provision too specific and introduce relatively narrow and insular provision, it is also true that some provision may be too general and perceived as lacking in relevance for individuals.

Contingency theories not only pose the problem of balancing general with particular needs, they also highlight the importance of differentiated provision. Once we accept the importance of contexts for leaders then we surely need to acknowledge in some way the different needs of leaders at any one time. These differences may be because of the different school contexts (primary, secondary, special schools; school size; school performance levels – failing, high performing, etc.) or, as we have attempted to do at the College, by leaders' career stage (i.e. emergent, established, entry to headship, experienced head). In short, differentiated leadership development becomes an obligation not an option. The only questions which remain to be resolved are:

• On what basis do we differentiate – school, career, both?
• How far do we take differentiation?

The second issue to highlight about context centres on what counts as context. I have already said that it is common for two aspects of context to be taken into account – organizational and career. However, there is at least a third issue which is acknowledged in several of the chapters in this book, namely the policy context.

In those educational systems which devolve responsibilities to schools, such as finances, staffing or curricular choice, then changes in school policies at state or national government level become of significant interest to school leaders. The policy environments in which school leaders operate are of growing concern to many of them. Certainly in England this is true, and elsewhere too. Yet whilst this can be stated with confidence, what is less certain is how do those who develop leaders prepare them for this aspect of their work? Do we include policy analysis as part of their development courses? Do we merely alert them to this change in their role?

There are no easy answers to these questions. Ironically, much may depend on particular policy contexts and how policy-makers wish to engage with their schools' leaders. Some may operate in a top-down way and regard leaders as recipients of policies they are to administer locally and in a compliant way. Others may seek more interactive forms of engagement. As ever it all depends . . .

Yet reliance on the stance of policy-makers is not total. Recent work by Michael Fullan (2003) into *system leadership* suggests a broadening of school leaders' perspective and responsibilities, a shift which may reshape thinking about school leadership and contexts. I shall return to this idea in the developing tomorrow's leaders section.

Distributed leadership

Distributed leadership is undoubtedly an idea which has found its time. Scholars and practitioners alike are talking about the idea. At NCSL we take a strong interest in the topic. We have said in our initial propositions about leadership that we believe leadership should be distributed. We have also commissioned reviews and research into the subject (see www.ncsl.org.uk/researchpublications). It is clear from several of the chapters here that our interest is shared by others, most notably Spillane (Chapter Three), who believes that it is not a question of whether leadership is distributed, but how.

Distributed leadership is not a new idea. It has been around for a long time, either as delegated or shared leadership. It is not a difficult idea either (Elmore 2000). It is essentially about sharing out – spreading or stretching out – leadership across the organization. However, there are some difficulties in spreading leadership across the school. One barrier is the belief in lone leadership. For a long time leadership was not the governing concept, rather it was 'the leader'. Leadership was always equated with an individual. There are countless stories and images which portray leadership in this way – heroes and heroines, charismatic individuals who save endangered communities, failing organizations or struggling schools. This belief in the power of the individual not only constrains leaders, it also holds many 'followers' in thrall too. They expect their leaders to be saints and saviours and when they do not live up to these expectations or images the followers are disappointed or critical of them.

Another barrier is that we tend to think of leaders as occupying organizational roles – the headteacher, deputy head, head of department and so on. In fact leadership is a function rather than a role. In any organization there will be many leaders. At different times, and in different circumstances and situations, individuals and teams will play a leading part, and on other occasions they will not. Leadership is spread across and throughout the school. It exists both formally through positions and roles, and needs also to be recognized as being informally exercised too.

A third barrier is whether those in senior positions can let go. Heads who hang on to leadership can deprive others of the one thing they need to become a leader. What they need is the opportunity to lead. Without this it is very hard to play a major part in the school. Those senior figures who do not create opportunities for others to lead parts of the school, or tasks and projects, are denying them to chance to exercise leadership. It does not matter how well trained and prepared you are, without the opportunity to lead you cannot really get started.

As far as NCSL is concerned the case for distributed leadership is based on three ideas:

1 The belief in leadership teams: belief in the power of one is giving way to a belief in the power of everyone.
2 As schools become more complex places to manage and lead, we need many more leaders than ever before.
3 Ensuring there are lots of leaders enables us to create pools of talented leaders. From these pools of talent we can draw and grow tomorrow's leaders.

There are a number of issues which arise from such a stance. First, having lots of leaders means we must ensure they work towards shared goals and follow the same pathways. It is no good having lots of leaders if they all go in different directions or compete with one another. Distributed leadership needs to be coordinated so that there is a shared sense of purpose.

Second, where leadership is shared and distributed we need to ask:

What is the sum total of all this leadership?

We know leaders make a difference but how do lots of leaders in the same school make a difference? What is their collective influence and impact? Unless we address this question and answer it empirically we may be strong on advocacy, but weak on saying how distributed leadership helps schools to serve their pupils.

The third point concerns the form leadership takes when it is distributed:

What is it that is distributed when a leadership is shared?

I ask this because much of the current interest in distributed leaders revolves around the nature of leadership as *process*. I am also interested in the *content* of such shared leadership. What do they actually concentrate on and make a difference to? I do not think we need lots of strategic leaders, but what schools do need is lots of leaders who can enhance the quality of learning and teaching throughout the school. The distinctive element of school leadership is that it focuses on learning and teaching. Therefore, when we talk about sharing leadership we ought to mean distributing learning-centred leadership. We should create and develop lots of leaders who influence and improve the quality of learning and teaching (Southworth 2004a).

Leading learning communities

It is also taken for granted in several of the chapters that making schools into learning communities is a good thing. I happen to agree with this outlook, and so too does the College, but this does not resolve some of the challenges to such a belief.

Stoll and Bolam (Chapter Four) emphasize the importance of schools becoming learning communities because it ensures they have the capacity to deal with change productively. They imply learning communities can respond to the external change forces which shape schools. They also infer that such schools treat organizational and individual change as a learning process.

Drawing on Bryk and his associate's work (1999) they argue that learning communities are characterized by high levels of relational trust. As others have argued, trust is the vital ingredient in developing 'social capital' (Hargreaves, D. 2001). Without social capital, intellectual capital – the professional craft knowledge of teachers, leaders and other professionals in a school – remains inaccessible. Twenty years ago when researching staff relationships in primary schools we identified the importance of trust and security in social relations and how these created the conditions for social and professional openness and sharing (Nias *et al.* 1989).

Perhaps what all of this points to is the need now to look really hard at the nature of community in schools. Community is one of those positive, affirming words, but it surely warrants closer examination of what it involves. Moreover, given that today community can take electronic and virtual forms and that there is increasing scope for networking, as NCSL's Networked Learning Communities project is revealing, we surely need to consider whether the very essence of community has changed from earlier configurations and definitions?

Mulford and Silins in their chapter (Chapter Ten) focus on leading learning organizations. They reinforce many of the points I have made above about distributed leadership and context. More than others they argue for broadening our notions of learning and, especially, achievement. They recognize and accept that school leadership is fastened to school improvement but believe this should not mean a narrow focus.

The idea of learning communities perhaps warrants a more critical review. There is also a need for quality evidence to show what they achieve and how they are created. Mulford and Silins provide us with a view of them in Australian secondary schools. We need to see if their findings transfer to other countries and school settings.

Leadership succession and sustainability

The chapters by Fink and Hargreaves (Chapters One and Two) make a powerful case for succession and sustainability. At NCSL we are taking the issues of succession and sustainability very seriously. We are exploring with researchers inside and outside education ways of dealing with these two challenges. For example, as suggested in the discussion about distributed leadership above, we regard the widespread sharing of leadership as an important idea in respect of sustaining leadership. The more leaders we have in schools the larger the pool of talent to draw from when we need to replenish the numbers of headteachers and principals.

We have also examined the topic of succession in terms of what lessons there are to learn from business and other public sector organizations. Hartle and Thomas, from the HayGroup, undertook a study for the College (2003) which addressed the challenges schools face when attempting to recruit high-quality staff to middle- and senior-management positions and reviewed the literature in this area and gathered data on leadership succession from organizations inside and outside education. They found that schools are facing a potential crisis in the recruitment and retention of leaders, but so too are many organizations in other sectors. They went on to report:

- Some organizations have developed successful practices which help them recruit, develop and retain sufficient numbers of leaders for future needs. The critical characteristics of those practices are that they are: integrated with other HR processes; operating within clearly defined frameworks; flexible and fluid; focused on the development of skills and behaviours.
- Schools can learn from the successful practices in other sectors but will need to adapt these practices to fit their distinctive culture and emerging models of school leadership.
- These new models of school leadership place a greater emphasis on distributed leadership, learner-centred leadership and collaborative leadership. They will have a significant impact on the leadership succession and leadership development practices adopted in schools.
- Many schools and some LEAs are employing innovative practices in developing their own leaders; however, the practice of structured leadership succession is not widespread in the schools sector.
- Leadership succession is about developing leadership talent at all levels and, as such, requires more attention and focus by all schools and LEAs.

They also argued that leadership talent development should be regarded as a key strategic issue. The development of staff to take on more senior roles should be seen by all school leaders, at all levels, as the major part of their leadership role. Collective and integrated action at national, local and school levels is required to meet the future demands for school leaders.

What the HayGroup report showed is that leadership succession and sustainability are inextricably bound up with leadership development. Instead of thinking of them as separate challenges, somehow set apart from leadership development activities, they are in fact all bound together. Therefore, in moving to look at leadership development in the next sub-section we are not leaving this issue behind, but carrying it forward.

Leadership development processes

Taken together the ten chapters have a great deal to say about developing leaders. I do not intend to try to review all that has already been said in this section. Rather, I intend to take a deliberately partial view and dwell on just a few aspects.

The first thing to note is the general tendency in this book towards school-based forms of leadership development. This is most evident in Crow's chapter on internships (Chapter Five), but others also promote the case for mentoring and coaching school leaders. At NCSL we have been moving along these lines too. Certainly we regard most leadership development as taking place in schools and therefore want to make on-the-job learning as effective as we can.

Work-based learning is one form of process learning and Stott and Sing Kong (Chapter Seven) make a strong case for such development. Indeed, Stott and Sing Kong describe how their innovative leadership learning 'elevates the significance of learning in the job' as well as in an intellectually stimulating environment. However, they then go on to show how they use a mix of learning opportunities – visits, journals, reading, interactive sessions with politicians and policy-makers and business attachments – to widen frames of reference by exposing the participants to a range of experiences and thereby challenging their taken-for-granted assumptions. Whilst the content of their programme differs from what we do at NCSL, there is one general similarity and that is in terms of offering a blend of learning experiences. Such a rich mix of experiences is growing in popularity and it extends the notion of experiential learning. It includes learning in the workplace but supplements it in a number of ways, as shown in the chapter by Paterson and West-Burnham (Chapter Eight). Nor should the opportunities of e-learning be ignored, as Richardson counsels (Chapter Nine). In other words, what we can see across these chapters is the broadening of leadership learning. The leadership learning curriculum includes on-the-job learning plus a range of other experiences.

This breadth of learning opportunities links up to the previous discussion about leadership succession and sustainability. According to the HayGroup we should avoid adopting a 'one size fits all' approach to leadership identification, development and succession. Instead we should recognize that effective leadership succession starts with personal development and that emerging leaders can be supported and helped through the following tactics:

- increased focus on formal or informal coaching and mentoring programmes;
- a managed and flexible approach to job moves;
- a development-focused approach to role design;
- a formal way of creating on-the-job development opportunities;
- individual-driven development contracts.

They promote these proposals because effective leadership development activities include: on-the-job assignments; working with others; coaching; work-based assignments; and internal training. Coaching is particularly efficient as it is directly related to specific tasks in the workplace and requires little investment. The HayGroup report cites a study by the Centre for Organisational Research (2001) which identified the characteristics of high-impact leadership development systems. The characteristics are:

- action and experiential learning to make the learning process 'real';
- encouraging leaders to take responsibility for planning and implementing their own learning;
- encouraging development at three levels: self, team and organization;
- experiences that involve innovation, creativity, strategizing and thinking outside the box;
- building a culture that is supportive of leadership development at all levels;
- formal mentoring.

Together all these ideas show that leadership development today, inside and outside education is increasingly differentiated, needs-based and involves a range of carefully worked out combinations of workplace and off-site learning opportunities. Expressed another way, leadership development has never been more needed and more complex.

Creating the schools of the future

Although there is a wealth of thinking and experience about leadership development in the chapters, by comparison there is relatively little on schools of the future. Without doubt this is a difficult topic, not least because it is too easily thought of as predicting what schools will look like.

Predicting the future is an exercise in which almost all efforts fail. However, if we are preparing leaders we need to do so for today and tomorrow, as Dean Fink advises. Therefore, we do need to have a sense of what schools might be like in the future. But how do we do this? Work the College has embarked on with the Innovation Unit at the DfES and the OECD in Paris, as well as colleagues in Canada, The Netherlands and New Zealand, has enabled us to think through the pitfalls of futures thinking and to develop some tools to help leaders engage in it.

The toolkit project was launched in 2002 and is known as *FutureSight*. It offers the potential for policy-makers and school leaders to step outside the problems of the present in order to see the future of learning and schooling in new ways. The *FutureSight* process involves participants in three modules. The first module enables them to engage with what is already known about trends in society and how these are likely to affect schools. For example these trends include such issues as changes in childhood and adolescence, demographic trends (e.g. migrations, population studies), the knowledge economy, technological advancements, shifts in values, inequality and social exclusion and changing family and community life. Participants are invited to share their perceptions and describe how they manifest themselves in schools.

The second module is based on six scenarios focused around maintaining the status quo, de-schooling or re-schooling. These challenge participants to think and respond to the scenarios, but without talking about the present or the desirability/probability of the scenarios. Later they are asked to consider possible, probable and preferred futures. Here they are not asked to adopt one of the six scenarios, but to combine them in new ways and to add to them.

The final module encourages participants to reflect on the differences between their current reality and their preferred futures and to identify the accelerators and brakes that will affect their future trajectory.

These materials remain in development at the time of publication. Nevertheless, what this project offers is a structured way of encouraging leaders to consider not only what is, but what might be; to move them from coping with the present and the immediacies of their tasks; and to begin to consider where we might be heading in the medium and longer term. It also invites leaders to consider how they might live with ambiguity.

This latter point has interested me for a long time, ever since I encountered Pascale and Athos' book *The Art of Japanese Management* (1983) in which they state:

> The inherent preferences of organizations are clarity, certainty and perfection. The inherent nature of human relationships involves ambiguity,

uncertainty and imperfection. How one honours, balances and integrates the needs of both is the real trick of management.

(Pascale and Athos 1983: 105)

Given the turbulent environments in which school leaders work today, where an array of change forces bear down on them and their schools, living with uncertainty and ambiguity is now even more critical. Furthermore, old style forms of prioritizing and planning may have outlived their usefulness. We need more flexible and organic forms of planning as a process rather than having a plan as product which lasts for three or five years at a stretch.

The point I am making is that leadership and management have always involved some measure of uncertainty. Today there may be even higher levels of instability given the ever changing worlds we live and work in. At a time characterized by change, individuals need to be adaptive leaders. Perhaps then the key skills needed by leaders today are:

1 Being able to cope with uncertainty and ambiguity.
2 At the same time, also having a sense of direction. According to Leithwood and Riehl (2003) this is one of the basic skills of leadership.
3 Being adaptive to changes inside and outside the school and responding productively to them.

No doubt there are others we could add to this list. However, my principal point is that in thinking about creating tomorrow's schools they are likely to be ones which are more dynamically responsive to their environments than those which exist today. Consequently leaders need to be prepared for this role.

Developing tomorrow's school leaders

The chapter by Stott and Sing Kong shows that in some systems careful thought has been given to preparing leaders for tomorrow's schools. This is an important development in its own right. Balancing out the needs of today with those of the future is a challenging task, but something we increasingly should do. Someone who is a deputy head and then moves on to headship may well be in a senior position for 10 to 15 years. We need to consider how they are prepared for the later years of leadership as well as the early years.

The College is tackling this issue in a number of related ways. One way is through the promotion of the idea that every leader is a learner. This is explicitly stated in our current strap line:

Every child in a well led school, every leader a learner.

Because individuals and teams who occupy leadership roles are going to be in such positions for a long time it is imperative they attend to their own development as well as that of their colleagues, the school and the pupils.

For this reason we have recently published a report entitled *Learning to Lead*. This report sets out our thinking about leadership development. It draws heavily on commissioned research and was the product of a series of think tank meetings throughout 2003 which included researchers, academics and leading thinkers from outside the College and the UK as well as the leadership team at NCSL. The report (NCSL 2004) describes the key elements of blended learning which are:

* Self-directed and learner-driven
* Interpersonal and collaborative, team and organizational learning
* Networking
* Support and challenge
* Needs assessed
* Problem-shaping and solving
* e-learning
* Celebration and acknowledgement

In terms of the areas of leadership learning the report states that these include:

* Leading learning and teaching
* Developing self and working with others
* Creating the future
* Managing the organization
* Strengthening community
* Accountability

In respect of creating the future the report states:

> Being a change leader is critical to 21st century educational leadership and crucial to building system and school capacity. Successful school leaders promote a shared vision of the future, underpinned by common purposes and values which will secure the commitment of a wide range of stakeholders. Successful leadership captures hearts and minds.
>
> (NCSL 2004: 8–9)

Such learning includes vision building and implementation, dealing with change and planning and strategic improvement.

The College has also developed a leadership development framework. This framework is an initial attempt to map the phases of leadership development. Although it has some shortcomings it also tries to show how once an individual has become a headteacher there is still more development needed. This is why the framework introduces two stages beyond entry to headship – advanced leadership and consultant leadership.

The idea of consultant leader has taken off recently in new ways. During 2003 1,000 experienced primary headteachers in England were identified and trained to support 4,000 school leaders in respect of the national primary strategy for literacy and numeracy teaching and learning. These 1,000 primary consultant leaders work outside their own schools, for part of their time. They are an example of what Michael Fullan (2003) calls *system leadership*.

If we believe that a public education system is worth having and that this should be a high-quality system then:

> Improving the overall system will not happen just by endorsing the vision of a strong public school system; principals in particular must be cognizant that changing their schools and the system is a simultaneous proposition.
>
> (Fullan 2003: 4)

In other words, leading tomorrow's schools involves three things:

1 Leading the school you are appointed to and ensuring it is a high performing and improving school.
2 Being prepared to accept external support and challenge from a leader or leaders in other schools, as well as from other agents (e.g. the LEA, OfSTED).
3 Becoming a consultant leader to other schools for a period of time.

This extension of the reach of individual leaders to beyond their schools is very likely to simultaneously enhance their leadership of their own school. By working with other schools and their leaders the consultant will very probably benefit and bring back into their own school new ideas and ways of working. Therefore, system leadership involves mutual and reciprocal gains for all participants. Nevertheless, it also marks a radical development of the role and remit of headteachers. It extends their responsibilities beyond the school boundary and marks a new sense of collaboration which transcends peer sharing to include professional advice and challenge. It could create not only a far more networked and interactive system, but also a networked *learning* system.

It is this vision of a networked system which is currently driving education policy thinking. The goal of system-wide connectivity and leadership which is *stretched* across the whole system, not just within a school, echoes some of the thinking of Spillane and his associates about distributed leadership within schools. Leading tomorrow's schools involves participating in distributed system leadership.

For this to happen additional forms of leadership learning will be needed and the ideas set out in this chapter could all be configured to enable system leadership as well as school leadership. Yet system leadership also requires leaders to have a sense of what some refer to as the 'big picture'. I take this to mean being aware of policy thinking and other trends which influence schools. Therefore, some approach to futures thinking will be an essential ingredient, as will looking outside the education system and national boundaries.

Another way of saying this is to return to what I said earlier about the importance of contexts. The idea of system leadership essentially alters the definition of context for school leaders. It moves them to think about outside their schools as well as inside them. One of the dangers in any organization is becoming too 'inside focused' – that is too internally focused and parochial. System leadership may help us to avoid this danger.

However, there is another risk it could introduce, that of some leaders becoming too outside oriented. Some leaders may never be in their own schools. That is why the work we are doing on how leaders influence what happens in classrooms is an important corollary to system leadership. We need to ensure that within all schools there is effective leadership of learning and teaching, as well as leadership of the organization, its direction and school-wide improvement efforts.

Learning-centred leadership focuses on how leaders exercise influence on classroom practices and student learning outcomes. It also implicitly acknowledges that in the future more learning in schools will follow constructivist principles and that the transmission model of teaching will be used less. If this proves to be an accurate assessment of where we are heading, then leaders will need not only to be learners themselves, but more knowledgeable about new forms of learning, assessment and pedagogy. And leaders will have to lead the change process from where learning and teaching currently are in their schools, to the new emphases and forms they are likely to take by 2010 or whenever the change forces begin to impact on schools and classrooms.

It is crucial that the development of leaders embraces their leadership of learning – as it will be in the not too distant future as well as today. Indeed, we may need to emphasize the importance of ensuring all students are intelligent learners, as well as knowledgeable across a range of subjects and skill areas.

Developing leaders for tomorrow's schools therefore involves a new blend of skills and knowledge. Much that leaders already know and can do will continue, but there will be new contexts and situations, as well as new emphases in learning and the curriculum. At the same time leaders need to be able to deal productively with uncertainty and lead change processes in flexible ways. The scope of their leadership will shift too, as more attention to system-wide development is fostered. Existing development processes will continue to be relevant, but these may also be adapted and applied in new ways, as we can see in the case of Singapore.

Conclusion

Without doubt all the contributions to this book provide much food for thought. Separately and together they offer ideas and insights into leadership, its development and its direction. They also show that leadership thinking, practice and development are interrelated and moving along at some pace.

One challenge for all involved in the field will be to sustain the pace of development. Another will be to meet the needs of practitioners and policymakers alike. Unless we can do all this then the current interest in and emphasis upon leadership could wane. The current decade marks a fertile and productive period in school leadership and management thinking, research and practice. However, unless many of the ideas reported in this volume can be translated into effective programmes and activities then the prospects for leadership development will not be so rosy. That is why in this chapter I have tried to show how the NCSL is responding to the expectations of our stakeholders and clients. What the College does is not the only way forward and it may turn out not to have been the best way forward. I have simply offered our actions as illustrations of the ways we have interpreted latest thinking and leading-edge practices.

Nevertheless, it is equally important that there is some sense of response and responsiveness. Leadership development involves a large investment of public money and practitioner time and energy. We must use these investments wisely and carefully. And we must ensure that in so doing we sustain the contemporary belief in leadership as a key lever in developing schools and the school system.

Leadership development has never been more highly regarded. The stakes have never been higher too. All who participate in leadership development – as sponsors, designers, deliverers or delegates – need to appreciate that this is a time when the context favours us. We are expected to make a positive difference. The enthusiasm for leadership and its development which is apparent throughout all the chapters in this book must be harnessed and shown to have made a difference to the quality of schooling and to children's lives and learning. That is why the stakes are high; not for ourselves, but those we seek to serve.

Bibliography

Bryk, A., Camburn, E. and Louis, K.S. (1999) Professional community in Chicago elementary schools: facilitating factors and organisational consequences, *Educational Administration Quarterly*, 35 (supplement): 751–81.

Centre for Organisation Research (2001) *High Impact Leadership Development*. www.cfor.org

Elmore, R. (2000) *Building a New Structure for School Leadership*. The Albert Shanker Institute.

Fullan, M. (2003) *The Moral Imperative of School Leadership*. Thousand Oaks CA: Corwin Press.

Hargreaves, D. (2001) A capital theory of school effectiveness and improvement, *British Educational Research Journal*, 27(4): 487–503.

Hartle, F. and Thomas, K./NCSL (2003) *Growing Tomorrow's School Leaders – the challenge*. Nottingham: NCSL.

Leithwood, K., Jantzi, D. and Steinbach, R. (1999) *Changing Leadership for Changing Times*. Buckingham: Open University Press.

Leithwood, K. and Riehl, C. (2003) *What we know about successful school leadership: A report by division A of AERA*. Philadelphia PA: Laboratory for Student Success, Temple University [also available through NCSL].

NCSL, (2004) *Learning to Lead*. Nottingham: NCSL.

Nias, J., Southworth, G. and Yeomans, R. (1989) *Staff Relationships in the Primary Schools: The study of school cultures*. London: Cassell.

Pascale, R.T. and Athos, A.G. (1983) *The Art of Japanese Management*. London: Penguin Books.

Southworth, G. (2004). *Primary School Leadership in Context: Leading small, medium and large sized schools*. London: RoutledgeFalmer.

Southworth, G., (2004a) How leaders influence what happens in classrooms, in *Learning-centred Leadership Materials, section 2*, Nottingham: NCSL.

Index

Related books from Open University Press
Purchase from www.openup.co.uk or order through your local bookseller

BUILDING LEADERSHIP CAPACITY FOR SCHOOL IMPROVEMENT

Alma Harris and Linda Lambert

- What form of leadership promotes school improvement?
- How do schools build leadership capacity?
- How do schools sustain improvement in changing times?

This book offers a new perspective on the relationship between leadership and school improvement. It emphasizes the importance of maximizing the leadership capabilities of all those within the organization and offers guidance about the way in which this is achieved. Drawing upon the latest research evidence concerning schools improvement, it is a practical guide to building leadership capacity for those working in schools.

Through case study illustrations the authors demonstrate how leadership capacity can be built in schools in very different contexts. Practical material is provided to assist schools in generating the internal capacity for change and development. The central message of this book is one of investing in leadership at all levels within the organization to maintain and sustain school improvement.

Contents
Preface – Foreword by David Jackson (NCSL) – Introduction – What is leadership capacity? – Capacity building connects with leadership – Building leadership capacity: The role of the head – How to build leadership capacity: Manor Primary School – How to build leadership capacity: Rookwood Comprehensive School – How to build leadership capacity: Highfields School – Building leadership capacity for sustained school improvement – Building leadership capacity for school improvement: The role of the LEA – Building leadership capacity for school improvement: The role of professional development – Questions and a few answers – Appendices – Bibliography – Index.

128pp   0 335 21178 X (Paperback)   Not available in North America

LEADERSHIP, GENDER AND CULTURE IN EDUCATION
MALE AND FEMALE PERSPECTIVES

John Collard and Cecilia Reynolds (eds)

This edited collection contains chapters by some of the world's leading scholars on gender and educational leadership. The chapters draw on research on men and women leaders in elementary, secondary and postsecondary schools in Australia, Canada, New Zealand, Sweden, the United Kingdom and the United States.

The authors counter essentialist claims about leaders that are based on biological, psychological and/or sociological theories that stress gender difference. Similarities between men and women and differences within gender groups are highlighted in this book. There are numerous discussions that employ sophisticated understandings of gender relations and leadership discourses in today's globalized context. Early scholarship on gender and leadership is supplemented here with more nuanced theories and explanations of how gender, race and class, for example, operate in connected and changing ways to affect the leadership experiences of men and women who work in different educational settings.

Contents

Contributors

Sandra Acker, Marie Battiste, Jill Blackmore, Cryss Brunner, John Collard, Marian Court, Anna Davis, Karin Franzen, Margaret Grogan, Olof Johannson, James Koschoreck, Betty Merchant, Cecilia Reynolds.

256pp   0 335 21440 1 (Paperback)   0 335 21441 X (Hardback)

EDUCATION MANAGEMENT IN MANAGERIALIST TIMES
BEYOND THE TEXTUAL APOLOGISTS

Martin Thrupp and Robert Willmott

This important and provocative book is not another 'how to' educational management text. Instead it offers a critical review of the extensive educational management literature itself.

The main concern of the authors is that educational management texts do not do enough to encourage school leaders and teachers to challenge social inequality or the market and managerial reforms of the last decade. They demonstrate this problem through detailed analyses of texts in the areas of educational marketing, school improvement, development planning and strategic human resource management, school leadership and school change.

For academics and students, *Education Management in Managerialist Times* offers a critical guide to existing educational management texts and makes a strong case for redefining educational management along more socially and politically informed lines. The book also offers practitioners alternative management strategies intended to contest, rather than support, managerialism, while being realistic about the context within which those who lead and manage schools currently have to work.

This controversial new title brings a new insight to the educational management debate.

Contents
Part one: Background – Introduction: what's wrong with education management? – The market, neo-liberalism and the new managerialism – Inequality, education reform and the response of education management writers – Reading the textual apologists – Part two: The textual apologists – Educational marketing – School improvement – School development planning and strategic human resource management – School leadership – School change – Part three: Conclusion – Education management: where to now? – References – Index.

224pp   0 335 21028 7 (Paperback)   0 335 21029 5 (Hardback)

CHANGING LEADERSHIP FOR CHANGING TIMES

Kenneth Leithwood, Doris Jantzi and Rosanne Steinbach

Envisioning the nature of schools of the future is more art than science. But the response of today's schools to challenges presented by such forces as technology, changing demographics, and government austerity offer useful clues. As a minimum, schools will need to be able to thrive on uncertainty, have considerably greater capacities for collective problem solving than they do at present, and meet a much wider array of student needs. *Changing Leadership for Changing Times* examines the types of leadership that are likely to be productive in creating and sustaining such schools. Based on a long term study of 'transformational' leadership in school restructuring contexts, the chapters in this book offer a highly readable account of such leadership grounded in a substantial body of empirical evidence.

Contents
Part one: The context for changing leadership – Changing leadership: a menu of possibilities – Transformational leadership as a place to begin – Part two: Transformational school leadership – Transformational leadership at Central Ontario Secondary School – Setting directions: vision, goals, and high expectations – Developing people: individualized support, intellectual stimulation and modelling – Redesigning the organization: culture, structure, policy and community relationships – Part three: Beyond transformational leadership: broadening and deepening the approach – The problem-solving processes of transformational leaders – Fostering teacher leadership – Building teachers' commitment to change – Creating the conditions for growth in teachers' professional knowledge and skill – Leadership for organizational learning – Maintaining emotional balance – Conclusion: future schools and leaders' values – References – Appendix – Index.

272pp   0 335 19522 9 (Paperback)   0 335 19523 7 (Hardback)

EDUCATIONAL LEADERSHIP AND LEARNING
PRACTICE, POLICY AND RESEARCH

Sue Law and Derek Glover

... it sets out both the theory and the everyday realities that lie behind the Government's 'improving leadership' agenda

T.E.S. Friday

Educational leaders – whether in schools, colleges or higher education – are challenged with steering unprecedented change; educational management has never been more demanding. Within the context of a new 'learning age' and the Teacher Training Agency's National Standards, this book explores many of the key issues facing those both aspiring to and already involved in leadership and management, whether at middle or senior levels.

While focusing particularly on schools and colleges, this book evaluates issues increasingly central to leadership in a variety of professional educational settings, for example school improvement, innovation, teamwork, organizational culture, professional development, motivation and the nature of leadership. In identifying key concepts, it scrutinizes possible management strategies within a changing policy context that is increasingly focused around standards, accountability and reputation.

The book utilizes research evidence to illuminate the practices, challenges and problems facing educationists and endeavours to overcome the perceived gap between practice and research to create an integrated approach to leadership and management development: one which both supports and stimulates managers' professional development aspirations.

Contents
Acknowledgements – List of abbreviations – Part one: Leading and managing – The context for educational leadership – Developing leadership and management effectiveness – Managing ourselves and leading others – Motivating and managing others – Leading effective teams – Part two: Changing and learning – Effective communication – Organizational cultures – Managing change and creating opportunities – Educational improvement, inspection and effectiveness – Leading and managing in learning organizations – Part three: Tasks and responsibilities – Managing staff and promoting quality – Managing resources and finance – Managing stakeholder relationships and partnerships – Leading and managing professional development – Postscript – Bibliography – Indexes.

208pp   0 335 19752 3 (Paperback)